for the Latino/a students
at Tufts - especially
the Dominicans!

Deborah Pacini H

*B*achata

Raulín Rodríguez, by Deborah Pacini Hernandez

Bachata

A Social History of a Dominican Popular Music

Deborah
Pacini Hernandez

Temple University Press
Philadelphia

Temple University Press, Philadelphia 19122
Copyright © 1995 by Deborah Pacini Hernandez. All rights reserved
Published 1995
Printed in the United States of America

∞ The paper used in this book meets the requirements of the American National
Standard for Information Sciences—Permanence of Paper for Printed Library
Materials, ANSI Z39.48-1984

Text design by Ellen Dawson.

Library of Congress Cataloging-in-Publication Data
Pacini Hernandez, Deborah.
    Bachata : a social history of a Dominican popular music /
Deborah Pacini Hernandez.
        p.   cm.
    Includes bibliographical references, discography, and index.
    ISBN 1-56639-299-3. — ISBN 1-56639-300-0 (pbk.)
    1. Bachata—History and criticism.   2. Popular music—Dominican
Republic—History and criticism.   3. Dominican Republic—Social
conditions.   1. Title.
ML3486.D65P3   1995
781.64'097293—dc20   94-29477

Portions of Chapter 1 were published in the *Latin American Music Review* in "Social
identity and class in bachata, an emerging Dominican popular music" (vol. 10,
no. 1, Spring/Summer 1989), pp. 69–91. By permission of the University of Texas
Press. Copyright © by the University of Texas Press, 2100 Comal, Austin, Texas 78722.

Portions of Chapter 2 were published in *Studies in Latin American Popular Culture*
in "Dominican popular music under the Trujillo dictatorship" (vol. 12, 1993), pp.
127–40.

Portions of Chapter 2 appeared in the *Latin American Music Review* as "*La lucha
sonora*: Dominican popular music in the post-Trujillo era" (vol. 12, no. 2, Fall/
Winter 1991), pp. 105–23. By permission of the University of Texas Press.
Copyright © by the University of Texas Press, 2100 Comal, Austin, Texas 78722.

Portions of Chapter 5 were published in *Popular Music* as "*Cantando la cama vacía*:
Love, sex and gender relationships in Dominican bachata" (vol. 9, no. 3, 1990),
pp. 351–67. By permission of Cambridge University Press.

Portions of Chapter 6 appeared in *Popular Music* as "Bachata: From the margins
to the mainstream" (vol. 11, no. 3, 1992), pp. 359–64. By permission of Cambridge
University Press.

Contents

Photo galleries follow pp. 63, 141, and 217

Acknowledgments

One of the great advantages and pleasures of working with popular music is that so many people enjoy it—not just listening and dancing to it, but reading and thinking and talking about it as well. The memories, experiences, ideas, enthusiasm of such people, for whom music is an integral part of life, have made this book possible, and I would like to acknowledge their contributions here.

By now, there are a great many people to thank, because this project has extended over ten years. Considering them chronologically takes me back to the mid 1980s, when I first undertook this research as a graduate student in anthropology at Cornell University. There, my committee members Billie Jean Isbell (anthropology), Martin Hatch (ethnomusicology), Charlotte Heth (ethnomusicology), and Tom Holloway (Latin American history) gave me valuable guidance throughout the sometimes unconventional directions my work took. I am grateful that they never tried to shoehorn me into scholarship that conflicted with my own interests and talents; the result of that freedom is my broad, interdisciplinary approach to anthropology and ethnomusicology, which is, I believe, my most valuable accomplishment and asset. Friends and colleagues in Ithaca also provided me with intellectual support and companionship, among them Mary Jo Dudley, Martha Carvalho, Lourdes Brache, Ann Peters, Chris Franquemont, Elayne Zorn, Claudio Buchwald, Bill Fisher, and Mike Leavy. As for institutional support for my graduate research on Dominican popular music, I want to thank Cornell's Latin American Studies Program for a pre-dissertation research fellowship, and the Fulbright-Hayes program for a doctoral dissertation research fellowship.

This book owes most to those in the Dominican Republic who

shared their information and insights with me when I was conducting my fieldwork on bachata and merengue in 1986 and 1987. Indeed, because little if anything had been published on bachata at the time, the dissertation on which this book is based could literally not have been written were it not for the generosity of people either involved with or interested in popular music who took the time to talk to me. Some people I spoke to only once or twice, but with others I had repeated conversations, and they deserve special mention. Bachata musicians Luis Segura, Tony Santos, and Blas Durán stand out in my mind as being particularly generous with their time and hospitality. Luis Dias, an extraordinarily versatile musician and cultural observer, contributed stimulating and insightful comments on all sorts of music and their role in Dominican society. Arístides Incháustegui, a professional singer and music historian, was also generous with information he has collected over years of studying the Dominican music industry. Radhames Aracena, who granted me several lengthy and invaluable interviews, as well as free access to Radio Guarachita's facilities, also deserves mention, as do Tony Díaz, Radio Guarachita's station manager, and disc jockey Jorge Sarit. Miguel Matos, then a medical student, amateur mechanic, and enthusiastic fan of all sorts of popular music, helped me with innumerable logistical difficulties. Sociologist Lusitania Martínez provided me, in the initial months of my residence in Santo Domingo, with indispensable advice and guidance on negotiating Dominican society, and later on, with a warm friendship that I still value. Above all, I want to thank Juan Valoy, a talented plastic artist, musician, and brilliant cultural observer, who was a good friend as well as an extraordinarily insightful commentator on barrio culture—his culture. The reflections and memories of all these Dominican contributors appear throughout this book, although lamentably—because of space constraints—not in the Spanish they were spoken in. It is my sincere hope that my translations adequately communicate the strength and vitality of their voices.

A 1994 follow-up visit to the Dominican Republic put me in contact with another group of people to add to my list of Dominicans who have generously contributed to this project. Bachata producers José Luis and Rafael Mañón and musicians Sonia Silvestre, Víctor Víctor, and Raulín Rodríguez provided me with valuable insights and information on recent developments in bachata. Journalist Juan de la Cruz Triffolio shared his extensive collection of articles on bachata that began appearing in the late 1980s and allowed me to reproduce some of his photographic material. Documentary film maker René Fortunato also generously shared his newspaper and photographic archives with me and connected me with key people, greatly expanding the productivity of an all too brief trip. One of these people was concert producer Tati Olmos. When the camera

I had taken with me to collect additional pictures for this book broke down the day I arrived in Santo Domingo, Tati put me in contact with a friend of hers, videographer Peyi Guzmán, who, incredibly, loaned his Nikon camera to me for two weeks, without even knowing me; my heartfelt thanks to both of them.

I also want to express my deepest gratitude to several of my colleagues who have supported this project in various ways over the last ten years. Martha Ellen Davis began advising me on an informal basis since I first contacted her in 1984, carefully reading and commenting on funding proposals and, later, thesis chapters, and providing me with invaluable field experience by inviting me to assist her in some of her video projects in the Dominican Republic. Moreover, I suppose this book might not have been written had she not encouraged me to switch the focus of my research to bachata when I was still in the field. Charlie Keil has been one of my most consistent supporters, and I am deeply grateful to him not only for his persistent urging to get the book done, but also for his careful reading of the thesis and his thoughtful suggestions for revising it as a book. I also want to thank Paul Austerlitz for reading the final manuscript; a number of last-minute improvements were made thanks to his knowledgeable comments. At the University of Florida's Center for Latin American Studies, I have enjoyed support and encouragement from several of my colleagues, including Charles Perrone and Amelia Simpson, both of whom read portions of the material in this book, and Helen Safa, who shared her as yet unpublished materials on women in the Dominican Republic. I am particularly grateful to Terry McCoy for generously giving me a research leave in order to complete this book. I want also to extend my heartfelt thanks to Barbara Firoozye for her outstanding job copy editing the manuscript and to Jenny French and Doris Braendel, my editors at Temple University Press, whose always sympathetic and constructive guidance helped me through the production process.

Finally, I want to thank my family, beginning with my father and mother, who watched, not always patiently and often with dismay, as I took some unexpected turns, but who were always supportive of my academic endeavors. Special thanks go to my daughter Radha and my son Tai, whose growing up has been indelibly colored by both my work in academia and my interests in Caribbean music and culture. They uncomplainingly left their friends in Ithaca in order to accompany me to the Dominican Republic while I did fieldwork, and they bravely confronted a new school and friends in a language they knew only superficially. As I wrote first the dissertation and later this book, they often had to put up with a chaotic household, dinners late, and papers and books chronically strewn all over the house. On the other hand, I trust they will have benefited by observing that learning can be a sociable and meaningful experience. Finally, I want to thank Reebee Garofalo, whose entrance into our lives has enriched the three of us in countless ways. I am deeply indebted to him for his many contributions to this book, which have included reading and commenting on chapters, talking me through theoretical and organizational brambles that came up along the way, providing invaluable computer support, assisting me on my 1994 field trip to the Dominican Republic, and last but not least, intuitively understanding and generously providing appropriate measures of both the companionship and space I needed in order to get it done. Reebee, Radha, and Tai, this book's for you.

Introduction

The myth of the Caribbean paradise is strong: my plans to travel to Santo Domingo, the capital of the Dominican Republic, for dissertation research on popular music in 1985 were met with a curious mixture of incredulity, disapproval, and envy by graduate student colleagues, especially those who had to endure all sorts of discomforts and deprivations when doing fieldwork in less hospitable places. This myth, however, does not take into account the equally aggravating problems peculiar to living in a tropical city: oppressive heat and humidity exacerbated by daily worsening electrical and water shortages. The constant electrical blackouts left fans motionless, food in the refrigerator rotting, and traffic snarled under inoperative stoplights. Water was scarce too, but even when it was available, it could not be pumped without electrical power, leaving entire neighborhoods of this steamy coastal Caribbean city of 1.5 million inhabitants without showers or flushing toilets, often for days at a time. Frequent rains temporarily relieved the summer heat, but when they came it was in torrents, transforming streets into rivers of black water that stalled cars and trapped pedestrians in whatever dry spots they could find. These were, of course, minor personal discomforts compared to the much worse, spiritually distressing specter of poverty, despair, racial discrimination, government corruption and repression, and a host of other social, economic, and political problems endemic to this part of the Caribbean.

While fieldwork in the Dominican Republic was not idyllic, it was, nonetheless, an agreeable and exciting place to work. The country's landscape is beautiful and varied, containing four mountain ranges, semiarid deserts, lush farmlands, and long strands of palm-fringed beaches. While it has suffered considerable environmental damage of all sorts, the Dominican Republic still retains much of its original natural beauty. But the best part about doing fieldwork in the Dominican Republic was its people, who are on the whole friendly, spontaneous, generous, and hospitable, and most of whom have an exuberant love of music. Not that this nation is a land of "happy natives," but I think Dominicans themselves would agree that one of the salient characteristics of their culture is the almost universal love of music and dance. Furthermore, Dominicans love to talk about music, which made my research truly enjoyable. Music is an important and highly esteemed part of the cultural baggage shared by most ordinary Dominicans. More than that, it is considered part of their very genetic makeup: I was told repeatedly, with great pride, that Dominicans carry their music *en la sangre* (in their blood).

And indeed, music is a ubiquitous feature of the daily lives of ordinary Dominicans. Almost every neighborhood store, every bus, taxi, and private car, has a radio going throughout the day. It is common to see people, young people in particular, burst into spontaneous dance on the street when a favorite musical piece or phrase happens to be playing on a nearby sound system. Music is such a vital part of their consciousness that sometimes they even dance without any audible music; with sheer pleasure they dance to the rhythms of music playing only in their heads. People of all ages pay attention to whatever is happening on the music scene, and it is not at all uncommon to hear passengers in the *públicos* (collective taxis) exchanging commentaries on whatever song is being played on the radio. Because Dominicans so highly value—and fully enjoy—discussing music, talking with a foreigner about their music seemed to be perceived as merely an unusual (but therefore interesting) variation on a common theme. In this sense, my project was, indeed, ideal, because I never had to cope with people misunderstanding my subject matter, nor being suspicious of my motives.

While my interest in Dominican popular music as a whole has remained a constant over the years, the focus of my research underwent major changes along the way, which explains, in part, the rather broad scope of this book. My initial research on the popular music of the Dominican Republic dated to 1983, when I began to consider a research project on merengue, the most popular dance music of the Dominican Republic. At that time it was beginning to compete successfully with salsa among Latin American and Latino audiences yet had received little academic attention in the United States. In the summer of 1984 I made a brief field trip to that country to conduct preliminary research, visiting both rural and urban areas. Most of what I heard on the radio was merengue played by large commercial *orquestas* (orchestras), which included saxophones, trombones, trumpets, congas, keyboards, and electric bass guitar, as well as the traditional *güira*, a metallic scraper (to be distinguished from the

Cuban and Puerto Rican gourd *güiro*), and *tambora*, a two-headed drum played horizontally, with the hand on one head and with a stick on the other. I also heard plenty of salsa (a hot dance music, based on Cuban *son* rhythms, that was developed by Spanish-Caribbean musicians residing in New York City in the mid-to-late 1960s) and *balada* (an internationally oriented, highly commercial form of romantic music characterized by elaborate arrangements, production, and publicity, whose most well known exponent is Julio Iglesias). I heard little, however, of the traditional *merengue típico*, which is associated with rural culture and played by small ensembles known as *conjuntos*, composed of accordion, güira, tambora, and sometimes a *marimbula* (thumb bass). Based on these observations, I prepared a research proposal for a project that would explore the relationship between both forms of merengue, paying particular attention to how the cleavage between the two styles reflected class and regional divisions in Dominican society.

In 1986 I received a Fulbright-Hayes doctoral dissertation grant for my fieldwork in the Dominican Republic. Shortly after I arrived in Santo Domingo, I began analyzing local radio programming. While most stations were playing the same lineup of merengue, salsa, balada, and U.S. rock I had heard earlier, I tuned into one station that was playing guitar music that sounded vaguely like old Cuban music. When I asked some friends about it, they responded, "That's not Cuban music, that's bachata!" They told me bachata was a guitar-based Dominican form of music listened to and made by uneducated *campesinos* (country people) and the urban poor. Considering themselves politically progressive intellectuals, they tried to describe the music with as much seriousness as possible, but their attitude revealed a contradictory mixture of good-humored acceptance of a popular form of expressive culture and a thinly disguised disdain for its musical and textual crudeness.

I had been told that one of the country's principal radio stations, Radio Guarachita, was well known for playing merengue típico and that it targeted a very specific audience—campesinos and the very poor residents of the city, most of whom were migrants from rural areas. But when I visited Radio Guarachita I found that, while the station's audience was indeed composed of the social groups I had expected, merengue típico was played only on a daily half-hour show at 5:00 P.M. and on Sunday afternoons. Instead, Radio Guarachita's programming was based almost exclusively on a music the disc jockeys called bachata or *música de amargue*. I realized that the music I had mistaken as Cuban was bachata being played by Radio Guarachita.

Curious, I began asking questions about bachata and learned that while it was popular among the rural and urban poor, bachata was not considered a significant musical form worthy of attention by the music industry, journalists, or academics. Developments in merengue, in contrast, were followed by the media as closely as fluctuations in the price of sugar. In order to get a more concrete idea of what music was actually selling best among the country's poorer classes, I prepared a small questionnaire and visited Avenida Duarte, the principal street in the Santo Domingo working-class shopping district, where records were sold in makeshift booths located along the sidewalks. I made it clear to the record vendors at the outset that I was not interested in buying music, but rather in obtaining information for a survey I was conducting, hoping they wouldn't alter their answers in order to encourage a sale. I began by asking the vendors what kind of music sold most. Unanimously, they told me it was merengue. I then asked which music sold best after merengue and was usually told it was balada. When I persisted, asking which music sold next best, the answer was salsa or rock, not necessarily in that order. Not one of the vendors mentioned bachata. When I finally asked specifically whether they sold bachata, they responded, "Oh yes," inevitably breaking into a big smile, "we sell more bachata than anything else!" Why did none of these vendors mention bachata before I brought it up? Perhaps because they correctly identified me as foreign, they assumed I wouldn't know about bachata or care about it if I did. Or perhaps they were trying to hide the fact that a principal source of their income was the disreputable bachata, which I would be sure to disapprove of; Dominicans are a proud people, who want foreigners to think well of them.

After conducting the vendor survey in the working-class district, I visited record stores in the more elegant commercial districts, the Calle el Conde and the upper-middle-class shopping mall, Plaza Naco. With the occasional exception of a few LPs by the most well known bachata interpreters, Leonardo Paniagua and Luis Segura, no bachata was sold. This didn't make economic sense: if a music has a sizable market, why wouldn't they sell recordings of it? One employee replied to this question by saying that they didn't stock it because they didn't want the kind of people who bought bachata coming into the store. Another told me simply that they didn't stock bachata because the vendors along the Avenida Duarte fulfilled that demand. Capitalist enterprises, however, are not usually picky about who buys their products, nor generous about sharing markets.

Somewhat later I had another experience confirming my observation that Dominicans were reluctant to accept bachata as a legitimate music form and that listening to bachata was considered incompatible with their desired self-presentation. I was browsing in a store when the salesgirl noticed I was carrying a bag that obviously contained records. She asked me what I had bought, and I told her it was bachata. She laughed incredulously, but I insisted it was true and opened the bag so she could see for herself. She thereupon called over two of her colleagues and announced to them, somewhat triumphantly, "See, she is foreign, and she likes bachata. She bought these records to take back to *los países* (as they call the United States), so you see, bachata really is not just for campesinos, even foreigners like it." It was obvious that they had previously had an argument about the merits of bachata and that one of the disputants had insisted the music was worthless and fit only for campesinos.

I was also intrigued by the diversity of opinions on bachata's origins: some people I asked said it had always been played in the Dominican Republic, others said it came from Puerto Rico, others said from Cuba, while still others said there was no such thing as bachata, it was just the traditional Cuban bolero played by untrained rural musicians. There was consensus only on the fact that the music was associated with a particular class of people, *la gente baja*, that is, low-class people, who were often stereotyped as maids and watchmen, undesirable occupations held by people from the lowest strata of Dominican society. It became clear to me that bachata was as popular—at least in terms of the number of listeners—as the far more well known and universally respected merengue; nevertheless, because its low social status prevented its dissemination through the usual channels of musical distribution, an informal music economy had been developed by its practitioners to meet public demand. The bachata economy, however, was not independent of the formal Dominican music industry, but rather, it occupied a marginal position within it that corresponded to the marginal position its constituency occupied in the Dominican social and economic hierarchy.

Economic marginality and social rejection of a music associated with marginality, however, need not always go together: Jamaican reggae, for example, is associated with the poorest sectors of Jamaican society, yet reggae is certainly well known and is valued—at least as a source of dollars if not for its musical or social value—by Jamaican society as a whole. Similarly, rap music may be associated with the U.S. black, urban underclass, but it has undeniably become one of the most widely disseminated and influential styles of popular music in recent memory. It became clear to me that a dialogue, uttered in a highly symbolic language unique to expressive culture, was going on between rural and urban regions, between socio-economic classes, and between different perceptions of the processes of social transformation that were occurring in the Dominican Republic. The more I looked, the more I saw bachata's potential to serve as a lens through which to view unique relationships between popular music, social identity, and class in the Dominican Republic. I gradually began spending more time at Radio Guarachita and along the Avenida Duarte, and with time, my curiosity and interest in bachata overcame my resolve to complete the research project I had already started: several months into my fieldwork, I left aside my research on merengue and dedicated my full attention to bachata.

Refocusing my research affected my work in fundamental ways, but fortunately the months of work I'd done on merengue were not in vain; one cannot make sense out of bachata's marginal position in the Dominican popular music landscape without understanding the configuration of the center, which in this case was occupied by merengue. While the majority of merengue típico's audience were peasants and working-class people from the Cibao region, orquesta merengue's popularity was nationwide and crossed class lines—although the bulk of its audience was solidly urban and working class. Merengue was big business in the Dominican Republic, however, so researching it had meant going to some of the centers of Dominican social and economic power: the country's principal radio and television stations, major newspapers, publicity agencies, record companies, and the various institutes of social research and culture, all of which had long taken an active interest in merengue. Outside of the musicians themselves, most of the people whose work revolved around merengue (e.g., producers, promoters, journalists), as well as those in the larger entertainment industry in which merengue played a major role, were middle class, or at least they identified with that group. In view of the attention merengue was receiving from the media on a daily basis, it was sometimes difficult for me to gain access to well-known musicians and music industry personnel; they had little interest in an academic enterprise such as mine, which was unlikely to result in worthwhile publicity or economic benefits. In contrast, the *bachateros* (musicians who play bachata) and those involved in bachata production and distribution were people of humble rural origins for whom the traditional values of hospitality were still important, and they were extraordinarily generous with their time and attention. Surprised and pleased that an outsider took an interest in their much-maligned music, they were eager to talk to me about it, which made my work correspondingly enjoyable.

Because for decades merengue has been considered a symbol of Dominican national identity, a great deal of material has been published on it—books, dissertations, magazine articles, reminiscences by elderly musicians, and so on. In contrast, published materials of any sort on bachata or on its related guitar-based genres were extremely limited. Andrés Rivera Payano published an article on bachata in 1983 in the Santo Domingo variety magazine ¡Ahora! Luis Manuel Brito included an appendix on bachata in his 1984 thesis on merengue; this appendix appeared as an article in ¡Ahora! in 1985 but was omitted from the thesis when it was published as a book in 1987. I also found a few references to rural recreational guitar music that were helpful in providing some historical depth to my discussion of bachata's antecedents. However, other than these, there was little I could learn from library research.

My data collection, then, depended on directly observing musical performances, listening to recorded bachata, and interviewing dozens of musicians and fans, which together allowed me to analyze the four principal components of music—the music itself, the performers, the audience, and the social context. I also explored an additional component critical to contemporary musical activity—the music business, composed of people who may not participate directly in music making, but who play determinative roles in recording, broadcasting, and distribution. As a result, I spent a great deal of time with record producers, record vendors, recording engineers, radio disc jockeys, and others involved in the production and distribution of bachata, asking them not only what they knew about bachata's history but how bachata functioned as a business, who controlled its production and distribution, and how it articulated with other commercially popular musics such as merengue and salsa.

I discovered certain places that were particularly favorable for encountering people involved in bachata, where I could elicit valuable information and opinions if I simply lingered long enough. One of my most fruitful "field sites" was the Avenida Duarte, which had street record vendors on practically every block. Busy as they were with shoppers stopping constantly at their stalls, these vendors were always willing to talk. As a bonus, I was able to observe what the customers bought, what they commented upon, and so on. Other useful sites were the recording studios, especially Estudios EMCA, which at the time was the studio most bachateros were using. There, I was not only able to find musicians who were normally difficult to locate (most lived in peripheral areas of the city and many had no telephones), but I was also able to observe them playing, although in a setting that was quite different from bachata's usual performance venues such as neighborhood clubs or bars. Recording sessions tended to be casual, with plenty of minor interruptions that gave me the opportunity to ask questions. Moreover, the constant electrical blackouts provided unexpected opportunities for lengthy conversations while everyone waited for the power to return. The other important site worthy of mention was the broadcast studio of Radio Guarachita, which had been expressly designed to accommodate visitors: the announcer's console was located on a platform within a *radioteatro* (radio theater) equipped with seating for audiences. I spent hours sitting in the radioteatro, asking the disc jockey questions while a record was on the air and taking advantage of the stream of Guarachita's obviously poor, low-class listeners who came into the studio to make requests or simply to observe the broadcast.

I did not concentrate in depth on any particular neighborhood or community; most of the people I talked to were dispersed all over the sprawling city of Santo Domingo, and most lived in shantytowns, slums, or poor working-class *barrios* (neighborhoods). These various types of neighborhoods are not alike. As Helen Safa notes, "Slums are usually located in the center of the city, close to the central business district, and consist of once adequate structures which have been converted from their original use to tenements housing many times their anticipated occupancy. Shanties, on the other hand, are from the outset inadequate structures; most are rather flimsily constructed with makeshift materials by unskilled labor provided by the owner and his friends. Thus, where slums are a form of blight or deterioration characteristic of highly industrialized cities, shantytowns are commonly found in the pre-industrial cities of developing areas where marginal public lands still exist on the urban fringe" (Safa 1974: 2). The houses in Santo Domingo's working-class barrios, on the other hand, are neither shanties nor converted structures, but cheaply built wood or concrete block houses, densely packed together. Compared to the shantytowns, working-class barrios are well integrated into the city's infrastructure, being connected to electricity, water, and other public works, although in some barrios these services are so irregular and the population density so high that conditions are not much better than in the shantytowns.

I spent the most time in a relatively new shantytown called Guaricano, located just outside Santo Domingo behind the principal garbage dump, also called Guaricano. This was by no means a proper community study, but the time I spent there gave me a basic understanding of the role of music in a Santo Domingo shantytown. Visits to other shantytowns and barrios—Zurza, Gualey, Villa Francisca, Villa Consuelo, La Fe—allowed me to compare conditions in the different types of neighborhoods; some, such as Villa Consuelo, were older and better integrated into the city, while others, such as Zurza, were somewhat newer, poorer, and less integrated. Guaricano, on the other hand, was the newest and poorest of these and provided the best view into a neighborhood whose residents were most clearly in transition from rural to urban life.

Finally, I interviewed a variety of educated and widely recognized intellectuals, who provided insight into how the country's cultural elites have viewed bachata in relationship to other popular musics. There were a number of (mostly amateur) Dominican music historians who may not have published anything on bachata, but whose opinions were useful additions to the material I was collecting from those working directly with bachata. I also interviewed a variety of social scientists with experience working with urban migrants; their insights confirmed—and on occasion contradicted—the conclusions I was developing from first-hand observation.

While most of my work was in Santo Domingo, the city from which most bachata is disseminated to the rest of the country, I also observed and interviewed people in diverse rural settings: in the southwest in San Juan de la Maguana, in the Cibao in Salcedo and Puerto Plata, and along the north coast in Las Terrenas, Samaná. Nevertheless, I emphasize that my research is heavily weighted in favor of bachata's urban Santo Domingo settings. I hope that future research will focus more on rural contexts, where bachata is just as popular as in the city.

Aside from the interviews, my most important source of information came from attending live bachata performances; however, at the time these were not at all easy to find in Santo Domingo. They were never advertised in the newspapers, on television, or on major radio stations. Radio Guarachita sometimes announced live performances by musicians who were under contract to the station owner's record label, Discos la Guarachita. In order to locate performances by non-Guarachita artists, I had to ask the musicians themselves to tell me when and where they were playing. The most frequent "musical events" that Santo Domingo's shantytown residents attended were not, however, live; instead, they depended on recorded music. Listening (and/or dancing) to music could be as informal as listening to a radio in a taxi or at the *colmado* (neighborhood store); or it could take place in small neighborhood *barras* (bars) or nightclubs; or at home, on radio or record players. I obtained a great deal of information on how bachata was perceived by its listeners and how listening to music articulated with other aspects of social life by frequenting colmados and barras and keeping my eyes and ears open.

The results of my field research on a music that at the time was largely confined within the poorest neighborhoods in Santo Domingo were influenced in large part by who I was and how people perceived me. My father is a native of Barranquilla, Colombia, where I spent my childhood, and where I have resided or visited intermittently over the past twenty years. Barranquilla, like other areas on the north coast of Colombia, is part of the Caribbean culturally as well as historically, economically, and demographically, so it was relatively easy for me to adjust and fit into Dominican culture. My identity was, of course, shaped as much by my extended residence in the United States, my mother's home country; but like other bicultural persons I enjoy a flexible cultural and national identity and am able to emphasize one culture/nationality over the other when I please, without being either a liar or an impostor. When doing fieldwork, I usually introduced myself as Colombian rather than as a *norteamericana*. Most Dominicans are fiercely nationalistic and may resent the United States for its constant interference in their internal affairs (as well as the affairs of their Latin American and Caribbean neighbors), but they seem to genuinely admire the United States culturally, so saying I was from the United States would not have caused me any major problems. But being fluent in Spanish and saying I was from Barranquilla, Colombia, identified me—to some extent, at least—as part of the Caribbean cultural family. This was an important advantage, because it counteracted several other conspicuous indicators of my foreignness: I enjoyed the much-envied privilege of being a citizen of a wealthy and powerful country, I had light skin, and because I owned expensive equipment, I was perceived as rich—and by comparison to most of the people I worked with, I suppose I was.

In addition, I was a single mother of two children, who at the time were ten and twelve. My two principal commitments—to the research and to the children—were often at odds with each other. On the one hand, the nature of my fieldwork demanded that I spend much of my time in the poorer sectors of Santo Domingo, sometimes late at night to attend performances. On the other hand, I did not feel it was fair to impose the hardships of living in a working-class neighborhood on my children, who were in the Dominican Republic through no choice of their own, and particularly because no matter where I lived I would be out of the house for long periods of time. I myself had lived on a shoestring and traveled in all sorts of conditions in Colombia when I was still married to my children's Colombian father, so I understood the sort of physical difficulties and cultural dislocation such a decision could inflict on them. Knowing I couldn't be around to mediate their adjustment to such conditions, I rented a comfortable apartment in a bourgeois section of Santo Domingo and enrolled the children in Dominican private schools. In order to move back and forth between my home and my field sites at any time of day or night, I invested in a battered old four-wheel-drive Daihatsu and drove to where I needed to go. This mobility bridged at least the physical distance between home and field sites.

What this arrangement meant, however, was that I never fully shared the living conditions of the people I was working with: I spent long hours in barrios, but I always returned home to a comfortable apartment and all the amenities Dominican middle-class life has to offer. This is, of course, a painful confession for an anthropologist to make, because part of what we are supposed to do is live among those we are trying to understand, and I myself had previously regarded researchers who did not do so with some contempt. Looking for the silver lining, however, I believe that living among middle-class Dominicans and working among lower-class Dominicans gave me a better understanding of the social and cultural extremes characterizing Dominican society, many of which are expressed in the relationship between merengue and bachata. Certain characteristics of barrio culture would perhaps not have seemed as salient if I had not known what middle-class Dominican life was like as well.

Just to give one example, one of the most distinctive features of barrio life is the ubiquity of sound—all kinds of sound. Because houses tend to be small and cramped, people spend much of their waking time on the street. Some are at leisure: children playing baseball with sticks and empty milk cartons, men playing dominoes, women combing and styling each others' hair. Others are at work: ambulatory vendors calling their wares, women selling fried food cooked on small charcoal stoves to passers-by, shoemakers exercising their trade on the sidewalks, mechanics working under cars parked next to the curb. Behind all the sounds produced by these activities, music—originating either from portable radios or record players—can almost always be heard emanating from houses or cars or from the ubiquitous colmados. Often several of these sound sources compete with each other at the same time, creating a veritable cacophony, but no one seems to mind: sound, after all, is vibration, and vibration is movement, and movement is life.

Bourgeois neighborhoods, on the contrary, are quiet, very quiet. There are far fewer colmados than in the barrio, and these keep their radios discreetly lowered. Houses are spaced farther apart, separated from one another by iron fences whose doors are guarded by uniformed and armed *guachimanes*—"Spanglish" for watchmen. Children sometimes play in the street, but usually under the watchful eyes of nursemaids. A few ambulatory vendors go by, but middle-class Dominicans are suspicious of allowing strangers into their homes, so most tend to shop in Santo Domingo's modern supermarkets instead. The music that sometimes drifts from houses and apartments tends to be rock music and orquesta merengue. In these neighborhoods, loud sounds indicate vulgarity, while silence indicates refined culture and social distinction. Clearly, both unorganized sound (street sounds) and organized sound (music) have different meanings to different classes.

Being a single woman was probably my most conspicuous feature, and it worked both as an advantage and as a disadvantage. On one hand, almost all of the persons involved in the music industry were men, who could not quite figure out how to relate to a foreign, single white woman conducting interviews about the disreputable bachata. They were always courteous, however, as required by custom; on the other hand, sometimes they did not take me seriously and hesitated to converse with me on a one-to-one basis. It often took repeated visits before I could engage in the kind of conversation useful to my research. This tendency to keep me at a distance, however, was more characteristic of urban professional types than it was of people of rural origins.

More delicate was the problem of dealing with the subtle sexual tensions between men and women in the Dominican Republic, where cross-gender friendships are not common; women can perhaps be superior socio-economically, or can be perceived as inferior sexually, but they are seldom equals. Being white and foreign placed me immediately in the "superior" category socio-economically, and I was treated with a certain deference and distance. However, being single rendered me "inferior" because, not having the protection of a man, I was considered exposed to their sexual superiority. (Men almost always asked if I was married, and against the advice of a colleague who suggested I wear a wedding ring, I always admitted to being divorced.) Most men did not actually make propositions, but more often than not, as I talked with them, there was a subtle (and sometimes not so subtle) undercurrent of psychic probing, as I became the object of their sexual scrutiny and appraisal. Thus I had to balance my informants' simultaneous tendencies—to distance and to intrude—in order to establish a dialogue and avoid being trapped by interactions dictated by traditional Dominican sexual politics.

Most of my research, such as interviewing musicians, street record vendors, record promoters, and so on, took place by day, and I was able to work alone without incident. It would have been extremely difficult, if not dangerous, however, to go by myself to live performances of bachata, which, at least in the capital city of Santo Domingo, took place only in cabarets and bars where it was essential to be accompanied by a man. Some of these establishments lacked most of the amenities typical of an urban nightclub but were not disreputable; they were simply modest neighborhood clubs patronized by local residents. Others, however, were in fact brothels, in which there could be no conceivable justification for the presence of a single woman attending a performance just to hear the music. Fortunately I had the companionship of my friend Juan Valoy, which provided me the opportunity to attend live performances. Because of our shared interests in popular culture and music, he accompanied me to bars and nightclubs, and we spent many pleasant evenings and Sunday afternoons drinking beer, listening to music, and talking to musicians. (Although I was again reminded, as I gingerly waded into the less than hygienic "ladies' rooms," that not all fieldwork in the Caribbean is particularly agreeable.)

Because bachata was so thoroughly rejected and stigmatized by mainstream Dominican society, I entitled my dissertation "Music of Marginality: Social Identity and Class in Dominican Bachata." Less than five years later, however, Juan Luis Guerra, a well-respected musician known for his sophisticated merengue arrangements, released a recording entitled *Bachata rosa*, whose worldwide success swept aside the barriers that had kept bachata out of the musical mainstream. Today, bachata is a socially acceptable, even trendy genre of music. Nevertheless, it would be a mistake and a disservice to bachata's originators to focus too much attention on Guerra, who, in historical terms, is a Johnny-come-lately to bachata's long and difficult trajectory, as well as an outsider who never shared the experience of poverty and desperation that nourished the genre. Therefore, while this introduction must properly acknowledge the largely positive impact that Guerra and other Dominican musicians producing modernized versions of bachata known as *tecno-bachata* have had upon the genre, this book was designed to explore the music created by street-level bachateros, who, since the 1960s, have resisted the efforts of a hostile society to prevent their music from being heard beyond the confines of the shantytown.

As a result of the profound changes that have taken place in bachata's status since the release of *Bachata rosa* in 1991, the point of reference from which I approached the subject in 1989 is now obsolete. Bachata's change in fortune does not, of course, change the validity of my observations in 1987, but it has forced me to reframe many of my arguments. I must acknowledge the likelihood that now, unlike the situation in 1989, many of my readers have already heard about bachata, even though they might not know what bachata is or where it comes from. I can no longer describe bachata as a socially despised outlaw genre, and I had to change the title of the book. I also had to extensively revise my definitions. In many cases, things changed so completely that in certain descriptive passages I had to change all the verbs from the present to the past tense; for example, in 1989 I discussed bachata dissemination in terms of records because bachata circulated mostly as vinyl 45 RPMs; now, vinyl records have been completely discontinued and bachata is being released only on cassettes and CDs. Finally I had to add an additional chapter, based on a field trip I took to the Dominican Republic in early 1994, in order to bring the book up to date and to analyze the profound changes that occurred since I last visited the Dominican Republic in 1988.

In spite of all these necessary changes, the book still reflects my original conviction that bachata is historically situated and economically generated and that sense and meaning can be discerned in the changing relationships between the Dominican Republic's various social classes and the country's popular music system, in which bachata has been only one of many possible musical choices. Nevertheless, while I offer a variety of social and economic reasons for bachata's popularity among the country's poorest citizens, I want to insist that ultimately it has survived and flourished because it gives its listeners that which music is best at giving—physical, emotional and psychic pleasure.

Bachata

DOMINICAN REPUBLIC

ATLANTIC OCEAN

CARIBBEAN SEA

HAITI

SANTO DOMINGO

Monte
Cristi

Dajabon

Mao

Sabaneta

Puerto
Plata

Santiago

Moca

Salcedo

San Francisco
de Macoris

Nagua

Samana

La Vega

Cotui

Monte
Plata

Bonao

Hato Mayor

El Seybo

Higuey

San Pedro
de Macoris

La Romana

Comendador

San Juan

Enriquillo Lake

Azua

San
Cristobal

Bani

Jimani

Neyba

Barahona

Pedernales

LEGEND

⊠ Cities

■ Capital

Map by René Ledesma

Chapter One

*D*efining Bachata

*U*ntil recently, bachata was a musical pariah in its country of origin, the Dominican Republic. Since its emergence in the early 1960s, bachata, closely associated with poor rural migrants residing in urban shantytowns, was considered too crude, too vulgar, and too musically rustic to be allowed entrance into the mainstream musical landscape. As recently as 1988, no matter how many copies a bachata record may have sold—and some bachata hits sold far more than most records by socially acceptable merengue orquestas—no bachata record ever appeared on a published hit parade list, received airplay on FM radio stations in the country's capital, Santo Domingo, or were sold in the principal record stores. Bachata musicians appeared only rarely on television, and they performed only in working-class clubs in the capital. In contrast, even second rate merengue orquestas were given lavish publicity and promotion, and they entertained at posh private clubs and nightclubs.

Now, only a few years later, the previously stigmatized bachata has been embraced by all classes of Dominican society, to the extent that trend-conscious musicians of all stripes are rushing to record in the now commercially viable bachata idiom. Bachata musicians now appear almost daily on the popular noon-hour television variety shows. Bachata records are included in the programming of major Santo Domingo FM stations and can be purchased in the city's best music stores. Favorably disposed essays and commentaries on bachata and bachata musicians are being published at an ever-growing rate by the country's leading newspapers. Outside the country, bachata has become practically a household word throughout Latin America, and even in the United States and Europe, anyone who follows Latin American music even casually is likely to have heard about Dominican bachata. Dominicans, once appalled at the rudeness and vulgarity of bachata, are now surprised—and proud—to see that bachata has acquired an international profile, bringing the music of the Dominican Republic to the attention of worldwide audiences.

Almost by definition, popular music undergoes constant change, as musicians, songs, and musical styles appear in the mass-mediated public arena and then recede from view just as quickly when consumers embrace the next musical innovation. Changes in the social status and mass dissemination of genres rooted in the musical practices of the poor, however, always reflect transformations in the larger social context, although they are usually launched by individuals who are able to successfully translate these class-bound musics to broader mass audiences by providing them with a veneer of social respectability. In the United States, for example, rhythm-and-blues music was generally confined within the African-American community until a young white southerner named Elvis Presley introduced it to white audiences in the mid-1950s. In the Dominican Republic, it was a talented young musician named Juan Luis Guerra who was responsible for taking bachata out of obscurity and introducing it to diverse audiences both in the Dominican Republic and abroad. In 1991 Guerra and his vocal group 4:40 released a recording entitled *Bachata rosa* (KCD-136/BMG 3230), which has been one of the most successful recordings in the recent history of Latin music, selling over 3.5 million copies worldwide and winning a Grammy in the Latin Tropical category in 1992. This recording single-handedly brought the lowly and despised bachata to the attention of Latin music fans worldwide and endowed it with respectability in its country of origin.

The resemblance between the accomplishments of Presley and Guerra, however, is only superficial. Elvis Presley may not have been black, but he was poor and southern, and to some extent he shared the same cultural milieu of rhythm and blues' African-American originators. Guerra, by contrast, was far removed from the social and material realities of the desperately poor bachateros, whose musical style he interpreted. His background is solidly middle class: his mother was a lawyer, his father a civil servant, and his friends and relatives were all from the more comfortable layers of Dominican society. He studied music at the National Conservatory and later received advanced musical training at Boston's Berklee College of Music (Tejeda 1993). His 1985 album *Mudanza y acarreo*, which contained complex and sophisticated interpretations of a variety of Dominican regional musics, had established him as one of the country's most accomplished musicians. Indeed, when he released *Bachata rosa* in 1991, some Dominicans were scandalized that such a talented and promising musician was dabbling in the disreputable bachata.

Prior to 1991, bachata had been characterized by an acoustic guitar-centered ensemble, with percussion provided by bongo drums and maracas. Its lyrics were typically concerned with love in all its various manifestations, were expressed in vernacular language, and often utilized bawdy double entendres. It was sung in an unpolished, over-emotional, almost sobbing style. Bachata recordings lacked sophisticated production, and they were marketed through an informal promotion and distribution system that overlapped but was distinct from the promotion and distribution system of other popular musics such as merengue, balada, salsa, and rock. One of bachata's most notable characteristics was extra-musical: the low social status of both musicians and audience, who were either campesinos or urban migrants of rural origins, and the extent to which it was rejected and marginalized by Dominican "polite society" and the music industry that catered to them.

It was precisely because of bachata's low social status that Guerra's experiments with the bachata genre in *Bachata rosa* made such an impact on the Dominican musical landscape. Guerra was not the first Dominican musician of his social class to experiment with the previously despised bachata idiom: avant-garde musicians Sonia Silvestre and Luis Dias[1] had released a handful of sophisticated bachatas called tecno-bachatas in the late 1980s with moderate success within the country. It was the success of *Bachata rosa*, however, that firmly established bachata's social acceptability and encouraged Dominican mainstream musicians to begin dabbling in bachata—although in sophisticated "tecno" versions.

Of the ten songs in Guerra's album, four were considered bachatas: the title song "Bachata rosa," "Burbujas de amor" (Bubbles of love), "Estrellitas y duendes" (Little stars and fairies), and "Como abeja al panal" (As a bee to the hive). These songs were categorized as bachatas because they were played with the typical bachata instrumentation of guitar, maracas, and bongos—although the arrangements were enhanced by synthesizers—and Guerra sang the romantic lyrics with the heightened emotion typical of bachata singers. The lyrics of "Burbujas de amor" also relied on the sexual double entendre favored by street-level bachateros—although in this song, the imagery of a man longing to immerse himself in a fish tank (i.e., a woman's body) did not reflect particularly well the impoverished material world of shantytown dwellers, where home furnishings were unlikely to include a fish tank. In fact, Guerra's elegant, urbane compositions were far removed from the stark simplicity of bachatas by street-level musicians like Tony Santos and Blas Durán, whose lyrics were devoid of sophisticated musical embellishments and poetic imagery; this, of course, is what made Guerra's bachatas so appealing to middle-class audiences.

Bachata rosa's success certainly gave bachata a new social respectability; nevertheless, Guerra and other *tecno-bachateros* like Dias and Silvestre were not solely responsible for its success. While the country's cultural establishment may not have been paying attention to bachata prior to *Bachata rosa*, stylistic changes that had been developing at the grass-roots level were being well received by a younger generation of Dominicans attracted by bachata's earthy vitality. Today, bachata is still defined primarily by the guitar-centered ensemble, but younger bachata musicians have switched from acoustic to electric guitars, incorporated the electric bass and synthesizers, and are using sophisticated mixers to improve the sound of their music. Bachata songs have increased considerably in tempo and are now far more lively and danceable than a decade ago, and, moreover, bachata ensembles are playing guitar-based merengues that are competing successfully with merengue orquestas.

As a result of these changes, bachata now includes several style variants, a more socially diverse group of musicians, and occupies a broader range of commercial and social contexts, which have made bachata much more difficult to define than even a decade ago. Why, for example, were Guerra's songs categorized as bachatas if they sounded so different from the music of bachateros such as Durán or Santos? How do we account for the fact that one bachata song sounds like a Mexican *ranchera*, another like a *bolero*, another like Puerto Rican *jíbaro* music, while another is clearly a merengue? What does all music called bachata have in common?

Answering these questions is no small task. A broad set of features, such as the guitar-based ensemble, helps us to begin describing bachata; but there seem to be no deeper configurations, such as a particular rhythmic signature, that clearly and unequivocally distinguishes bachata from other similar forms of guitar-based music. In terms of style, bachata has only recently been recognized as a genre distinct from the antecedent genres out of which it grew; and there has been some disagreement as to what bachata's essential characteristics are: whether they are musical (e.g., rhythmic patterns, instrumentation, singing style), or, as some (including myself) have claimed, extra-musical as well (e.g., the music's social context, the language and content of lyrics, or the social status of the musicians). In this chapter, I will address these stylistic questions by first exploring bachata's musical and social origins and then describing the range of characteristics that contribute to making a bachata a bachata.

Musical and Social Antecedents

The Dominican Republic is a small country—its population of 6.5 million inhabitants occupies approximately three-quarters (48,464 square kilometers) of the island of Hispaniola, which it shares with Haiti. Its economy has long been primarily agricultural, although this has changed rapidly in the past decade as a result of free-trade zones established in response to the Caribbean Basin Initiative and a rapidly expanding tourist industry. For years economic development was hampered both by constant interference from the United States and by internal political divisions and corruption, and the thirty-one-year Trujillo dictatorship (1930–61) further isolated the country from developments occurring in the rest of the region. Today it has a relatively low economic and political profile on the international stage, particularly when compared to its mainland Latin American neighbors such as Mexico.

The music that today is called bachata emerged from and belongs to a long-standing Pan–Latin American tradition of guitar music, *música de guitarra*, which was typically played by trios or quartets comprised of one or two guitars (or other related stringed instrument such as the smaller *requinto*), with percussion provided by maracas and/or other instruments such as *claves* (hardwood sticks used for percussion), bongo drums, or a gourd *güiro* scraper. Sometimes a large thumb bass called marimba or marimbula was included as well. When bachata emerged in the early 1960s, it was part of an important subcategory of guitar music, romantic guitar music—as distinguished from guitar music intended primarily for dancing such as the Cuban *son* or *guaracha*—although in later decades, as musicians began speeding up the rhythm and dancers developed a new dance step, bachata began to be considered dance music as well. The most popular and widespread genre of romantic guitar music in this century, and the most influential for the development of bachata, was the Cuban bolero (not to be confused with the unrelated Spanish bolero). Bachata musicians, however, also drew upon other genres of música de guitarra that accomplished guitarists would be familiar with, including Mexican *rancheras* and *corridos*, Cuban *son*, *guaracha*, and *guajira*, Puerto Rican *plena* and *jíbaro* music, and the Colombian-Ecuadorian *vals campesino* and *pasillo*—as well as the Dominican *merengue*, which was originally guitar-based.

The Cuban bolero developed in the nineteenth century out of previously existing genres such as the *danzón* and the *contradanza*, from which it received its characteristic four-four time (Rico Salazar 1988: 15–18). In the late nineteenth century a wave of Cubans fleeing the Wars of Independence (1895–98) migrated to the Dominican Republic, particularly the Cibao region (Castillo 1979), where they introduced Cuban music—the guaracha, rumba, and, of particular relevance to this study, son and bolero. The renowned Cuban musician Sindo Garay, for example, who specialized in boleros, immigrated temporarily to the Puerto Plata region, befriending and playing together with Danda Lockward, a well known early twentieth-century Dominican guitarist (Juan Lockward, interview). Lockward and other Dominican musicians like him adopted the bolero form but composed their own versions, leading Dominican musicologist Bernarda Jorge to insist that while the Dominican bolero owes a debt to Cuba, its development within the country has endowed it with Dominican qualities: "Overlying the often noted musical models from abroad, some autochthonous genres of sentimental character make their appearance. The bolero, the work of popular [i.e., from the popular classes] troubadours who spontaneously created verses and music, flourished in the first two decades [of the century]" (Jorge 1982a: 93–94, translation mine). Most of these early Dominican *boleristas*, like the bachateros who followed them decades later, were of humble rural origins and played *de oído* (by ear); Lockward, for example, a shoemaker by profession, played by ear, as did Chepe Bedú, another contemporary of Lockward and Garay who composed simplified versions of the Cuban bolero (Jorge 1982a: 94).

In the early twentieth century the Cuban bolero spread all over Latin America, where it was typically played by guitar-based duos, trios, and quartets. Over the course of the thirties, forties, and fifties, however, the Cuban bolero was elaborated into what John Storm Roberts (1985: 23) calls an "international Latin" style, orchestrated with pianos and stringed and wind instruments, over time bearing less and less resemblance to its guitar-based antecedents. Although both the acoustic and the international styles of bolero continued to share the same name, the social context of the international style bolero—the elegant salon or night club—was very different from the mostly rural context of the traditional guitar-based versions. The bolero reached the height of its international popularity during the 1950s (Pérez Sanjurjo 1986; Galán 1983), just prior to the time when bachata began to emerge as a distinct genre in the Dominican Republic. The precursor of bachata, however, was not the international style of bolero, but rather the original bolero played by guitar trios or quartets comprised of one or two guitars, bongos, and maracas.

The Cuban bolero also took root in Mexico, where it developed into two styles: the more international variety was called *romántico*, danceable tunes played in the urban music hall; the *bolero ranchero*, on the other hand, was typically played by mariachi conjuntos, was sung only, and was associated with the rural segments of the population (Kahl 1980). One of the most famous interpreters of the Mexican style of bolero was the Trío los Panchos, who played boleros rancheros in the early stages of their career but later adopted the more international style of bolero (Roberts 1985: 23). Los Panchos' boleros rancheros greatly influenced the generation of rural guitar musicians who pioneered the bachata genre.

The Cuban son was also a staple in the repertoires of the guitar-based ensembles out of which bachata emerged. A hybrid of Afro-Cuban and rural Hispanic-derived genres, the son is said to have first appeared in eastern Cuba in the late nineteenth century (Manuel 1988: 30). It was introduced to the Dominican Republic at the same time as the bolero, and it has since been kept alive and active both by the trios and quartets who play all sorts of música de guitarra, as well as by groups specializing in son; many of the latter are still found in the Cibao region as well as in certain municipalities in the south such as Villa Mella and San Pedro de Macorís. The instrumentation used for playing son consisted of stringed instruments (either the guitar, the mandolin-like *laúd*, or the *tres*, a type of guitar with three single or double courses of strings) and percussion instruments, most typically bongo drums, claves, maracas, and the marimbula (or marimba) (Manuel 1988: 30; see also Díaz Ayala 1981; Boggs 1992). With the exception of the tres, the instruments used for playing son were the same used for playing boleros and the other guitar-based musics mentioned above; later, the same instrumentation would be used in bachata ensembles as well. The son influence on bachata was not nearly as significant as the bolero's—at least until the 1980s, when bachata musicians began incorporating the livelier son rhythm into their compositions to make them more danceable.

Before the development of a Dominican recording industry and the spread of the mass media, guitar-based trios and quartets were almost indispensable for a variety of informal recreational events such as Sunday afternoon parties known as *pasadías* and spontaneous gatherings that took place in back yards, living rooms, or in the street that were known as *bachatas*. Dictionaries of Latin American Spanish define the term *bachata* as *juerga, jolgorio,* or *parranda,* all of which denote fun, merriment, a good time, or a spree; but in the Dominican Republic, in addition to the emotional quality of fun and enjoyment suggested by the dictionary definition, it referred specifically to get-togethers that included music, drink, and food. The musicians who played at bachatas were usually local, friends and neighbors of the host, although sometimes reputed musicians from farther away might be brought in for a special occasion. Musicians were normally recompensed only with food and drink, but a little money might be given as well. Parties were usually held on Saturday night and would go on until dawn, at which time a traditional soup, the *sancocho,* was served to the remaining guests. Because the music played at these gatherings was so often played on guitars (although accordion-based ensembles were also common), the guitar-based music recorded in the 1960s and 1970s by musicians of rural origins came to be known as bachata.

The following passage, written in 1927 by the Dominican folklorist Julio Arzeno (1892–1932), provides us with a rare description of a rural bachata:

> On Saturday, or the last day of the week, when night falls, our popular troubadour requires only a guitar, a tambourine, and the indis-

pensable maracas to enjoy himself with the dance and improvised party called BACHATA, where commentary on all happenings is king and ruler, using for it an extemporized bolero; and not only for the sheer pleasure of singing about a momentary passion or easy romantic conquest, but any current event or incident, will cause him to become absorbed in the mute poetry of plastic beauty: the dance that he loves with delirium, with devotional worship, and poetic love. . . . They practice this art empirically, without knowledge of theory; they learn by memory the various pieces that are in fashion, with which they construct their repertoire, but they also improvise lovely songs. . . . When they don't know the bolero or the guaracha, they sing and dance musics with a rough and romantic flavor, although with tranquil grace, whose lyrics allude always to some anecdote or popularly known event, repeating at length and insistently their insubstantial and unconnected couplets that for their simplicity become epigrammatic. . . . The jocular tone adds animation and charm to these wholesome gatherings of popular celebration, because the improvisation makes fun of everything. The important thing for them is to rhyme while dancing, although childishly. (Arzeno 1927: 102–3, translation mine)

The word *bachata* also had certain class associations; upper-class parties would never be called bachatas. In his book *Al amor del bohío* (1927), Ramón Emilio Jiménez, a distinguished Dominican "man of letters" and "writer of manners," described a bachata in terms that reflect how such gatherings were associated by the elite with low-class debauchery and dissipation:

The "bachata" is a center of attraction for all the men, where the social classes of those who attend them are leveled and where the coarsest and libertarian forms of democracy predominate. The most elegant figures of the barrio are there, daring and audacious. The setting of these dissolute pleasures is a small living room impregnated by odors that seem conjured to challenge decency. . . . In an adjoining room a guitarist plucks and unleashes into the contaminated air of the house [a] blazing street-level couplet, to which a singer with a well-established reputation as a "second" makes a duo, provisioned with a pair of spoons which he strikes to accompany the melody. (Jiménez 1927: 216–17, translation mine)

There has been considerable debate about whether the term *bachata* also referred to a specific dance or type of music that took place at these gatherings. Arístides Incháustegui notes that the Cuban musicologist Odilio Urfé affirmed that around the turn of the nineteenth century "the theatrical guaracha then cultivated in Santiago de Cuba was called bachata, which seems to indicate that in the Dominican Republic as well as in Cuba this term has in some ways served to refer not only to a festive environment, but also to a certain type of music interpreted in it" (Incháustegui 1990: 16, translation mine). Incháustegui offers as evidence for this theory an interview with Dominican composer Julio Alberto Hernández (b. 1900), who recollected that at bachatas "a cheerful and danceable music was played, invented mostly on the run by popular musicians at parties in the barrios, and . . . once he saw some scores of guarachas composed by Julio Acosta from La Vega, at the end of the last century, that had all the characteristics of the rhythms of the bachateros" (Incháustegui 1990: 16, translation mine). Hernández went on to speculate, "Before, they preferred to call guarachas what were really bachatas, to avoid the use of the latter term, which was considered in poor taste by people from high society" (ibid).

Dominican anthropologist Marcio Veloz Maggiolo, on the other hand, insists otherwise: "Bachata was never a musical genre. In our youthful years bachata was a street party, a reunion of musicians who sang between drinks and jokes, while in the midst of the gathering dancing happened on its own. . . . In a bachata, music appears as an accompaniment and never was the music itself called 'bachata' " (Veloz Maggiolo 1991: 7, translation mine). Journalist and music critic Juan Antonio Cruz Triffolio also states emphatically that bachata is a lively party but was never a musical genre (1987 and 1991). He cites Fernando Ortiz's *Nuevo cantauro de cubanismos* (1974), which suggests that the word *bachata* may be derived from the African words *cumbancha* and *cumbanchata* (both derived from *cumbé*) and contracted later to *bachata* and even *bacha*, all with the same meanings: orgy, spree, binge, chaotic and noisy merrymaking (Cruz Triffolio 1991). Even Incháustegui, in spite of his meticulously researched evidence that bachata may have been a musical genre, admits, "In any case, for many years, *haciendo una bachata* (making a bachata) in this country has meant getting together in private, generally poor, locations, with improvisational musicians: players of guitars, tambourines, maracas, marimbas (marimbulas) with steel tongues, and claves, sometimes substituted by striking spoons, and where spontaneity was the common denominator of these parties" (Incháustegui 1990: 16, translation mine).

The kind of music played at a bachata depended on whether the ensemble present was accordion- or guitar-based. Accordion-based ensembles—typically consisting of an accordion, güira, tambora, and sometimes a marimbula—were appropriate for certain genres of music, particularly the popular Dominican merengue and other genres such as *mangulina, carabiné,* and *priprí,* all of which were dance musics; they were not, however, well suited for interpreting romantic music. In contrast, guitar ensembles could interpret not only dance musics such as merengue and the Cuban son or guaracha, but also romantic music intended for listening or singing along, such as boleros and the Dominican *criolla,* a music similar to the bolero, but rhythmically distinct.[2]

Indeed, guitars were indispensable for playing romantic music. In the Dominican Republic, as in other Latin American countries, the tradition of romantic poetry expressed musically was inherited from its Spanish colonizers, for whom romantic song was an important component of courtship. Two forms of romantic musical expression, originating in Spain, influenced bachata musicians: the *décima* and the serenade. The décima is a verse form characterized by ten octosyllabic lines, with a number of possible traditional rhyming patterns. Décimas, which could express any sort of commentary, have been categorized into four principal groups according to subject matter: *en amor*—about love; *en queja*—complaints; *a lo divino*—supplication to the divine; and *en desprecio*—disparagement (Coopersmith 1949: 45). The décimas of love and supplication were used most in courtship and other romantic contexts and musical expressions such as the serenade. Décimas falling within the category of complaints and disparagement, however, were used to vent the less than romantic feelings that occur when love is frustrated. Décimas could be improvised or traditional, soliloquies or repartees, and they could be recited by both men and women (Valverde 1975: 79–83). While décimas need not be set to music, this widely known verse form provided rural composers with a universally understood rhythmic structure on which to base a wide range of commentary; even today, many bachata lyrics have verse structures similar to the classic décimas.

While the serenade, a particular form of musical performance used in courtship, was known throughout the country, it was practiced most frequently in the Cibao region, where both Spanish and Cuban influences were strongest. The music played by serenaders had to be as romantic and poetic as possible. The quintessentially romantic bolero was the favored music for these occasions, although other music such as a lyrical criolla or a sentimental tango might also be chosen; lively, danceable guitar music such as son or guaracha was, obviously, inappropriate for a midnight serenade. One elderly Dominican of rural origins recalled his youthful serenades as follows:

> Here the custom was to serenade with the guitar. Sometimes when we gave a serenade we would have quite a scare, because the parents would get up and they didn't want us to serenade the girl, because they found that wrong. One day a man got up—his name was Chalín—and he threw himself on us and cut our guitars into a thousand pieces; later he paid us for them. I had a lot of scares. Once they threw urine [from chamber pots] at us through the cracks and it fell into our eyes, because the parents didn't want the girls to get married, or if they were to marry they wanted it to be according to their wishes. In those days one used the guitar and records, because one couldn't talk to the girls. With the guitar one could sing them the record. Then the guitar would speak. (Ramón Alejo, interview)

In the largely oral culture of the Dominican countryside, the ability to play the guitar and sing well was highly valued, providing considerable motivation for young men to learn to play it. First, it provided a man with another tool in his array of strategies with which to court and win the attentions of young women. If he became skilled at playing, he would be called upon to play at bachatas, pasadías, and other social events at which, in addition to the appreciation and respect of the community, he would receive all the food and drink he desired. A further incentive was that the guitar was accessible to persons of slender means: unlike accordions, which were imported and quite costly, almost anyone could acquire a guitar, which could be homemade using local wood. Moreover, there were plenty of people with at least minimal skills available to teach a young man the basic techniques of guitar playing. The guitar, then, became the rural musician's instrument of choice. Most rural musicians could neither write nor read music, but favorite pieces of music were handed down orally. If they had the ability, rural guitar players also composed their own songs; if not, they could learn new songs, as Ramón Alejo mentioned above, from records heard on the radio or on juke-boxes—most of which were popular recordings imported from Cuba, Mexico, Puerto Rico, and Colombia. Over time, these guitar-based songs, whether old favorites, new ones, or songs learned from current recordings, became part of a diverse repertoire of guitar-based music shared by rural musicians.

In the early 1960s, thousands of peasants began migrating into the cities, primarily the capital, Santo Domingo, where most of them could find work only in such unskilled, low-status, and low-paying occupations as street vendors, maids, and security guards. Unable to afford proper housing, most of them squatted on vacant lands, resulting in a proliferation of shantytowns around the edges of the city. While forced to adapt to their new urban environment, the migrants' musical and social practices remained firmly rooted in rural traditions. Thus, when rural musicians began to record their own compositions in the early 1960s, their songs were almost indistinguishable from the familiar guitar-based musics that had inspired them—especially the long-popular bolero, but also guarachas, guajiras, rancheras, jíbaro music, vals, son, and the other genres mentioned above—and had long been listened to at rural social gatherings.

The guitar music recorded by musicians of rural origins in the early 1960s did not have a distinct name: it was sometimes referred to as bolero, or *bolero campesino* (country-style bolero), but more commonly, simply *música popular*. Their first recordings were perceived by the middle and upper classes, however, as little more than crude imitations of the stylish Cuban bolero by ignorant peasants who could not do any better. Indeed, these early recordings exhibited few of the features considered prestigious by a society that was rapidly urbanizing and modernizing, such as written arrangements, formally trained musicians, or high-status instruments such as saxophones or violins. As a result, it was disparagingly nicknamed *música cachivache* (lit., bauble, knickknack), a term marking the music as trivial and insignificant, and *música de guardia* (lit., guard's music). The latter term had originated during the dictatorship of Rafael Trujillo (1930–61) and was intended to invoke an image of low-rank soldiers in bars and brothels listening to low-quality guitar music—particularly musics like Mexican rancheras and corridos that extolled drinking, womanizing, and *machismo* (the glorification of male sexual prowess) (Rivera Payano 1983: 42). Two other derogatory names were also used for the guitar-based music played by rural musicians: *música cuaba* and *música de guardia cobrao*, the latter being a variation on música de guardia (Cruz Triffolio 1991): the term, which literally means "music of just-paid guards," elaborated on the image of policemen and guards by suggesting that on payday they were more likely to engage in vulgar and licentious behavior. These terms referred to music that was unschooled and rough in quality, however, not to a specific musical genre.

Among Dominicans there is considerable disagreement as to exactly when the term *bachata* came to refer to a particular kind of music. In the absence of any systematic research into the subject, there is a tendency for people to rely on their own memories, which vary according to their age, class, and where they grew up. According to bachata musicians themselves (and I prefer to accept their opinion), it was in the 1970s that the guitar-based music they recorded came to be identified by the term *bachata*, which by then had lost its more neutral connotation of an informal (if rowdy) backyard party and acquired an unmistakably negative cultural value implying rural backwardness and vulgarity. For example, on hearing one of these recordings, a middle- or upper-class person might say something like "¡Quítate esa bachata!" (Take that bachata off!). By using the term in this way, a style of guitar music made by poor rural musicians came to be synonymous with low quality. The condemnation fell not only upon the music and its performers, but upon its listeners as well; the term *bachatero*, used for anyone who liked the music as well as for the musicians, was equally derogatory.

In the late 1970s and 1980s, the worsening social and economic conditions of bachata's urban and rural poor constituency were clearly reflected in bachata. The instrumentation remained the same, but the tempo had become noticeably faster, and the formerly ultra-romantic lyrics inspired by the bolero became more and more concerned with drinking, womanizing, and male braggadocio; and increasingly, it began to express *desprecio* (disparagement) toward women. As bachata's popularity with the country's poorest citizens grew, the term *bachata*, which earlier had suggested rural backwardness and low social status, became loaded with a more complicated set of socially unacceptable features that included illicit sex, violence, heavy alcohol use, and disreputable social contexts such as seedy bars and brothels.

The naming of the guitar-based music recorded by musicians of rural origins as *bachata* presents an interesting contrast to the naming of emergent musics elsewhere. Charles Keil, for example, noted that when blues and polka styles began to emerge as distinct styles from a pool of earlier twentieth-century musical styles, "the very naming of musics as 'blues' or 'polka' is a declaration of consolidation" (Keil 1985: 126). Christopher Waterman came to the same conclusions when observing the emergence and naming of new twentieth-century African musics such as *highlife, juju, soukous* (Waterman 1990: 8). While bachata was indeed being consolidated as a style in the 1970s, in this instance the music was named not by bachata musicians or fans themselves, nor even by music industry people seeking marketing terms, but by the country's middle and upper classes, whose intentions were not to acknowledge a new style of music, but to trivialize and stigmatize it. Indeed, the naming was done quite against the will of bachata musicians themselves, who were well aware of how the name bachata was being used. Luis Segura, for example, noted: "Here people call it bachata, but I don't know what they want to imply with that. Because for me they are not bachatas, but a music that I consider is ours, what we call romantic bolero. I don't know why they give it that name here, because I never call it bachata, but romantic song" (interview). Leonardo Paniagua also believed his music was bolero, and denied that a music called bachata even existed: "Here people call the music that we play bachata. I do not acknowledge that. I haven't seen that word in any book, that this music is bachata. It doesn't exist. I would tell you not to put that word into practice" (interview).

By the 1980s, however, most bachata had increased its tempo so much and its lyrics had become so bawdy and raunchy, that it was clearly inappropriate to categorize it with the quintessentially romantic and poetic bolero, the protestations of Segura notwithstanding. Furthermore, the bolero's context had always been genteel, more traditional and refined—the salon, the informal family gathering, the serenade. Bachata's context, on the other hand—even the romantic music of Segura and Paniagua—was more likely to be bars or brothels in urban shantytowns. Bachata had clearly evolved into a distinctive style of music, and it needed a new name. Most bachateros understood this and accepted the term, if reluctantly, in the absence of anything better. Poor and working-class Dominicans also added the term *bachata* to their vocabulary and referred even to the widely admired Segura and Paniagua—with the greatest respect—, , bachateros, not as boleristas or baladistas.

In the early 1980s a few bachata musicians, especially those whose music was of the more romantic variety, made an effort to distance themselves from the negative images associated with the term *bachata* by coming up with a new name. They began referring to their music as *música de amargue* (music of bitterness), thereby emphasizing the feelings of nostalgia and suffering that characterized their music. They insisted that the term *bachata* applied only to the raunchier, more danceable music being made by some musicians; their own slower, romantic songs were to be called *canciones de amargue* (songs of bitterness). As Luis Segura asserted, "Esos son los que son bachatas, que van corriendo" (those are the bachatas, the fast ones) (interview). In contrast, Tony Santos, one of a younger generation of bachata musicians whose music was indeed faster and more sexually explicit than Segura's and Paniagua's, had no problem with the word *bachata*, although he did recognize the symbolic power of the words used to describe the music: "I'm not bothered if it's called bachata. But since names are always changing and making things nicer, *amargue* makes it more acceptable, more decent" (Santos, interview).

While the term *amargue* was indeed free of social stigma, it had limitations that prevented it from replacing *bachata*, which continued to be used by bachata's patrons themselves. First of all, the term *bachata* provided Dominicans with an appealing continuity between the traditional informal family and neighborhood parties of the same name and the musical genre that grew out of them; the newer term *amargue*, on the other hand, had no such historical resonances and evoked an unhappy state of mind. More importantly, the term *amargue* would not adequately describe those songs within bachateros' repertoires that were modeled after other guitar-based genres—particularly the merengue, but others such as the son and the ranchera as well—that were not based on the bolero and that were not necessarily romantic. In contrast, the term *bachata* could incorporate all these musical relatives, distant as they might have been; the very ambiguity of the term *bachata* provided the necessary flexibility for a still-emerging genre. This inclusiveness became particularly important in the 1990s, when almost all bachata musicians began including guitar-based merengues in their live as well as recorded repertoires. Rhythmically these were clearly merengues, but they could be comfortably accommodated within the boundaries of bachata because they were guitar based.

In 1989, I made a prediction about the term *bachata:* "I suspect that . . . if bachata filters through the class barriers that keep it marginalized from mainstream society, the word *bachata* will lose its negative connotations and will once again become at least more 'neutral'—if not a source of national pride—as Dominicans acknowledge the music as a unique feature of their national musical culture" (Pacini Hernandez 1989b: 40). Time proved me right: in the wake of Juan Luis Guerra's international success with *Bachata rosa* in 1990, all concerns about the term *bachata* have dissipated, and everybody, even Luis Segura, has accepted it because it no longer carries the weight of negative and derogatory connotations. Indeed, bachata is now being successfully promoted to mainstream audiences as a musical form endowed with both authenticity and exoticism. The word *amargue* is still used interchangeably with the word *bachata*, but less frequently.

As well-educated, middle-class musicians like Juan Luis Guerra continue to make sophisticated versions of bachata, nomenclature issues will almost certainly arise again. Their versions were initially distinguished from the low-status, street-level originals by being called *tecno-bachata* or *tecno-amargue*, a reference to their high-tech instrumentation and recording techniques. (Interestingly, street-level musicians, such as Blas Durán, who incorporated electric guitar and synthesizers into their ensembles were never referred to as tecno-bachateros.) Now, however, since the word *bachata* has been redeemed and marks trendiness rather than stigma, the prefix "tecno," which originally distinguished the two styles, appears to be disappearing. For example, a 1993 newspaper article announcing a performance of "classic" bachata songs by balada singer Anthony Ríos referred to him as a bachatero, not a tecno-bachatero. Similarly, articles on Juan Luis Guerra talk about his bachatas, not his tecno-bachatas. If Ríos' and Guerra's stylish and refined music continues to be called bachata, what then, should the gritty and earthy music made by bachateros such as Tony Santos and Blas Durán be called? Musicians from both sides of the social divide know their styles are profoundly different and instinctively use the words "ours" and "theirs" when talking about their own or others' music. Sonia Silvestre, for example, one of the pioneers of tecno-bachata, noted the differences between the two styles by saying, "Our bachata is a bit more schooled" (interview).

How these very different bachata styles will ultimately be defined and named remains to be seen, although most likely the name problem will be resolved not by musicians and fans themselves, but by producers and promoters requiring marketing terms to facilitate sales. However, it is possible to make some educated guesses by comparing bachata in its current moment of transition to that of rural merengue in the 1940s when merengue was "dressed up" by band leader and arranger Luis Alberti and introduced to polite society (see Chapter 2). At that juncture, the grass-roots style of merengue became modified by the word *típico* or else was referred to with the nickname *perico ripiao*, while the unmodified word *merengue* henceforth remained associated with the more modernized big-band versions. It is not unlikely, then, that the "original" street-level bachata will end up being renamed rather than the more recent style being developed and promoted by better socially and economically situated musicians and promoters. Looking at the recurring conflicts about nomenclature that have arisen throughout bachata's evolution, it seems clear that the debates about what to call the music have always expressed the various opinions about social status, prestige, and class of Dominicans from different social and economic positions competing to define the identity not only of the music but of its audience as well.

Stylistic and Social Contours

Underlying the vexing problem of what to call such different-sounding music as the boleros of Luis Segura, the merengues of Blas Durán, and the refined verses of Juan Luis Guerra is the more complex question of what exactly makes a bachata a bachata. Is bachata a musical genre or simply a particular style of playing and singing? If bachata is a genre, what should be included and what should be excluded from the category? Perhaps the most fruitful way to begin thinking about bachata is to consider it analogous to the musical categories *salsa* and *soul*, which are "generic" terms, as Baron points out, that capture a culture's "essence," but that can contain several musical styles (Baron 1977: 217). Salsa, for example, can include interpretations of Cuban *son, guaracha, guaguancó,* or *charanga,* Puerto Rican *bomba* or *plena,* Dominican *merengue,* or Colombian *cumbia.* If a genre is considered to be a category of music, while a style is a way of making music, then bachata can be considered a genre—a broad category of Dominican popular music—that contains within it several styles, or ways of interpreting that music. The term *amargue,* for example, can be considered a style within the broader category of bachata, referring specifically to the songs of romantic lament. Similarly, the terms *tecno-bachata* or *tecno-amargue* can refer to the high-tech, middle-class-oriented music of mainstream musicians who incorporate some of the elements associated with bachata such as the guitar-bongo-maracas instrumentation and an emotional singing style, even though they do not share the social context or street-level language and imagery of their lower-class counterparts.

Bachata, then, incorporates a number of styles and stylistic features, which I will describe at length in this section. Expressed in an elementary way, style is a way of doing something. Trying to understand or interpret the reasons people do things the way they do is, of course, one of the essential concerns of anthropologists, so there are, not surprisingly, almost as many theories and definitions of style as there are commentators on the subject. I will not try to add another to the list, but rather, I will cite some existing definitions that are relevant to this discussion because they take into consideration not only the music itself and how it is practiced, but also the influence of music's larger socio-economic context; they also recognize that style contains political as well as symbolic content.

David Coplan, in his work on South African popular music and performance, suggests that "style is itself an index of meaning, established collectively over time by artists and their audience. Styles provide a foundation, a vocabulary of forms, activities, and occasions which constitute and express social and cultural processes. Participants may apply a range of meanings to stylistic metaphors, yet there is a core of association and feeling that unites form and meaning in a shared identity" (Coplan 1985: 4). Manuel Peña, writing about Texas-Mexican conjunto and orquesta music, insists that musical style is inherently connected to its social context and must be meaningful to both producers and receivers of musical expression:

> Conceived as a discrete cultural system, musical style may be defined as a regularly occurring combination of sounds produced by vocal, instrumental and/or other means, arranged into recognizable patterns and situated within specific social contexts, wherein the style will acquire varying degrees of symbolic significance. The last point is especially critical for a culture-sensitive conception of style, because only when we recognize the symbolic dimension can we account for normative rules of composition and performance as well as evaluative criteria. As these rules accrue upon a given style, they gain a determinative role in the acceptance or rejection of modifications that innovative artists may introduce. Moreover, within its social context a musical style can associate with and reinforce other "crucial behavior patterns upon which the continuity of a culture hangs" (Lomax 1968: 8). (Peña 1985: 2)

Charles Keil and Christopher Waterman link their definitions of style even more strongly to notions of identity; although Keil sees community identity as helping to shape style, Waterman sees style as helping to shape community identity. Keil observes that "the presence of style indicates a strong community, an intense sociability that has been given shape through time, an assertion of control over collective feelings so powerful that any expressive innovator in a community will necessarily put his or her content into that shaping continuum and no other" (Keil 1985: 122). To Waterman, music can serve as "a system for the enactment and negotiation of emergent patterns of identity under conditions of pervasive demographic, political and economic change"; musical styles, he suggests, can be seen as "paradigmatic structures guiding the production of meaningful constellations of expressive features" (Waterman 1987: 2).

Anya Peterson Royce also associates style with identity, although she conceives of style even more broadly, as "the whole complex of features that people rely on to mark their identity . . . composed of symbols, forms, and underlying value orientations" (Royce 1982: 157). She conceives of "style" as analogous to "tradition," but she substitutes the former term for the latter because, she explains, tradition implies "something conservative and unchanging" (Royce 1982: 28), whereas style accommodates the continual and rapid change that characterizes music in modern urban societies. Within this definition, musical style is but one of many possible markers of identity and will be closely related to other associated cultural features such as recreational activities, use of language, attitudes towards sex, and so on, which similarly contribute to forming and maintaining group identity.

These definitions of style contain common themes, or motifs, that will become apparent in the detailed descriptions of bachata below and in the subsequent chapters of this book tracing bachata's development. First, style is intrinsically related to the social context in which music or any other expressive event takes place. Second, the patterning that produces identifiable ways of doing things reflects cultural meanings shared by all those who participate in a communicative event such as musical performance. Third, these meanings are related in fundamental ways to conceptions of identity—the ways people perceive and define themselves, especially in opposition to other groups of people. The obvious and inevitable corollary of these motifs is that changes within a social context are certain to find resonance in stylistic changes. We can also be certain that the ways these resonances are expressed will reflect the survival strategies as well as the perceptions and values of the social group experiencing the change.

In the case of bachata, any description of its styles must keep in mind the fact that bachata has emerged only recently, and it is still changing rapidly: witness the appearance of tecno-bachata and the transformation of bachata's social status within a roughly two-year period. In considering bachata's stylistic developments over the years, it is useful to keep in mind Keil's observations on the processes surrounding the emergence of musical styles: "An exclusion principle or focus on a sharply limited form or set of forms marks the beginning of a style, but it grows by inclusion, assimilating to its purposes the instruments, techniques, and ideas of significant other styles within earshot" (Keil 1985: 126). Applying Keil's description of emerging styles to bachata, we can see that bachata may indeed have begun as a rustic form of the Cuban bolero, but it was also permeated with a variety of influences and elements that were part of the larger Dominican musical landscape. Commenting on the problems of examining emerging styles in a context of mutually influencing and overlapping styles, Keil also observed that "analysts seeking cause and effect are placed in a long hall of fun-house mirrors and echo chambers filled with uncertainties" (Keil 1985: 124). The image of the fun house filled with mirrors is particularly apt for bachata, whose divergence from its related antecedent genres is still incomplete and too recent to permit the construction of a clearly defined genealogical tree. Given the number of descriptions I have already had to revise since I began writing this manuscript in 1987, I have no illusions[3] that some of the features I describe here may have disappeared and new ones may have been added by the time this book is read; thus I advise my readers to keep in mind that my comments are not intended to define a style, but rather to describe bachata at a particular period of time.

In organizing my descriptions of the specific musical and social features that constitute bachata, I have followed Charles Keil's analysis of U.S. blues (1966: 51–52), in which he posits four fundamental characteristics of musical style: structure, timbre and texture, content, and context. In terms of structure, the first thing to note is that bachata does not have any deep structural features like salsa's clave beat or the blues' four-four twelve-bar pattern: there is no one comparably standardized rhythm, chord pattern, or verse form in bachata, but rather a variety of rhythms, chord patterns, and verse forms reflecting its continuity with various antecedent genres. The closest thing to "classic" bachata could be likened to the romantic Cuban bolero, but many other bachata songs are modeled after the other Latin American guitar-based genres mentioned earlier. Since the late 1970s and 1980s even those bachatas still resembling the bolero tend to be much faster than their original models. In some cases, the bolero rhythm has simply been sped up, but in others, the rhythmic groove of the long-popular Cuban son has crept into the music, leading some observers to refer to the faster bachatas as being a form of *bolero-son* (Herrera 1991: 7; Víctor Víctor, personal communication).

While bachata does not have any signature rhythms, it does have a defining timbre and texture that are the outgrowth of two features: its instrumentation and its vocal style. A particular configuration of instruments is essential for a bachata to be a bachata: one or two guitars, maracas or güira, and bongos. Except for the fact that recently the güira is being used more frequently than the more traditional maraca, this instrumentation is virtually identical to that used by the sort of trios and quartets that played boleros and other guitar-based music familiar to bachateros. One guitar plays lead, embellishing by picking rather than strumming, and another plays rhythm. The bongo and maraca (or güira) players mark the typical four-four time rather discretely, although sometimes in musical breaks the bongo player might add a few flourishes; he never, however, executes a *descarga* (lit., a discharge—an energetic improvised solo) as occurs in the *montuno*[3] section in Cuban son and salsa. Traditionally, the lead guitar player also composed and sang lead, while the other musicians provided choruses, although as bachata groups have professionalized, some are now fronted by a vocalist who does not play, thereby relegating the lead guitar player to a secondary role. Old-time bachateros like Luis Segura and José Manuel Calderón, for example, compose, play lead guitar, and sing; more recent singers such as Tony Santos, Blas Durán, and Leonardo Paniagua, on the other hand, do not play instruments.

Bachata is essentially a vocal genre, meant to tell stories—there is no such thing as an instrumental bachata. Besides its characteristic guitar-led instrumentation, one of bachata's defining features is its highly emotional, sometimes almost sobbing, singing style. The vocal quality of bachata singers varies to the degree that the singer wishes to emphasize the emotion being expressed: pleading, exhorting, and despairing are expressed with a tightening of the voice, giving a tremulous quality to much of the singing. Some singers take this dramatic singing style to its limits; Luis Segura, for example, fairly weeps out his songs, earning him the nickname of "el Añoñaíto" (*ñoño* is a word used to refer to a whining, spoiled child; *añoñaíto* is a diminutive of this word). The vocal quality in songs that are not romantic, however (e.g., humorous double entendre songs or those which criticize women), is much more open and relaxed, and even more so when they express bravado. Bachata's vocals, like those of other rural musics (such as U.S. country and Colombian *carrilera*), are often sung in close harmony, usually in thirds. The backup vocal parts in bachata are often in call-and-response form; sometimes the backup singers simply repeat a phrase such as "no, no, no" between solo lines; at other times the chorus might repeat the last line of a verse, or the singer and vocalists might engage in a dialogue.

Further vocal variation is provided by spoken or cried-out phrases uttered by the soloist between verses. They can simply be exclamations, such as "¡romo!" (rum!), exhortations to a woman such as the classic "¡mami!" (mommy!), to specifically named friends, or to the listener in general. On recordings the spoken phrases are sometimes directed to the producer. For example, in a song entitled "Dímelo, dímelo" (Tell me, tell me) in which Sijo Osoria begs his woman to tell him why she is so mean to him, during the instrumental break he calls out to the producer, "Radhames Aracena, ¡dígale que me lo diga, aunque me muera de dolor!" (Radhames Aracena, tell her to tell me, even though I might die of pain!). These exclamations are outside the formal lyrical structure of the song and are typically uttered in more colloquial language and/or enunciation than are the lyrics themselves. Furthermore, they allow the singer to violate the narrative boundaries of the song and to manipulate concepts of space and time. So for example, when Sijo Osoria addresses producer Radhames Aracena in the song cited above, he breaks out of the narrative setting, in which he is pleading with his woman, and relocates himself in the studio—thereby telling listeners, most of whom know who Aracena is (see Chapter 3), that he is only performing. Yet by asking Aracena to intercede with the woman, he thereby links the narrative space of the song to the "real" space of the studio.

Another example of the sort of liberties bachata musicians take with song texts is the spoken dialogues between two persons that are sometimes inserted within the song texts themselves. These minidramas set the stage, so to speak, for an idea that the song texts will develop musically. In one song, "El mandamás" (The big shot), Olivo Acosta addresses Orlando Jiménez, a rival bachatero whose nickname is "el Pashá" (a Turkish title for a person of high rank). Acosta begins his song by calling out, "¡Orlando, a ti y que te dicen el Pashá!" (Orlando, so they call you the Pasha!). A voice answers, "Sí, ¿y qué?" (Yes, and so what?). Acosta continues, "Pero ¡ahora a mí me dicen el mandamás!" (Well, now they call *me* the big shot!), and then proceeds into the song verses in which he boasts of his physical prowess. Similarly, in one song by Marino Pérez called "El recuento de Marino" (Marino's retold story), which is a medley of his biggest hits, Pérez uses the dramatic device of having a woman talk to him in between each song segment in order to set up the next segment. After a verse taken from a song in which Pérez harshly criticizes a treacherous lover, a woman is heard crying. Pérez asks in a fawning voice, "¿Por qué tú lloras, mami?" (Why are you crying, mommy?). The woman whimpers, "Cántame una cosita más suave, papi" (Sing me something a little gentler, daddy), to which Pérez responds, "Sí, chichí, te la voy a cantar" (Yes, *chichí*, I'm going to sing it to you—*chichí* is a term of endearment usually used with children, but men also use it in order to express affection toward a woman); he then sings a verse from one of his more romantic songs. In addition to establishing songs' dramatic settings, these dialogues also serve to populate narrative spaces with other actors beyond the singer and the person(s) to whom a song is directed.

Bachata lyrics reflect the musicians' rural origins and, often, their poor educational backgrounds as well. Many (though by no means all) bachatas are written in the octosyllabic line pattern associated with the décima verse form long popular in rural areas. Lyrics often exhibit what mainstream society would call grammatical and pronunciation mistakes, although sometimes the irregularities are simply regionalisms. For example, people from the Cibao region end with an *i* words that properly should end with an *r*. Thus in one song, the singer, clearly from the Cibao, says "Voy a comprai un cañón" rather than "Voy a comprar un cañón" (I'm going to buy a cannon [gun]). Spelling errors also appear on record and cassette labels. Sometimes these mistakes are corrected in the studio by producers if they are better educated than the musicians. Often, however, the texts are recorded as they were composed, leading to charges by mainstream Dominicans that bachata musicians are ignorant and that they corrupt the Spanish language; for example, a woman writing a letter to the Santo Domingo newspaper *Listín Diario* in 1977 asserted:

> I am an educator who at present owns a record store and I have been able to observe that the major percentage of record sales are those we call bachatas. These records arrive with spelling mistakes on the record labels from the producing houses, especially Unidad Records, that are frankly disappointing. Mistakes like *me gusta la Vevida, Ben conmigo, Atras de quien Borvistes,* etc., [examples in which *v*'s and *b*'s are incorrectly used, *r* is substituted for *l*, adverbs are used as prepositions, and written accents are missing] are some of the ones we see constantly. You will realize that these records are mostly bought by people of the peasant class and persons of low academic level and they see these labels written this way and they think this is the way they are written correctly. This causes our language to be corrupted even more. (Cited in Brito 1985: 75, translation mine)

The pronunciation and grammatical infractions in bachata songs make little difference to their listeners, who are far more interested in what is being said and how it is expressed than whether it is being said in correct Spanish.

Before proceeding further with this discussion of bachata lyrics, it is necessary to emphasize the close relationship between bachata's style and its principal social context—urban shantytowns and poor working-class neighborhoods. Bachata musicians may be of rural origins, as are many of their listeners, but most of them reside in urban areas and have become adept at interpreting musically the urban experience for both their urban and rural listeners. Popular language in particular is one of the most important markers of barrio identity, and the ability to use language creatively is a highly valued skill.[4] Indeed, the most successful bachateros are those who best command a Dominican urban street language that offers a rich variety of words, phrases, and proverbs for expressing their thoughts and feelings, to which they add further nuances through subtle variations in intonation; in bachata, as in U.S. rap, language, spoken or sung, empowers a speaker: through the control of words, a speaker can construct alternative realities.

Arístides Incháustegui has suggested that in earlier times popular language, whether sung or spoken, was lyrical, lengthy, and poetic. In recent years, the popular language that has emerged from poor urban social contexts has become streamlined, more compact, with a wide range of cultural meaning contained in terse phrases, such as "¡Esto sí está rico, mami!" (This is really good, mommy!) or "¡Esa hembra está buena!" (That female is fine!), that are instantaneously understood by those who share barrio culture (interview). The word *hembra*, to give an example, literally means "female" but has class and sexual connotations as well, invoking a lower-class woman who possesses a sort of raw sexuality. One bachata fan, commenting on the ability of bachata musicians to express things concisely, told me, "Bachata says things like they feel them, they say things faster, not with theory like Julio Iglesias, but in action, in one shot." In the way bachateros compress multiple meanings into concise phrases, they resemble U.S. bluesmen:

> Usually each blues phrase consists of a fairly simple and concrete image, a trope or Negro idiom of some kind that stands for a complex set of associations and connotations. For example, the phrase "the eagle flies on Friday, and Saturday I go out to play" conjures up in a Negro listener's mind a multitude of activities associated with payday and the pleasures of Saturday night. . . . In other words, there are many stock phrases in the blues tradition plus slogans of the day that can be played off against each other to illustrate a particular theme or create a general mood. (Keil 1966: 52)

The tendency to manipulate language is a significant feature of bachata lyrics in general, but it is taken to its logical extreme in a widely used and popular narrative strategy, the *doble sentido* (double entendre), in which words and meanings are manipulated for humorous effect. These songs, like Dominican popular speech in general, are full of hidden or ambiguous meanings that subvert official meanings. Incháustegui attributes Dominicans' use of language to simultaneously conceal and reveal information to the effects of the repression characterizing the Trujillo regime: "During the Trujillo era words didn't work properly. So the Dominican became a specialist in speaking in masked messages. It was something so ingrained in our consciousness that you couldn't say things, that it entered our genes, and when children are born, they already know how to play with words. You will have a hard time getting a Dominican to give you a straight answer" (interview). Bachata lyrics also communicate indirectly through a creative use of imagery. Food products, food preparation, and eating provide bachateros with some of their most vivid metaphors, but other common features of barrio life are also used. For example, baseball, the most popular sport in the Dominican Republic, is often used as a metaphor for conflict or competition. In Bolívar Peralta's song "Tani bol" ("Spanglish" for time-out), he tells his woman that he is tired of playing (i.e., fighting), and he asks for *tani bol*.

In the barrio, the most creative use of language is placed in the service of humor. According to Jorge Cela, a Catholic priest who worked in Santo Domingo's shantytowns, humor, love, and suffering are the principal characteristics of barrio psychology; the ability to laugh at oneself and at one's romantic problems is an important strategy for survival (interview). Barrio humor is created by manipulating language in several ways, among them: turning things inside out; placing things out of their usual contexts; making unexpected comparisons; grossly exaggerating; and calling things by one name while meaning another (the double entendre). All of these techniques are used with great success in bachata texts; as one fan said of bachata, "Con las sonrisas la música penetra" (Music penetrates with smiles). I should point out that the extensive use of humor as a stylistic technique is a relatively recent development; in early bachatas the romantic themes were expressed in the more florid, poetic language that Incháustegui referred to above. Previously, the topical merengue típico was the most common idiom for expressing humor.

Bachateros are particularly imaginative in using words from the popular lexicon in the spoken exclamations that they interject into song texts. One such extremely popular phrase in 1986 was "¡Amarilis! ¡Echame agua!" (Amarilis, throw water on me!), with which Tony Santos introduced his song "Amarilis." In this song, Santos asks his lover Amarilis to throw water on him, i.e., have sexual relations with him, in order to cool him off. An additional level of humor derives from the image this phrase invokes, which all barrio residents would appreciate, that is, throwing water on copulating dogs that have become stuck together in order to separate them (Arístides Incháustegui, interview). Another example is Blas Durán's phrase at the beginning of "¿Qué será lo que quiere Juanita?" (What could Juanita want?), in which he calls out, "¡Juanita, desbarata guachimán!" (Juanita, *guachimán* demolisher). *Guachimán* is "Spanglish" for watchman; in this song the humor derives from the idea of a woman so sexually attractive that she can demolish an armed guard. Durán explains the phrase, "It's about a woman that I give everything to and she doesn't want to give me anything, so I tell her up front, 'Juanita, guachimán demolisher!' In other words, she is good, she is so good she even demolishes the watchman. I say it at performances and people laugh" (interview).

Durán also plays with his audience's social perceptions of the guachimán, an occupation held only by the very poor and serving only the very rich. The image of the guachimán, simultaneously powerless (because he is poor) and powerful (because he is armed), becomes a humorous reference to his own similar condition of power and powerlessness when it comes to women.

Humorous effects are also created by turning things inside out or by reversing their usual order in a hierarchy of values. For example, in one song "Homenaje a los borrachones" (Homage to drunks), Teodoro Reyes inverts the values of two activities normally proscribed—heavy drinking and prostitution—and celebrates them unabashedly. In other songs humor is created by hyperbole, either in the song text itself (e.g., a man bragging that no woman can sexually exhaust him) or by the singer's exaggerated intonation (e.g., the pitiful calls to mami or to chichí). On the other hand, sometimes the humor is created or emphasized through deliberate understatement. For example, the feigned innocence and sweetness with which Julio Angel sings his story describing himself as a hairdresser fixing women's hair in his double entendre song "El salón" (The salon)—although the song was more widely known as "El pajón" (The bush)—contrasts humorously with the outrageous sexual explicitness of the lyrics, in which the word for comb, *peine,* transparently stands in for *pene,* the word for penis.

The techniques described above are employed by bachateros to communicate their emotions and ideas in a way that is comprehensible to their listeners. It is often stated that bachateros compose the sort of lyrics they do because they are uneducated and ignorant and are incapable of writing any other way. In fact, bachateros write the way they do because they understand the importance of using a language shared and appreciated by their listeners, and because this language offers them a wider range of possibilities for creative expression. All bachata lyrics, whether they express erotic, romantic, or disillusioned love, or extol the pleasures of the bar, serve their listeners as a triggering device for thinking about the relationship between an individual and his or her world, whether it be the relationship between the individual and other persons, or between the individual and society. Most bachata songs are written on the basis of the composer's personal romantic experiences, which resonate with those of listeners who have had similar experiences. I was told by several informants that when they had an emotional problem, they would play or request a particular bachata with relevant lyrics, and they would listen to it repeatedly. The interpretations or solutions the songs propose may not be, according to our standards, the best ones, but they are perceived by their listeners as helpful in coping with difficult problems.

Clearly, bachata stories and the language and imagery with which they are expressed encode important information about class identity. Nevertheless, it does not follow automatically that because a music is associated with the poor the social meanings ascribed to it must be negative: for example, in Puerto Rico jíbaro music is proudly considered a symbol of the country's rural past and, moreover, of a certain independence of spirit. The social meanings ascribed to bachata, however, were neither spontaneous nor arbitrary, but were instead imposed upon the music in the 1970s, when competing economic groups wished to limit bachata's exposure to a wider market. Style, in other words, was used to mark—and fix—both the regional identity and the socio-economic position of bachata's listeners. The negative social connotations have not, however, been passively accepted by bachata's constituency, who evaluate the music according to the extent to which it speaks to their lives and emotional concerns. As a result, until very recently bachata was viewed by those who would suppress it and those who would resist such suppression—the contenders, of course, were located on opposite sides of class lines—as contested terrain over which the power to determine the meaning of musical styles would be decided.

In the 1990s bachata's musical and textual characteristics have become less predictable as new features have been added to the previously existing range of possibilities or are being used in different combinations. Many bachateros, for example, are relying less on sexual double entendre songs in order to improve their chances of getting their records played on the radio. The most significant changes in bachata, however—other than its new social respectability—have been in terms of instrumentation. While still guitar led, bachata is increasingly being played with hollow-body electric guitars rather than acoustic guitars, which has dramatically changed its timbre. Blas Durán's 1987 hit, the electric guitar-based bachata-merengue "Consejo a las mujeres," was the first to establish the commercial potential of using the electric guitar in bachata. In the final chapter of my 1989 dissertation, I speculated that Durán's success with an electric guitar-led bachata might inspire other bachateros to imitate him; again, time has proved me right—all the most successful bachata musicians since 1990 are using electric guitars. Some of the younger bachateros have also added to the characteristic texture produced by the guitar-bongo-maracas/güira ensemble by introducing other new instruments such as the electric bass and synthesizers. Moreover, they have improved on bachata's characteristic (although not deliberate) poor sound quality by using sound mixers.

Bachata's recent livelier sound corresponds to changes in its social functions. When it first emerged in the 1960s, it was, like its predecessor the bolero, primarily romantic—as opposed to dance-oriented—music. The distinction between dance and romantic music is more than the difference between fast and slow music. Romantic music is, in fact, frequently danced to, and the lyrics of dance music are often about love. But the function as well as the physical and emotional effects of dance and romantic music are quite different. In Latin America dance music is for having fun, for letting off steam, for showing off one's ability to move well, and it is more public and impersonal. It can, of course, play a role in courtship, in that body movement can express a person's sexual energy; but unlike romantic music, dance music is not intimate and does not deal directly with the emotional sphere. Romantic music, in contrast, provides a couple with an opportunity for close physical contact in a socially acceptable way, but more importantly it serves as surrogate voice for people who wish to publicly express personal emotions but who feel incapable of doing so themselves. For years, bachata's primary function was to articulate the experiences of male-female relationships. As a bachata dance has evolved, however, bachata has been moving from being an exclusively romantic music toward one that is also dance oriented. When a bachata ensemble plays a merengue, however, the dancers dance merengue. As a result, the term *bolero-bachata* is sometimes used to refer to those bachatas derived from the bolero or other guitar-based genres, and the term *bachata-merengue* (or *merengue-bachata*) for those danced as merengue.

Informally, some Dominicans have opined that the bachata dance style is an offshoot of the bolero dance, while others have claimed it is related to the son. The former seems a more likely explanation, given bachata's strong connections to the bolero tradition, although it is certainly true that the lively, syncopated bachata dance step probably owes something to the dancers' familiarity with the son's highly danceable groove. The bachata dance consists of an alternating "one-two-three-kick" pattern, in which the "kick" is a toe step or a small hop. Body movement is smooth and sinuous, but relatively reserved; a few dancers, however, exaggerate their hip and arm movements, displaying their choreographic skills in a way more reminiscent of salsa or merengue dancing. This more energetic style of dancing has become more common as bachata's tempos have sped up in recent years—although it is also possible that the dancers' preferences may have stimulated the changes in tempo rather than the other way around. Keil, for example, noted the role of dancing in shaping polka style: "It is in constant response to the expressed and implicit needs of the dancers passing before their eyes that tunes are chosen, tempos fixed, and the broad stream of musical style subtly elaborated from weekend night to weekend night in each polka locality over the years" (Keil 1985: 123).

The faster bolero-based bachatas are themselves quite danceable, but younger audiences have encouraged bachata musicians to include more merengues in their repertoires; as a result, bachata-merengues now comprise as much as half of many bachata ensembles' repertoire. It was largely in order to play merengues that many ensembles replaced the traditional maracas with the güira, which can be played to sound like a maraca, and therefore can be used both for bolero-bachatas as well as merengue-bachatas. The tambora, indispensable for merengue, has been added to the bachata ensemble, although it has not replaced the bongo, which is still essential for the bolero-bachatas.

The increasing popularity of these hybrid bachata-merengues represents a truly significant turn of events in the evolution of both genres. Since the late nineteenth century, when the accordion displaced the guitar as the principal instrument for merengue production, guitar-based me-

rengues were seldom heard outside of informal rural settings. By repopu-
larizing the guitar-based merengues, bachateros have brought merengue
back full circle to its original instrumentation—only now most of the guitars are electric. When bachateros play merengue with electric guitars,
they imitate the sound of the accordion or the saxophone in merengue
típico ensembles, thereby consolidating into one the Dominican Republic's two most popular rural-based music genres (Daisann Maclean, personal communication). Moreover, in addition to consolidating the two
sounds, their functions—merengue's as a dance music, bachata's as a romantic music—have been consolidated as well. Musician and producer
Víctor Víctor believes that this versatility will eventually give bachata a
competitive edge over both merengue and balada, each of which can be
only a dance music or a romantic music, respectively (personal communication).

Bachata's widening popularity and new social respectability have
also been changing the characteristic social contexts for listening to bachata. In terms of live performance, until the 1990s bachateros played
only in small, often seedy, neighborhood bars (many of which were also
brothels) located in the poorest sections of Santo Domingo, or in similar
establishments in provincial towns whose patrons, like the musicians
themselves, were persons of low socio-economic status. Occasionally,
well-known bachateros were contracted by provincial municipalities to
play at patron saints' festivals (*fiestas patronales*), which, because they were
outdoors and free, exposed bachateros to larger and more diverse audiences—in terms of class, gender, and age—than would be possible in bar
settings.

Live bachata performances were infrequent in urban areas, however,
because it was difficult for most bars in poor neighborhoods to afford
even the minimal cost of hiring a bachata ensemble. In addition, bachata
was excluded from FM radio and from television; therefore, one of the
few opportunities for publicly listening to bachata (although again only
recorded) was in neighborhood *colmados*. Colmados are neighborhood
grocery stores somewhat reminiscent of what we think of as mom-and-
pop grocery stores, although much smaller than their U.S. equivalents,
and far more numerous in any given area than would be the case here.[5] In
shantytowns and poor working-class barrios, colmados provided a public
place for exchanging news, information, ideas—and culture: women
tended to visit them several times a day to buy household necessities,
while men typically visited them in the evening and on weekends to buy
beer and cigarettes, and often to play dominoes on tables set up in front.
In order to enhance the colmado's social functions, colmado owners typically had some sort of sound system—most commonly a record player
and a small record collection—which they kept up-to-date by purchasing

a few carefully chosen bachata records on a regular basis. Colmados, then, served as key loci for the dissemination of bachata in urban areas—especially to women and children, who could not frequent the barras. Middle-class people, on the other hand, had little, if any, contact with bachata.

In the aftermath of bachata's debut into polite society in the early 1990s, however, bachata has begun transcending the boundaries of the shantytown. It is now receiving some airplay on major urban FM radio stations, and a handful of successful bachateros have been playing on television and at more upscale venues. Most bachateros, however, have continued to play in the same sort of undistinguished locations in which they played in the mid-1980s, although somewhat more middle-class venues are now open to them as well. Interestingly, although successful bachateros can now play in socially prestigious clubs and are making more money than they ever could have before, they continue to play in poor and working-class venues in order to maintain contact with their principal constituency, the poor.

Bachata performances as I observed them in the 1980s were fairly informal affairs, and the spatial and social distance between performers and audience was not very great. Most small clubs or bars did not have raised stages, and in between sets the musicians sat at tables with their friends, so that patrons could approach them if they wished. The stage area was relatively uncluttered, because bachata ensembles used little sound amplification equipment—usually only a small public-address system. Throughout bachata performances, *saludos* (greetings) were continually sent by the singer to friends in the audience, or on behalf of audience members who requested the singer to deliver it. These saludos served to establish personal connections between the musicians and audience, and to create a sense of community. The familiarity and informality of bachata performances contrasted with performances by merengue orquestas in elite venues, in which the musicians were presented as "stars" who were socially and spatially removed from their audience: they emerged from a backstage area rather than from the dance floor and played on raised stages surrounded by an imposing array of expensive-looking instruments, speakers, and wires.

In spite of their informality, bachata musicians—especially the singers—did distinguish themselves as professionals, usually through dress. Sometimes the entire band wore something that identified them as an ensemble, such as shirts of the same color; at other times only the lead singer dressed up. Because bachata musicians were poor, however, their clothing was usually inexpensive and, according to the dictates of urban fashion, unstylish—for example, polyester suits and ruffled shirts. Bachateros' lack of sophistication and elegance in dress, in fact, was yet another reason they were scorned by the fashion-conscious middle classes. In contrast, orquesta merengue musicians always appeared in coordinated outfits in the latest styles from New York, presenting a glamorous—and always corporate—image.

The typical bachata performance in the 1980s was fairly subdued in style, with emotion being expressed more by the singer's melodramatic vocal style than through theatrical gestures. One exception was Tony Santos, who was known for his flamboyant performance style: while singing, he would rip off his jacket, fling it into the crowd, unbutton his shirt, unfasten his belt buckle, and, during one particular song in which he desperately pleads with his woman not to leave him, he would throw himself on the floor, pounding his hands and feet—very much like a child having a temper tantrum. The audience loved this exaggerated display of emotion, and the younger women in the crowd screamed in delight. I also heard reports that another bachatero, the Solterito del Sur, had a similarly dramatic performance style, which included taking off his shirt, standing on tables, and, the story went, even urinating from the table. In general, however, except for some dramatic hand gestures by the lead singer to punctuate a particularly emotional song, the singers and musicians simply stood quietly and played their music. In contrast, performances by merengue orquestas were flashy and energetic spectacles: the lead singer and backup vocalists executed elaborate dance routines, and even the musicians performed some synchronized dance steps as they played.

Regarding more recent bachata performance styles, during my brief visit to the Dominican Republic in early 1994 I was able to observe one bachata performance that exemplified some of the directions bachata has been taking since 1990. The musician was Raulín Rodríguez, at the time the fastest-rising young bachatero, whose song "El dolor" (Pain) was considered by many to have been the most popular Dominican song released in 1993. Raulín's success had given him access to performance venues that had been unavailable to most of his predecessors: he had played many times on television, had completed a successful tour playing within various Dominican communities in the United States, and had even played in the nightclub of one of Santo Domingo's elite hotels. However, this particular performance took place in an unassuming venue in Sabana Perdida, a poor working-class suburb of Santo Domingo—a car wash. (Car washes, modeled after U.S. car washes, are a relatively new phenomenon in the Dominican Republic and were probably introduced by returning Dominican migrants; prior to that cars were typically washed at gas stations.) The car wash equipment had been moved neatly into a corner in order to make room for tables, chairs, and a dance floor—although the place had obviously been designed to double as a night spot, because it had a built-in bar in the front. It was a decidedly inelegant, but by no means disreputable event: the audience was well dressed if socially undistinguished, and the relatively steep cover charge—equivalent to about US$5—had excluded the very poor. In short, the location clearly spoke of Raulín's continuing connection to bachata's non-elite consumers, although he was drawing only the upper strata of that group.

In contrast to the rather informal and low-key bachata performances I had witnessed in the 1980s, Raulín was very professional. Well before Raulín himself arrived, a group of six young "roadies" came to set up the equipment, which included a new and expensive-looking sound reinforcement system. While modest compared to even amateur rock bands in the United States, this display of equipment for a bachata performance represented a remarkable development. When Raulín arrived (from his hometown, Montecristi, three hours away in the northwest), he sat down at a table with friends among the audience, just as bachata performers had always done before, and casually walked up to the stage without fanfare when it was time to begin playing. But this was almost the only aspect of his performance that resembled those of his predecessors. Even superficially, the band looked different. It was larger—seven musicians—and they were all very young; Raulín was twenty-two, and some of the others were even younger. Raulín was very well dressed in a stylishly cut suit, expensive shoes, and an impressive array of gold jewelry. His band members were not wearing identical band outfits, but they were dressed in hip casual clothing, looking like they had just gotten back from New York City (which they had). No one could accuse them of looking like hicks!

The band's instrumentation had also evolved dramatically from bachata ensembles' former simplicity. Both Raulín and the rhythm guitar player used hollow-body electric guitars, and Raulín had a special-effects pedal. An electric bass guitar had been added. The güira player—no old fashioned maracas here—simultaneously played a bass drum with his foot on some numbers. A fifth musician played a small synthesizer. The bongo player used sticks instead of his hands for the bolero-bachatas and a tambora for bachata-merengues. The most striking innovation, however, was the addition to the band lineup of a young woman—Raulín's sister—who sang backup vocals and danced. The idea of having an attractive young woman fronting the band to dance and sing backup parts had clearly been borrowed from merengue orquestas, but was a recent addition to the bachata ensemble, which added a new element of spectacle to the performance. Also notable was that the young man working the mixing board was located among the band rather than offstage, bringing the number of persons onstage to eight. Their repertoire, combining about equal numbers of fast bachatas and bachata-merengues, appealed greatly to the multigenerational audience, which packed the dance area for every song.

One of the reasons cited for Raulín's extraordinary popularity was that he makes a deliberate point of writing what are considered to be "nice" lyrics about romantic love, in imitation of the bachatero he most admires, Luis Segura. As a result, even though his music is lively and danceable, he has reestablished bachata's credentials as a romantic music to middle classes and the mass media. The reasons for Raulín's success go beyond his squeaky-clean romantic lyrics, however. During this 1994 performance, Raulín himself and the entire band exuded a contagious enthusiasm and dynamism that were a far cry from the subdued and somewhat depressed bachata performances I had attended in the 1980s. With their modern amplification equipment and expanded ensemble, the band's sound was strong and literally electric. Moreover, these young musicians were clearly not burdened by the same sort of social reproba-tion and obstacles to their careers that their predecessors had to endure. The combination of the band's youthful energy and confidence, and the fresh new sound of their electric guitar-based bachatas and merengues, reminded me of the energy that early rock and roll had in the 1950s, as it burst through the social barriers that had confined its parent, rhythm and blues.

Thematic Framework

The social history of bachata that follows is organized both chronologi-cally and thematically. In Chapter 2, I describe the preconditions for bacha-ta's emergence in the 1960s, exploring the relationship between popular music and the dictatorship of Rafael Trujillo and examining the historical, social, and musical seeds that were to bear musical fruit in the 1960s. In Chapter 3, I place the emergence of bachata within the context of a coun-try suddenly released from a repressive thirty-one-year dictatorship and the ensuing massive rural to urban migrations that sent thousands of peasants into urban areas. Unable to find employment, people of rural origins were condemned to working for subsistence in the informal sector and to residence in shantytowns, where traditional patterns of making music were transformed by the urban experience. In Chapter 4, I discuss the struggles for economic and political power that marked the Domini-can Republic as a whole in the 1970s and explore the ways that the compe-tition between promoters of various genres of popular music for musical hegemony represented the competing ideological interests of different sectors of society. In these struggles, bachata, associated with the coun-try's poorest and most dispossessed citizens, was accused of being musi-cally worthless and vulgar and was systematically excluded from the mass media, effectively pushing it to the margins of the popular music arena. Yet in spite of these obstacles, bachata's popularity continued to grow as it established a community of listeners who shared a culturally defined space shaped by the common experiences of overcrowding, severe economic hardship—and listening to bachata. In Chapter 5, I explore how issues of sex and gender were perceived and articulated by bachata's mostly male musicians in the context of worsening economic conditions that transformed traditional patterns of marriage and family. In Chapter 6, I describe how and why bachata, which by the 1980s was thoroughly disparaged and despised by mainstream society because of its explicit sexuality and its uncomfortably accurate reflections of shantytown culture, was transformed into a socially acceptable if not fashionable genre and even an icon of popular authenticity. In the concluding chapter, I broaden the discussion by raising some of the theoretical issues concerning emerging styles and how bachata confirms or contradicts the models proposed by other scholars writing about urban popular musics. Finally, I speculate on how bachata compares with other Latin American musics that have similarly originated among the very poor, some of which, like bachata, later crossed over into the mainstream.

While the book's overall organization is chronological, the various chapters are also thematically linked by a number of theoretical questions. In addressing these, I refer continually to the development of merengue, using its trajectory as a counterpoint and comparison to the development of bachata. For example, when merengue emerged in the nineteenth century, it too was denigrated by the dominant classes as vulgar and musically worthless, only to be later enshrined as a universally accepted symbol of national identity; is this likely to happen to bachata? Why has it been so difficult for bachata to compete with merengue, not only economically but symbolically? How have the changing economic and social relations of the music industry affected the development of both bachata and merengue? How did the widespread belief that bachata was musically and socially without value come into being, and whose interests did such determinations serve? What did bachata mean to its own constituency, and what did it mean to its detractors? Who has the power to determine the meaning of cultural products such as popular musics?

In answering these questions, it will become clear that bachata's appeal has rested precisely on its ability to articulate the needs and concerns of people being forced to adapt to the difficulties of the urban experience under conditions of extreme poverty. Over time, bachata has successfully expressed the cultural values, such as attitudes about sex, money, and power, that its practitioners and patrons have adopted in response to life on the margins of modern Dominican society. It has also served as a form of resistance for those excluded from Dominican mainstream culture: in expressing, in its own terms, the values and experiences of the urban shantytown, bachata has legitimized and helped to sustain a shared cultural identity for its constituency. Since its inception, bachata has consistently revealed a vitality, a sense of humor, and an affirmation of self—regardless of the singers' desperate socio-economic situation—that actively challenged the mainstream Dominican perception that bachata was a degenerate genre devoid of musical or social value. On the contrary, bachata has always been an expression of a subculture in transition, struggling to create new cultural coherences and to attain form, autonomy, and legitimacy within a hostile society.

Chapter Two

M usic and Dictatorship

*T*he greatest influence on the development of popular music in the Dominican Republic prior to 1961 was without question the dictatorship of Rafael Leonidas Trujillo. Dictators by definition exercise a high degree of control over the lives of their subject peoples, although typically they concentrate on political, economic, and military activities in the country; they tend to pay less attention to cultural affairs as long as these do not challenge or interfere with the regime. Rafael Trujillo, however, was different: he had an extraordinary impact on all aspects of the country's cultural life, including its music, throughout his thirty-one-year regime (1930–61), determining to a significant extent what music Dominicans could make, listen to, and buy.

Trujillo's favorite music was merengue, which had been a popular form of music since the nineteenth century. His direct involvement with merengue, despite its previous popularity, profoundly affected the nature of its development during the three decades he was in power. Moreover, because of his interference in musical production, he also severely inhibited the development of the Dominican popular music industry. Even bachata, which did not emerge as a distinct genre until after Trujillo's death, was affected indirectly but significantly by the political, economic, and cultural configurations that took shape during the dictatorship. This chapter will explore in detail the various ways Trujillo and his family influenced the Dominican popular music landscape out of which bachata emerged in the 1960s.

The Trujillato: Origins and Characteristics

Rafael Trujillo was born in 1891 into a lower-middle-class family from San Cristóbal, a town near Santo Domingo. As a young man Trujillo joined the Dominican constabulary, the Guardia Nacional Dominicana, which had been set up in 1917 by U.S. occupation forces to serve as a local police force. By the time the Marines withdrew from the country in 1924, Trujillo had risen through the ranks and had assumed leadership of the Guardia Nacional. Internal political turmoil, which had long plagued the country (and had been cited as a justification for the U.S. 1916–24 occupation), continued unabated after the withdrawal of the Marines, creating the conditions for Trujillo—through a variety of intrigues and strategies that included murder and rigged elections—to seize power in 1930 (Black 1986; Crassweiler 1966).

Once in power, Trujillo set about to acquire absolute political power. His first target was the civil service, long the nation's largest source of employment. The country's prior experience had proved that a government unable to provide enough civil-service jobs could not maintain public support. Yet the country was in debt, and Trujillo could not borrow money to cover the salaries for the civil servants he needed to insure his support. His solution was to decree that no public office could be held by a person not belonging to the Partido Dominicano, his personal political party, which he founded in 1931. Because in the Dominican system political parties were charged with nominating persons for government positions such as the Supreme Court and the Senate, Trujillo thereby gained control of the upper levels of the government as well. He then added the proviso that all public employees, from the lowest to the highest, were required to pay 10 percent of their salary to the Partido Dominicano. The 10 percent, deducted directly from all government paychecks, provided the Partido Dominicano with an enormous budget establishing it as a powerful and influential quasi-governmental organization: it distributed food and other types of social assistance, it constructed office buildings all over the country, it organized meetings and rallies, it even loaned money to the national government (Bosch 1986b: 388–89). In addition to these measures, which devastated competing political parties, opponents and critics were harassed, imprisoned, and assassinated by the armed forces. In this way, Trujillo—ambitious, greedy, and ruthless—managed to acquire absolute power over the country that he maintained until he was assassinated in 1961.

Trujillo also used his power to turn the country's economic system to his own personal advantage, obtaining monopolistic control of key sectors through a combination of governmental decree and physical intimidation of competitors. For example, Dominicans had always consumed sea salt, which had been easily produced along the country's extensive Caribbean shoreline. Trujillo purchased the country's only source of rock salt and promptly declared sea salt illegal, citing environmental damage to the coast as justification. He then quintupled the cost of salt, and within a short period of time his wealth increased several fold (Bosch 1986b: 390). He also gained monopolistic control over the sales in the capital of other goods such as tobacco and meat, as well as services such as insurance, which was required by law—although only his company was authorized to provide it. With the wealth generated by these enterprises he established new industries such as cement, paint, and shoe factories. He also purchased controlling interests in the foreign-owned sugar plantations and banks, reducing foreign influence to a minimum; when Trujillo died in 1961 only four important U.S. companies remained in the country. As Juan Bosch points out, Trujillo became "the owner of political, military and economic control. . . . The Dominican state was his personal enterprise" (Bosch 1986: 404–5, translation mine).

Trujillo and the Development of Merengue

Like others of his class, Rafael Trujillo loved vernacular music and dance, but his favorite was merengue. When he came to power in 1930, merengue was only one of a variety of regional recreational music styles existing in the countryside—for example, *mangulina, carabiné, pripri, sarandunga,* and several variants of merengue, including the *pambiche,* the accordion-based *merengue cibaeño* (merengue from the Cibao region), and merengue played with guitars. A wide variety of guitar-based musics were also popular in rural areas; some of these, such as bolero, son, and guaracha, originated elsewhere in the Spanish Caribbean. Other primarily sacred genres such as *salve* and *música de palos* were also used as recreational music after or in between ritual performances (Martha Ellen Davis, personal communication). The accordion-based merengue was most popular among the lighter-skinned peasants from the Cibao, a region that was also home to the country's traditional elite. The Cibaeñan elite, for their part, had little use for the local merengue, which they considered irredeemably vulgar, preferring instead foreign music considered more appropriate to "refined" culture, such as fox-trots from the United States, or Cuban rumbas.

The origins of merengue are much disputed; in addition to the Dominican Republic itself, Cuba, Puerto Rico, and Haiti have all been mentioned as possible birthplaces. No one, however, disputes that merengue's principal development has been in the Dominican Republic. Some accounts report that the merengue was first danced in 1844 in the northwest region of the country, near the Haitian border, during the Dominican Republic's struggle to defeat the occupying Haitians (Coopersmith 1949). If the merengue was, in fact, first observed in the northwest region of the country, it would lend weight to arguments that it may have descended from the Haitian *meringue* (Austerlitz 1986: 14); this suggestion, however, has been hotly contested by those Dominicans who would deny any Haitian influence on their national music. The first printed references to the merengue appeared in some 1855 Santo Domingo newspaper articles that decried the fact that the vulgar merengue was being danced in polite society (Jorge 1982a: 31).

The earliest merengues were played with guitars or related string instruments (Jorge 1982a: 62; Austerlitz 1986: 24). It was not until the 1870s, when the accordion was introduced into the Dominican Republic, that the accordion became the principal instrument of merengue ensembles from the Cibao region—although when accordions were unavailable, guitars continued to be used to play merengue. In other regions of the country, such as the east and southwest, merengue was played largely with guitars. Whether played with guitars or accordion, however, merengue remained essentially a rural music, whose principal performance contexts were family parties, community celebrations such as fiestas patronales, or related to other recreational events such as cockfights (Alberti 1975: 69).

During the U.S. occupation of the country between 1916 and 1924, popular music from the United States lost favor with the elite. A few fox-trots were in fact played in elite salons but, as Dominican band leader Luis Alberti has stressed, only those with a Latin flavor: "They had prohibited the performance and dance of American music in their salons; neither were the musicians interested in maintaining that kind of danceable musical number in their repertoires. 'My man' was the name of the first fox-trot that could break and penetrate that patriotic barrier; it imposed itself on an environment hostile to this music because of its French origin and because the melody had a completely Latin flavor" (Alberti 1975: 33, translation mine).

The merengue, once scorned by the elite because it was so rooted in vernacular culture, for the same reason became a symbol of national identity (Black 1986: 23). Nevertheless, before the merengue could enter polite society, it needed to be "dressed up" appropriately. This process took a few years, as composers searched for a way to transform merengue from a rural folk form to urban salon music. In 1918, a formally trained composer, Juan Francisco García, published the first arrangement of a merengue, although it was intended to be heard in a concert hall or salon rather than danced to. Later, composer Julio Alberto Hernández followed García's example of basing arrangements on folk merengues, although unlike García, Hernández added lyrics as well (Austerlitz 1986: 45; Jorge 1982a: 102). These efforts were not immediately appreciated: in 1922, when a merengue was played in a Puerto Plata social club, some members were so scandalized they walked out. "In the Commercial Club of Puerto Plata, those present at the dance left the salon in repudiation of the audacity of playing a popular and vulgar tune in such a distinguished place" (Lizardo 1978, translation mine).

This same year, however, Juan Espínola introduced a merengue—this time for dancing—into an elite club in La Vega, where it was well received by the members (Austerlitz 1986: 47). With the "refinements" provided by formally trained composers and arrangers, the merengue gradually made an entrance into the upper classes. After the Marines withdrew from the country, however, the merengue returned to being an index of class rather than national identity; and by the time Trujillo came to power in 1930, the merengue was once again principally associated with rural areas and customs—or, in urban areas, with low-class bars and brothels—and was generally considered unacceptable by the upper classes.

Guitar-based merengues were typical of the southeast region of the country where Trujillo was born, but he had come into contact with the accordion-based Cibaeñan form during military campaigns, and it had become his music of preference. He astutely recognized merengue's potential for attracting attention and support from his main power base, the campesinos, who at the time represented 82 percent of the country's total population (Duarte 1980: 191). During his successful campaign for the presidency in 1930, he traveled throughout the countryside accompanied by Cibaeñan merengue ensembles that sang to the future glories his election would bring (Austerlitz 1993: 78).

While the populace as a whole responded favorably to the musical propaganda, the upper classes scorned not only the music but the general himself for their low-class origins. Merengue composer Luis Alberti recalls the response of the elite to the rural merengue: "In the social dances that he attended, he always requested merengues, because it was his favorite music. Because society had proscribed the merengue, and now there was another motive to dislike it, [i.e.,] political sentiments, as soon as Trujillo turned his back they forgot about the merengue" (Alberti 1975: 74–75, translation mine).

Backed by his ill-gotten wealth and increasing power, Trujillo eventually insinuated himself into Dominican high society—although he did not thereupon abandon his preference for the rural merengue cibaeño in favor of the more "refined" and international tastes of the elite. Instead, he decided to refashion the merengue so that it would better reflect his new social context and, furthermore, turn it into a symbol of the power and modernity of his regime. In 1936 Trujillo hired Luis Alberti's band Lira del Yaque and took it to the capital, Ciudad Trujillo—as he had renamed Santo Domingo. Alberti had attracted the dictator's attention in 1932 when he added the traditional güira, tambora, and accordion to the jazz band ensemble[1] and included arrangements of folk merengues—and original merengues as well—as a regular feature of the band's repertoire (Alberti 1975: 34). According to Rafael Colón, who sang for Alberti's orquesta, Trujillo took great personal interest in the band, taking note any time there was a change in personnel (Cruz Triffolio 1988) and in 1942 naming it after himself: Orquesta Generalísimo Trujillo (which after his death was again renamed Orquesta Santa Cecilia) (Alberti 1975: 58).

Dominican sociologist Teófilo Barreiro commented on merengue's transformation:

> Trujillo introduced the merengue to strengthen his class position. So that there would be a typical Dominican music, the merengue was transformed into a kind of salon music. An orchestra was formed, which he himself contracted and shaped, which was the Orquesta Santa Cecilia. Subsequently the merengue of the dictatorship was a merengue that was cultured, refined, harmonic, sophisticated, appropriate for a particular way of dancing it, a merengue in which the lyrics were poetic—they rhymed adequately, because Trujillo didn't allow things to be done poorly. (Interview)

Joseíto Mateo, a merengue singer just beginning his career at the time, witnessed the impact of Alberti's band: "Alberti went straight to the [*sic*] society. He had an elite band, sponsored by Trujillo, who brought it to the salons, so when we saw them, they looked fine. Also, he was a great musician. This was another class of merengue" (cited by Austerlitz 1986: 63). Alberti may not have been the first to incorporate elements of folk merengue into an urban dance band, but because he was backed by Trujillo and became so widely known, he has been credited with being most responsible for permanently establishing merengue as the national music of the Dominican Republic (Austerlitz 1993: 79–80).

Trujillo's influence on merengue was not limited to changes in musical style; he also transformed merengue's social position by literally forcing it upon the elite. Rafael Colón recalled that no one was allowed to leave a dance at which the Orquesta Generalísimo Trujillo was playing until Trujillo himself left—even on one occasion when the party went on for more than twenty-four hours (Cruz Triffolio 1988). As Miniño observed, "The merengue was one of the means that the tyrant used to break the resistance of the social elite, who had previously rejected him, this being a subtle way of imposing one class upon another" (Miniño 1983: 17, translation mine). Band leader Rafael Solano noted the changes in social attitudes toward merengue by recalling the time when his orquesta arrived at an elite social club in Santiago. They parked the car in front of the club and attempted to enter in order to set up. An irate member came out and berated them for presuming to use the front door, sending them around to the servants' entrance in the back. Years later, when Solano was director of the Orquesta Angelita (named after one of Trujillo's daughters), the orquesta was engaged to play at the same club. This time they were met at the door by the members, who escorted them inside, offered them drinks, toasted them—and did not neglect to send back greetings to the general (Rafael Solano, 1987 conference presentation).

As if Trujillo's support alone was not enough to give the merengue a significant boost, Trujillo's brother José Arismendi, commonly known as Petán, also loved music and founded a top-notch band called the Orquesta San José that played regularly in a luxurious ballroom located inside the broadcasting studios of the country's leading radio station, La Voz Dominicana—which he owned. It is said that Petán and Rafael Trujillo competed with each other through their respective orquestas, and one story has it that Rafael once became incensed when Petán outfitted his band with new uniforms grander than those of Rafael's (García 1985: 191–96). There was no question, however, that the Trujillo brothers' bands were the finest in the country, and the Trujillo era is still remembered as the golden age of the merengue orquestas.

Trujillo, then, succeeded in isolating one regional rural music form, the merengue cibaeño, and introducing it to all regions of the country and to all classes of Dominican society. Under his tutelage, the merengue became, once again—this time permanently—a symbol of national identity. As Teófilo Barreiro remarked, "After Trujillo established that merengue was the national dance, the person who didn't dance merengue was not Dominican" (interview). Yet while Trujillo successfully transformed the merengue into the country's national music, he did not thereby eliminate merengue's class associations: on the contrary, his support of the large dance bands encouraged a class-based cleavage that developed between the small traditional, rural conjuntos and the large orquestas—a cleavage which remains to this day. He did continue to support some traditional merengue conjuntos, such as those of Ñico Lora and Toño Abreu (Austerlitz 1986: 58), but he lavished far more money and attention on the merengue orquestas, which, unlike the conjuntos, played regularly in the most fashionable clubs and hotels and on Petán's radio station, La Voz Dominicana.

As the increasingly sophisticated urban orquestas were elevated into high society, a name was needed to distinguish their merengue from its lower-class predecessor played by merengue conjuntos. Because the word *merengue* had become a symbol of the country's modern nationhood, it is not altogether surprising that the newer urban merengue de orquesta, associated with the dominant classes, kept the well-known and established name *merengue;* the merengue cibaeño, on the other hand, was henceforth referred to by urbanites as "perico ripiao" or as "merengue típico." The origins of the term *perico ripiao* are open to conjecture, although a common explanation is that it referred to the name of a Santiago bar/brothel in the early 1930s and later came to refer to the sort of rural accordion music that was played there (Miniño 1983: 39; Austerlitz 1986: 61).

At the same time that Trujillo was promoting the merengue typical of the largely white Cibao region, he suppressed musics that exhibited strong African characteristics. Even before his rise to power, Dominican culture was already notably Iberocentric and, in the aftermath of the twenty-two-year occupation by Haiti (1822–44), rabidly anti-Haitian. Trujillo himself was Afrophobic in spite of (or perhaps out of shame at) having a Haitian grandmother. In 1937, under the pretext of protecting the country's border areas from occupation by Haitian squatters, he ordered the execution of all Haitians living in Dominican territory (Moya 1992: 519). The resulting massacre took the lives of thousands of dark-skinned persons (estimates range from a low of about 12,000 to a high of 40,000), many of whom were Dominican. Under these conditions, those elements of Dominican rural folk culture that exhibited any traces of African and/or Haitian descent such as *vodú* (which even previously had been rejected and denigrated by Dominican society) were either abandoned or driven underground (see Davis 1987: 33–48).

On the other hand, one of the happier consequences of Trujillo's enthusiasm for music was that he founded and supported municipal bands, as well as academies of music in the larger provincial towns all over the country (Coopersmith 1949: 35). These municipal bands served several important functions in the musical life of the country as a whole; their performances in town squares on Sunday afternoons provided townspeople with free musical entertainment in a common public space.[2] Moreover, they provided formally trained national composers with an outlet and audience for their compositions. In turn, the existence of these provincial audiences encouraged composers to incorporate vernacular musical idioms into their compositions. Finally, these bands provided a generation of musicians with formal musical training and experience. Many musicians who began their careers in provincial bands later went on to play in merengue orquestas.

Trujillo's interest in merengue cannot be explained as simply reflecting his love of music. Under his tutelage Dominican popular music responded to a very specific agenda: propaganda (Jorge 1982b: 76–77). He first used merengue in his 1930 political campaign; but even after he seized power and up until his death, he continued to use music, particularly merengue, to indoctrinate and control the populace. No criticism of the regime—explicit or implicit—was tolerated in music (or any other media).

Very, very few composers/singers tried making even veiled commentaries on the dictatorship, and these usually had serious consequences; for example, a composer was imprisoned because of his song "La miseria" (Misery). The famous Dominican tenor Eduardo Brito also dared to sing a song called "Esclavo soy" (A slave I am), lamenting a poor Dominican's terrible working conditions. Brito died young, supposedly of mental disease, although many believed Brito was done away with by Trujillo.

Since its inception, merengue had been a vehicle for social commentary of all sorts, so this severe form of censorship represented a radical departure from its original form and function. Worse still was that musicians could not even maintain a discrete silence, but instead had to prove their loyalty by composing songs praising Trujillo and his every action. Some Trujillista songs were composed "voluntarily," while others were commissioned directly by Trujillo's political party, the Partido Dominicano. Not all pro-Trujillo compositions were recorded; some were sold in sheet music for live musical performances. The music glorifying Trujillo, however, was not a separate category of music under the exclusive control of the Partido Dominicano, but rather was considered part of the "normal" production of the country's music industry, and both recordings and sheet music were sold through regular commercial channels as well as through the Partido Dominicano. (The partido also gave away free recordings to foreign visitors as proof of the regime's popularity.) All Dominicans were required to listen and dance to Trujillista music, and all record vendors had to stock it, to be sold to people who, willingly or not, sought to include Trujillista songs in their collections. Francisco Amaro, who distributed records during the 1950s, recalls: "In any party you might have, you'd almost always have to have a [pro-Trujillo] record, even if you didn't play it. Or even if you played it only once. Because if you didn't play it, it was as if you didn't identify [with the regime]" (interview).

In the course of the thirty-one-year Trujillo regime thousands of merengues extolling the dictator and his activities were produced, not by a few slavish followers of the dictator, but by all Dominican composers of any stature who did not go into exile. An anthology of songs from the period entitled *Antología musical de la era de Trujillo 1930–1960* contains three hundred of what were considered the best of these merengues, many of which were written by the country's leading composers of both popular and classical music (Rivera González n.d.). The titles of these songs reveal the depths of submission and triviality to which the composers were forced to stoop: "Veneremos a Trujillo" (We venerate Trujillo) (1949); "Trujillo es grande e inmortal" (Trujillo is great and immortal) (1953); "Gloria al benefactor" (Glory to the benefactor) (1932); "Pedimos la reelección" (We want reelection) (1946); "El embajador-at-large" (The ambassador-at-large) (1941); "Trujillo protector de choferes" (Trujillo, protector of chauffeurs) (1950). Other merengues served to publish the regime's views on national or world events, resulting in such forgettable titles as: "El censo de 1950" (The census of 1950) (1950) and "La deuda externa" (The foreign debt) (1954).

Luis Alberti's merengue "Najayo," a paean to Trujillo's country home, is a typical example of pro-Trujillo merengues—and is still considered a classic.

Najayo

Es Najayo bello, sitio ideal	Beautiful Najayo, ideal place
Residencia veraniega de Trujillo	Summer residence of Trujillo
Es un precioso paisaje natural	Its lovely natural landscape
Engrandece la grandeza por su brillo	Exalts greatness with its brilliance
La casita que lo adorna de marfil	The little marble house adorning it
Embellece ese paisaje natural	Beautifies that natural landscape
Engalana la floresta del vecino	It enhances the neighboring woods
El lugar donde descansa el general	The place where the general rests
Que viva Trujillo	Long live Trujillo
Hombre sin igual	Man without equal
Que viva Trujillo	Long live Trujillo
Nuestro general	Our general
Trujillo Molina	Trujillo Molina
Dios me lo bendiga	May God bless him for me
Así dice la gente	So say the people
Trujillo que viva	Long live Trujillo
General estrella	Stellar general
Eso digo yo	That's what I say
Trujillo en la tierra	On earth, Trujillo
Y en el cielo Dios	And in heaven, God

In spite of the obsequious titles and lyrics, some of these songs were, in fact, widely popular because the music itself was good. Francisco Amaro recalls one that was a major hit: "Pedro Pérez made a record about politics that was called 'Era gloriosa' (Glorious era). The record was really popular—they sold like hotcakes! They made two or three political numbers like that that sold a lot; because they were danceable, people bought them" (interview).

To some Dominicans in exile, however, the merengue could not so easily be disassociated from the dictatorship. The following passage by Nicolás Silfa, writing about his exile in New York during Trujillo's regime, is a scathing attack on merengue and its relationship to the dictator. It also expresses an unmistakable contempt for merengue's (and by implication, Trujillo's) low-class origins:

At 11 o'clock in the morning the parade passed in front of us. . . . They caused laughter and shame and compassion. We were Dominicans! The ridiculous group of our compatriots, in their large majority obligated to participate in that spectacle, gave the impression that Trujillo's consul in New York had collected all the güiras, tambourines, and goatskin drums in the city in order to put together that sad show. That crazed gang circulated through the most aristocratic city of the United States, seeming to have emerged from the most remote and uncivilized regions of the globe. The troupe moved down the wide avenues, playing out of tune the latest variations of merengues that had been written to render homage to the dictator. The few passersby who were strolling in the street in the inclement weather burst out laughing, not understanding the language and much less the strange music. Everything was transformed into güiras and more güiras, tambourines and more tambourines, tamboras and more tamboras. (Silfa 1980: 373–74, translation mine)

The Dominican Music Industry in the Trujillo Era

Trujillo's influence on Dominican popular music was by no means limited to supporting bands and certain musical genres, or even to controlling the lyrical content of songs: his long regime spanned almost the entire period during which the country's broadcast and recording technologies were established and developed, and indelibly marked their evolution with his imprint. As a result of his power over the country's mass media he determined what Dominicans could hear on the radio, what could be recorded and who could record it, what could be sold and what could be bought.

While in some ways the growth of the Dominican recording and broadcast industries resembled that of their counterparts in other third-world countries, in other ways their development was unique and in many cases anomalous. It is important to keep this in mind, because the peculiar configuration of the mass media inherited by the country after Trujillo's death shaped bachata and its subsequent development. Moreover, it insured the hegemonic position of the music that was to be bachata's principal competitor—merengue. Tracing the development of the Dominican music industry helps to illuminate the struggles between contending groups in Dominican society for access and control over the media, not simply for economic motives, but for the power to determine the construction of social and national identities, and to assign value and meaning to various forms of cultural expression.

Radio Broadcasting

Throughout most of Trujillo's regime, radio was the principal medium of mass communication. The beginnings of radio broadcasting in the Dominican Republic were, like Trujillo's own career, linked to the 1916–24 U.S. occupation. The first radio equipment to arrive in the country was brought by the Marines, who used it in their efforts to locate and destroy guerrilla resistance in the eastern region (Collado 1985). A pioneer in Dominican radio broadcasting, Frank Hatton Guerrero (of mixed Irish and Dominican descent), was one of the Dominicans engaged by the U.S. armed forces to serve as interpreters and intermediaries. Hatton had learned about radio while studying in the United States before the occupation, but it is unclear whether he actually worked with any U.S. radio-telegraphic equipment. In 1924, while the Marines were still in the country, Hatton established a small radio station, HIH, from which he broadcast Spanish versions of baseball and boxing events he heard on U.S. radio. After the Marines withdrew, he expanded his operation, and in 1927 his station, renamed HIZ, became the country's first commercial station (Homero León Díaz, interview).

By the time Trujillo became president in 1930, the country had at least three radio stations.[3] One of these, HIX, had been established in 1928 and was the official government station. Although I did not find any documentation to this effect, it is probably safe to assume that Trujillo used it for political purposes as soon as he took power. Trujillo continued to allow private stations to operate, and at least three more stations were established during the 1930s. In 1935 Trujillo founded his own radio station, La Voz del Partido Dominicano, which was the exclusive organ of his political party, the Partido Dominicano. While this station was dedicated primarily to propagating the activities of the Partido Dominicano, its programming included music, sports, humor, drama, and *novelas* (romantic serials) and therefore competed with the existing radio stations for the attention of the Dominican public (León Díaz 1982).

Trujillo was fully aware of the power of radio, and insisted on controlling it. The resulting censorship in the media—as in all other aspects of the country's life—stunted the cultural development of an entire generation of Dominicans. Some censorship was explicit: for example, one decree required newscasters to keep copies of their broadcasts for one year so that they could be examined at any time for subversive material; another required announcers to obtain a license—issued by the government, of course. But most censorship was what radio broadcaster Homero León Díaz called *auto-censura* (self-censorship); people simply knew what they could and could not say. Self-censorship seems to have been effective, because Trujillo closed down only two stations for political reasons during his thirty-one-year regime (Homero León Díaz, interview).

Of course with Trujillo it was not always easy to predict what would offend him. The combination of Trujillo's absolute power and his paranoia exerted a chilling effect on broadcasting, as the following anecdote told by León Díaz illustrates. He recalled that radio newscasters often got their news from international radio. One day a newscaster reported something he had heard on a French radio station—that President Roosevelt was fishing in Dominican waters. Shortly afterwards, the newscaster was taken into custody and questioned about where he had gotten the story. Trujillo was angry because he heard the story on the radio before hearing it from his own intelligence agency; as a result he decreed that newscasters could not broadcast anything that had not first been published by the newspapers. León Díaz recalled another incident: when a disc jockey broadcast a Chinese record given to him by a friend, Trujillo thought it was a coded message for the opposition and jailed the disc jockey until he could prove that the song was simply in Chinese and did not contain subversive material (interview).

In 1942 Trujillo's brother Petán founded a radio station called La Voz del Yuna in the provincial city of Bonao. Sometime between 1947 and 1948, he moved the station to Santo Domingo and changed its name to La Voz Dominicana. Thereafter, endowed with the best equipment Petán's considerable wealth could acquire and enhanced by the power and prestige that accompanied Trujillo ownership, it became the country's most important radio station until after the fall of the Trujillos in 1961.

Petán, reports León Díaz, loved music, and while he was an unsavory character in every other respect, he valued both musicians as well as radio personnel, paying them well and establishing schools for voice training and for radio announcers. He believed that musicians' principal occupation was performance—*live* performance—and that records should be used only when musicians were physically incapable of performing. La Voz Dominicana, then, broadcast its entire twelve hours of daily programming live. Beginning in 1953 La Voz Dominicana also began sponsoring an annual week-long festival called La Semana Aniversaria (Anniversary Week), for which foreign musicians were invited to the Dominican Republic to perform live on the air (Lora Medrano 1984: 83–84). When I asked León Díaz why Petán would choose such a grueling method of running a radio station, he replied, "chifladuras del dueño" (the owner's lunacy) (interview).

The effect on the musicians, however, was devastating, because even though they were paid adequately, they were on exclusive contract with the station and could not perform or record without Petán's permission. Because La Voz Dominicana did not record music—which would have run contrary to Petán's insistence on exclusivity and on live performance—the musicians were effectively prevented from recording. As we shall see below, some musicians did in fact record with a few intrepid producers, but not on a scale which would have permitted them to become major recording stars as had their peers in other Spanish Caribbean countries, nor to reap the profits thereof.

The Dominican Republic's central location in the Caribbean basin and the relatively clear airwaves that existed before 1960 meant that in addition to the national radio stations, Dominicans could also tune in to radio stations from elsewhere, including Cuba, Puerto Rico, Colombia, Mexico, and the United States. During most of his regime Trujillo permitted the population to listen to foreign radio, so Dominicans were able to hear music broadcast from these countries—although by most accounts, Cuban radio was by far the most well liked. The foreign radio stations were quite popular, which meant that local radio stations had to compete not only with La Voz Dominicana, which monopolized the best national musicians, but with foreign radio stations as well. Because, as I will explain below, there was little recorded Dominican music available, Dominican radio programming depended on imported recorded music—mostly Cuban, Mexican, Colombian, Puerto Rican, and North American.

Listening to foreign radio became less acceptable as the 1950s progressed, when the opposition—especially the exile community in Cuba—was becoming more worrisome to the regime; after the Cuban Revolution in 1959, it became a punishable crime to listen to Cuban radio. Many Dominicans recall that Trujillo's security forces used to drive through neighborhoods in Volkswagen bugs known as *cepillos* listening for the sounds of forbidden radio, and even today some associate the sound of the VW bug with state repression.

Recording

Like radio broadcasting, recording began early in the Dominican Republic, but its development was similarly paralyzed by the interference of the Trujillo family. A complete and autonomous recording industry, which included all stages from recording to pressing to distribution, did not emerge within the country until the late 1950s, far later than in other Spanish Caribbean countries.

The first recordings of Dominican musicians were made in the late 1920s by the U.S.-based Columbia and Victor Talking Machine companies, both of which sold phonographs in the Dominican Republic and were competing for the Dominican market.[4] In 1927 Columbia recorded the Puerto Rican Trío Borinquen, whose lead singer was the Dominican Antonio Mesa, in its New York studios.[5] In 1928 Victor made the first recordings of Dominican musicians within the Dominican Republic itself, at the government radio station HIX in Santo Domingo (the selections included a merengue, two boleros, two criollas, and a *canción*, a song form similar to the criolla and the bolero). Because of the primitive recording facilities at HIX and the destructive effects of tropical heat and humidity on the wax cylinders that were used for recording at the time, these recordings were of very poor quality, so Victor abandoned the idea of recording in the country; henceforth Victor recorded Dominican artists only in their New York studio (Incháustegui 1987).

For the next two decades, all recording of Dominican musicians was done in New York. There were two exceptions, which are more interesting as unusual anecdotes than as milestones in Dominican recording. The first occurred in 1936 when Juan Salazar Hernández, an engineer at HIN (La Voz del Partido Dominicano), manufactured a recording device made out of spare parts that included a steering wheel, watch parts, and pieces of a sewing machine (Incháustegui 1987). Because of its limited recording capacities, the principal purpose of this equipment was to record radio commercials, but it was also used to record a few merengues. The second exceptional recording event occurred in 1940, when Leopold Stokowski, who was making a world tour with his orchestra aboard a transatlantic ship, visited the Dominican Republic and made some recordings of Luis Alberti's orquesta in a small recording studio that was on board (Incháustegui 1987). Alberti sent the masters abroad for pressing and released them under the Alberti label, which, Incháustegui observed, were the only significant Dominican recordings made during the early 1940s (Incháustegui, interview).

Recording in the Dominican Republic itself did not really begin until 1944, when Frank Hatton brought the first Fairchild recording equipment to the country and installed it in his radio station, HIZ. Hatton's equipment recorded directly onto acetate discs, which was adequate for radio commercials—which they were intended for—but inefficient for recording discs to be sold to the public, because each acetate disc was an "original" (Homero León Díaz, interview). The technological limitations of this recording equipment, then, did not allow anything beyond extremely limited distribution.

In 1946 Petán Trujillo brought another Fairchild to the country for recording the musicians he had on contract with La Voz Dominicana (Homero León Díaz, interview) and founded the Dominican Recording Company, which was to release these recordings on the Caracol label (Incháustegui 1987). In order to eliminate any competition with his brother's new company, Rafael Trujillo promptly forbade the importation of foreign recordings. Petán, however, lacked the enthusiasm and know-how to properly commercialize the recordings of his musicians, so that only two 78 RPM records were ever released under the Caracol label. Because the recording venture languished, after a year or two Trujillo again permitted merchants to import foreign records (Radhames Aracena, interview). Throughout the entire decade of the 1940s, then, while other Latin American countries were recording national and regional musics of all types, there was practically no record production in the Dominican Republic.

It was not until the early 1950s that Frank Hatton imported the first truly modern recording equipment to the country: an Ampex that recorded onto magnetic tape, from which multiple copies of a recording could be made. Hatton purchased this equipment in order to record radio commercials and novelas and never got involved personally in recording and distributing music. He did, however, rent the equipment to others, which allowed a number of individuals to cautiously venture into the commercial recording of Dominican musicians. Among these new producers were band leaders Luis Alberti and Antonio Morel, and businessmen Julio Tonos, Francisco Amaro, Babín Echevarría, and Radhames Aracena (Incháustegui 1987). But it must be emphasized that these were small enterprises, whose entrepreneurial (and courageous) owners recorded and released records whenever possible, but by no means were they well-developed "record companies" as we think of them. Furthermore, the country still did not have any record manufacturing facilities, and master tapes still needed to be sent to the United States for stamping and pressing.

Because Petán had the best Dominican musicians on contract with La Voz Dominicana and had little interest in recording them for commercial purposes, these musicians did not have the same opportunities to record (or to benefit from recording) that they would have had in another country. The fact that Dominican musicians had to travel abroad to record, however, also meant that they had an opportunity to remain in exile—and several did. One notable example was Billo Frómeta, who took his Ciudad Trujillo Jazz Band on a tour to Venezuela and stayed there. (In Venezuela Frómeta formed a band called Billo's Caracas Boys, which became one of the major pioneering groups of the salsa style in the Spanish Caribbean [Rondón 1980].) Other Dominican musicians to record in exile were Negrito Chapuseaux, Simó Damirón, and Angel Viloria, all of whom were responsible for introducing the merengue to the United States and Europe.

Throughout the 1950s, then, a national recording industry of sorts did exist, but it was small, timid, and incomplete, a fact that can be largely attributed to the inhibiting influence of the Trujillo family. No one wanted to attract the attention of the Trujillos, nor appear to compete with them, and Petán's participation in the music business actively discouraged people from entering that arena except with extreme caution. As music historian Miguel Holguín recalls, "Our development is atypical, it doesn't reflect what should have been or what was in other places. It was such an iron dictatorship, so ghastly, that if it occurred to me, for example, to make flutes, I'd think that maybe Petán might be thinking about something similar, or he might take an interest in it, and that would make me forget the flutes—just thinking that Petán might disapprove" (interview).

The case of Francisco Amaro, one of the first entrepreneurs to attempt to commercialize Dominican recordings, illustrates the influence of the dictatorship on the country's national recording industry. Amaro entered the record business at the end of the 1940s, renting "pickups" (portable sound systems that included a turntable, amplifier, speakers, and record collection) for political rallies sponsored by Trujillo's Partido Dominicano as well as for family parties: "At parties, 'pickups' were used; you rented them. For each person who entered, the man paid one peso, women paid fifty cents or nothing. So they had their parties, and they sold beverages, because there weren't any nightclubs or discotheques then. They were popular parties, for the common people, not the middle class" (Francisco Amaro, interview).

Later, however, when Amaro noticed the eagerness of his customers to buy the records from him, he stopped renting the pick-ups and decided to sell records instead. Amaro explains the demand: "In those days, around 1949–50, there was no recording here. All the music came from abroad, everyone listened to foreign radio stations. People listened to Cuba, to BBC in London, and so on. So the music that came out there would end up here. When the record came here, there was already a demand" (Amaro, interview).

At the time, the major international labels were handled by dealers who had obtained exclusive rights over local sales. Nevertheless, a friend of Amaro's, a local disc jockey named Din Soler who had traveled to Cuba, connected Amaro with a small label in Cuba called Panart and advised him on which records were likely to sell well in the Dominican Republic. Amaro began importing Cuban and later Puerto Rican records, which he sold to local radio stations. Subsequently, he established contact with the owner of a record company in Puerto Rico who urged him to record Dominican musicians himself and to send the tapes to Puerto Rico, where they would be forwarded to New York for pressing. The Puerto Rican company agreed to return a portion of the recordings to Amaro and keep the remainder for sale in Puerto Rico. Amaro replied that there were no recording studios in the Dominican Republic, but his friend insisted there had to be one that recorded radio commercials or novelas and encouraged him to request permission to use the equipment for recording music. Amaro approached Frank Hatton, who agreed to let him use HIZ's equipment.

Dominican musicians—especially the most prominent ones who were under contract to Petán's La Voz Dominicana—were understandably frustrated at their inability to record. One of them, Luis Kalaff, agreed to record for Amaro just for the pleasure of hearing himself on a record. The recording sold well, and Amaro hesitantly began recording other musicians including Lucía Félix and Antonio Morel. Often he recorded at the request of the musicians, who were so anxious to hear themselves on discs that as payment they required only a few copies of the records to give to friends. With time, more and more musicians recorded for Amaro, although they later began to demand some sort of compensation: "They saw that there were profits. What I did was give them things, dinner, drink, things like that, but little money" (Francisco Amaro, interview).

HIZ's recording equipment, intended for recording novelas and commercials rather than music, had only one microphone, so recordings from this period were of small ensembles rather than of the larger urban orquestas. Amaro recalls these early recordings: "They sounded acceptable, they were passable, but it [HIZ's recording equipment] wasn't any good for big orchestras. Conjuntos típicos, merengue conjuntos, guitar trios, but not big ensembles" (interview).

The few Dominican musicians who recorded in this period were those who had already established a name for themselves through live performances or through live broadcasts on La Voz Dominicana, and whose records were guaranteed public acceptance; for example, Juan Lockward, the son of Danda Lockward and a favorite of the Trujillos, recorded during this period. It was not the kind of context, however, in which unknown musicians could rent a recording studio, find a radio station to play their records, and thereby hope to establish careers in the music business. An elderly Dominican guitarist recalled:

> In Trujillo's time there were few singers who had made a record, because you had to receive the approval of too many juries, too many tests; spend two or three years performing in a broadcast studio and be listened to by many important musicians like Papa Molina, Don Goyo Rivas, who directed the Orquesta Santa Cecilia for many years. Then, if you didn't meet these requirements to make a record and if you didn't have the approval of Petán Trujillo, who would dare to make a record without the permission of Trujillo? (Interview)

What remains a mystery is how the recording business was able to survive at all under the shadow of the Trujillos. Yet in spite of these conditions, Amaro and other local entrepreneurs such as Julio Tonos and Antonio Morel used Hatton's studios, sent the tapes abroad for pressing, and released the records under their own labels. Amaro eventually recorded most of Petán's musicians, all of them at Hatton's studio, although sometimes he changed the names of the musicians on the label, so Petán would not know who was playing. Petán initially either didn't notice the recordings or looked the other way; Miguel Pichardo, a studio engineer active in the late 1950s, recalls that these labels were small enough that they didn't attract the attention of the Trujillos (Miguel Pichardo, interview).

Nevertheless, Amaro and the other recording entrepreneurs like him were always vulnerable to the unpredictable and potentially deadly wrath of the Trujillos. Amaro recalls that one day in 1955 Petán recognized the voice of Nicolás Casimiro, one of his (Petán's) favorite singers, on a radio station that was not La Voz Dominicana. The Trujillos had made a number of recordings of Casimiro for their personal use, but they had not been released or even broadcast on La Voz Dominicana. When Petán heard Amaro's recordings of Casimiro on the radio, he was enraged and sent his guards to arrest Amaro for having had the audacity to record his "personal" musician. During the interrogation, Petán learned that Amaro had recorded many other of La Voz Dominicana's musicians as well. Amaro, terrified for his life, nevertheless managed to convince Petán that he was only trying to promote Dominican musicians; and in a desperate strategic move, he suggested to Petán that there was money to be made in recording and that they should go into business together. Petán agreed, and from then on Amaro rented the recording equipment from La Voz Dominicana rather than HIZ and, additionally, paid Petán a share of the profits (Francisco Amaro, interview).

It was not until 1959 that the first record-manufacturing factory, Fábrica Dominicana de Discos, began pressing 45 RPMs in the country. Incháustegui credits the founding of the factory to Pedro Pablo Bonilla (Incháustegui 1987). Record producer Radhames Aracena, on the other hand, reports that the factory was actually owned by the wife of Rafael Trujillo's son, Radhames Trujillo. Aracena claims that the Trujillos had offered him the "opportunity" to go into the business with them before Bonilla got involved but that he declined, expressing lack of interest, but in fact not wanting to do business with the Trujillos. Subsequently, Aracena says that the Trujillos approached Bonilla to establish and run the business but that control of the company remained in Trujillo's hands. (Aracena claims that Bonilla later served again as front man for the Trujillos, appearing as the owner of a television station [Channel 4], which was actually a Trujillo enterprise.) Aracena's version, in which the Trujillo's were the actual owners of the new record company, is borne out by the fact that shortly after the company was established, the importation of foreign records was forbidden.

Record Distribution

In spite of the Trujillo family's interest in music, with the exception of the brief periods when Petán tried to establish the Caracol label in 1946 and in 1959 when Fábrica Dominicana de Discos was founded, neither Trujillo nor his family sought to profit from record sales. As a result, there were fewer obstacles to record distribution than there were to other aspects of the music business. Moreover, given the lack of serious competition from a national recording industry, imported records enjoyed a definite advantage. As a result, imported records played a far larger role in the Dominican musical landscape than in other Latin American countries whose national recording industries competed more actively and effectively with music from abroad.

At the time, each of the major international labels had strengths in the music of a certain country; for example, RCA distributed some of the most popular Mexican artists such as María Luisa Landín and Luis Alcaraz, while Columbia distributed some of the more successful Puerto Rican artists. These record companies gave exclusive licensing agreements for their entire catalogue to a handful of wealthy, urban-based merchants within the Dominican Republic. Thus for example, García Gautier's store Odix handled all RCA distribution in the Dominican Republic; other dealers who wanted to sell RCA records could not negotiate directly with RCA, but had to buy from Odix (Radhames Aracena, interview).

Recorded music was much in demand in urban lower-class contexts, where parties depending on rented sound systems called pickups had largely replaced the informal gatherings with live music such as bachatas and pasadías that were common in rural areas. Jukeboxes, known in the Dominican Republic as *velloneras*, were also a tremendous stimulus to Dominican record vendors. The term *vellonera* came from the word *vello*, meaning hair, referring to the shock of hair between the horns of the buffalo on U.S. nickels used to operate them; jukeboxes were also known as *traganíkels*, or "nickel-swallowers." In the 1950s almost every *colmado* (neighborhood store) and *barra* (bar) throughout the country was equipped with a jukebox—many of which were 78 RPM models that had been unloaded cheaply on the Dominican Republic by Puerto Ricans after they had purchased the newer 45 RPM machines. Trujillo's brother-in-law Francisco Martínez de Alba imported thousands of these jukeboxes and placed them in colmados, free of charge, in exchange for 50 percent of the earnings. It was a highly desirable arrangement, because the jukeboxes did not require any capital investment by the owner of the colmado except for the cost of buying records (Radhames Aracena, interview).

In rural areas, whether for reasons of aesthetic preferences or simply availability, songs remained popular far longer than they did in urban areas. Music historian Miguel Holguín recalled that "rural people used to come from the countryside in order to exchange with the cafes, the restaurants. In other words, when the records had been listened to too much in the city, they sold them to people from the countryside, where they continued to listen to old songs." Radhames Aracena, who distributed records in the 1950s, also observed that in the countryside as records wore out, they were often replaced by other recordings of the same song. After the international recording companies ceased releasing new artists and songs in the older 78 RPM format, Aracena astutely continued to reorder new pressings of older, long-popular music specifically for rural jukeboxes; although on each record jacket he printed the phrase "Acostúmbrate a comprar los discos pequeños" (Get used to buying the little records) in order to prepare his customers for the inevitable disappearance of 78 RPM records.

Colmados were ubiquitous in towns and cities, and even in rural areas where more than a few houses clustered together: as far back as the late 1930s there were almost 14,000 of these commercial establishments in the country, an enormous number of shops for a population of little more than 1.5 million persons (Bosch 1986b: 399). Because the stores were so numerous and accessible, people visited them frequently to buy small quantities of groceries and, in doing so, could encounter friends and listen to whatever music happened to be on the jukebox. The jukeboxes placed in colmados throughout the country transformed these small grocery stores into important loci of musical dissemination—particularly to poor people not likely to own sound equipment—by providing a public social context for listening and dancing to music, and for discussing music as well. Colmados' musical functions persisted well into the post-Trujillo era, even after jukeboxes were later replaced by record players.

Other entertainment establishments—barras and their close relatives, cabarets, cantinas, and *burdeles* (various words for bars associated with prostitution)—were also important sites of musical transmission, because they too had jukeboxes, although they would be more likely than the colmados to have occasional live entertainment. An anecdote related in a retrospective article on the Trujillo era in a 1983 issue of ¡*Ahora!* illustrates the economic importance of these establishments, as well as how the financial interests of the dictator's family determined public policy decisions:

> The dictator Rafael L. Trujillo Molina ordered the closure of all houses of prostitution in the country . . . but when the complaints began to come in and he realized that the income from taxes on alcoholic beverages was diminishing, he reopened them. This event took place in 1957. I remember that in my natal town they closed the only two there were, but soon afterwards, we could again hear at night, after the electric plant closed down, the sounds of the güira, tambora, and accordion that emerged from them. When the dictator closed the cabarets, they began to send back the jukeboxes, which were sold exclusively by Mr. Francisco Martínez de Alba, his brother-in-law. The ice factories stopped making sales, furniture was being returned from the houses of prostitution and the brothels, and the prostitutes began going back to their hometowns. The sale of rum, cigarettes, and beer diminished considerably, and then it was seen that the measure was an error. (Cordero Regalado 1983: 4, translation mine)

Radhames Aracena and Empresas Guarachita

One of the individuals who successfully imported and distributed records in the Dominican Republic during the Trujillo era was Radhames Aracena, who merits special attention in this chapter for several reasons. Aracena began as a small-time radio disc jockey and record vendor but was able to create a profitable multifaceted company called Empresas Guarachita (Guarachita Enterprises)—which today includes all aspects of record production, from recording to manufacture to promotion to retail sales. Aracena's success story aptly illustrates the unusual combination of constraints and opportunities encountered by music-business entrepreneurs during the Trujillo regime. Aracena was also a major distributor of those guitar-based musics popular in rural areas that were bachata's antecedents. Later, in the post-Trujillo era, Aracena became the most successful bachata producer in the country. Finally, Radhames Aracena and his Empresas Guarachita have had an enormous impact on the Dominican music industry in general and on bachata in particular, and he will be referred to frequently in the chapters that follow. In order to maintain the chronological continuity of this book, material on Radhames Aracena's early career, during the Trujillo era, is included here; the later development of Guarachita in the post-Trujillo era is discussed in detail in Chapter 3.

Radhames Aracena was born in 1930 to a family of modest means in Santiago, although his family migrated to the capital, then known as Ciudad Trujillo, when he was very young. At the age of 18, while he was still in high school, he approached Homero León Díaz, director of radio station HIN, La Voz del Trópico, requesting an opportunity to work as an announcer. Díaz, struck by the young man's enthusiasm, agreed to let him work at HIN on an informal basis. After four years at HIN, Aracena was offered a job at HIZ by its owner, Frank Hatton, who had been impressed by Aracena's announcing style. After two years at HIZ he moved to HI5K, a new station at the time, where he eked out a living working as a news announcer. Noticing that the station had no program at noon, Aracena requested and received permission to use that hour of radio time.

From the beginning Aracena displayed the combination of cultural astuteness, entrepreneurial skills, and showmanship that contributed to his later success. With the earnings he received from the noon-hour music program's sponsors, he purchased an additional half hour of radio time. In the first hour he played a variety of popular music. Realizing, however, that the show following his was a popular sports program, he gambled that even if he filled most of his half hour with commercials, people wouldn't change the radio dial if they were sufficiently entertained. Because he charged very little for the commercials, his sponsors tended to be small neighborhood businesses, such as auto repair shops and colmados, that his audience was likely to be familiar with. People liked the music he played in the first hour and did not mind listening to the lively and folksy commercials while they waited for the sports show to come on. He called the show "La campana comercial" (The commercial bell), referring to the bell sound he produced by banging on a metal rod he hung from the ceiling in order to enliven the show.

In 1955 these successful strategies caught the attention of Ramón Pacheco, who invited Aracena to direct a radio station he had just purchased called Onda Musical. Aracena agreed, under the conditions that he be paid in radio time rather than cash and that he be allowed to make certain changes in the announcing format. At the time, radio announcing was considered a serious business, and the booth was supposed to be a perfectly soundless, neutral environment. Aracena, however, introduced sound—all sorts of sounds—into the announcers booth: to Pacheco's dismay Aracena installed a telephone in the booth and took live requests from the public by putting the telephone receiver up to the microphone. Moreover, rejecting the usual formal, deadpan style used by other radio announcers, Aracena animated his voice, varying its volume, speed, pitch, and intensity. At first his innovations were considered by some to be tasteless and inappropriate, but he was undeniably successful in attracting an audience. Today, these ideas are standard practice in radio broadcasting, and Aracena is frequently credited with being the father of the modern Dominican disc jockey.

Aracena's ability to recognize and creatively use the power of sound to attract attention indicated his ability to perceive a historical moment, a public need, and a cultural preference. A growing number of rural migrants who had been forced off the land by Trujillo had begun to move into Santo Domingo during the 1950s. The cultural traditions of these mostly illiterate rural migrants were largely oral. Aracena, who effectively used sound effects as recognition and triggering devices, clearly appealed to the growing numbers of rural migrants tuning in to his show—and to the advertisers of products and services directed at these groups as well (Brea 1975).

In 1955 Aracena also tried his hand at producing records. Like Francisco Amaro, he rented the facilities at HIZ and sent the masters abroad for pressing. His earliest records were in homage to Trujillo, which, in addition to proving his loyalty to the regime, earned him some money. The first song he recorded was entitled "Trujillo, feria y pelota" (Trujillo the fair and baseball), by the popular merenguero Luis Kalaff y los Alegres Dominicanos. Shortly afterwards Aracena recorded a típico accordionist named Guandulito whom he had discovered playing on the street, thus launching Guandulito's career as one of the best-known típico accordionists in the country. Aracena also recorded, among others, Antonio Morel and a local group called Los Ahijados closely modeled after the Cuban *son* duo Los Compadres.

Early on Aracena had wanted to go into record distribution, but he was barely making a living as an announcer and had no capital with which to acquire a distributorship for an international label. Around 1954, while he was working as an announcer for HI5K, a Dominican baseball team returning from a playoff against Mexico brought back with them some Mexican records, including Pedro Infante's hit song "Cien años" (One hundred years). Local disc jockeys obtained the records and played them on the radio, and they became extraordinarily popular; Aracena remembers that people wanted to hear Infante's song so badly they were offering disc jockeys money to play it on the air. No one, however, had acquired the distribution rights, and the records could not be purchased in the country.

Aracena, certain that his instincts about music could pay off, decided to try to convince Pedro Infante's Mexican record company, Peerless, to give him distribution rights for the Dominican Republic. Making a calculated gamble, he wrote Peerless on the stationary of his father's small importing firm (without his father's knowledge), pretending to have economic resources he by no means had. Peerless, convinced of his financial solvency, sent the records on credit. When the unexpected shipment of records arrived at customs, Aracena's father was shocked and angry, but—perhaps because he had no alternative—he lent his son the money to pay for the records. On July 14, 1955, Aracena opened up a small record store near El Conde, calling it Tienda de Discos la Guarachita (Guarachita Record Store), *guarachita* being the diminutive of the word *guaracha*, a form of Cuban popular music. Because Aracena had very little capital, he rented the partitioned living room of a house belonging to an elderly widow in which to locate his store, and he borrowed an old record player so he could play the music into the street. The only records for sale in this new store were the Peerless records Aracena had recently received from Mexico. Despite that, he invested in a large ad in a local newspaper to announce the opening of the store and the sale of Pedro Infante records.

Aracena's recollection of the day he opened up his store illustrates how little escaped the personal attention of the Trujillos. One of the Trujillo brothers came by in a big car and, on seeing the small size of the business, exclaimed, "¡Anda, pero yo veo el anuncio en el periódico y pienso que es algo de otro mundo! ¿Y esta cocina es la Guarachita?" (Come on, I see an ad in the paper and I think it's something from another world! This kitchen is Guarachita?) Nevertheless, he bought some records, thereby giving his stamp of approval to the store (Radhames Aracena, interview).

Aracena's business instincts proved sound. Using the profits from the successful sale of the Peerless recordings, Aracena began obtaining distributorships from other small foreign record companies, one of which, Panamericana de Discos, had the exclusive rights to the tremendously popular bolero singer Lucho Gatica (he also got Nat King Cole with this deal). He also obtained a contract with Discos Fuentes, a Colombian label with a subsidiary in Miami, that handled the music of Colombian and Ecuadorian vals campesino musicians such as Julio Jaramillo, Olimpo Cárdenas, Lucho Bowen, Duo Villafuerte, Los Pamperos, and others whose guitar-based music was widely popular in the Dominican Republic.

Success breeds success, and over time Aracena was able to acquire contracts with more important companies dealing with Latin American music such as Ansonia, Seeco, Valverde, and even, eventually, major labels such as RCA, CBS, and London. (The previous RCA distributor, García Gautier, had become more interested in selling electrical appliances than records and did not oppose the transfer of the distributorship to Aracena.) With these distributorships Aracena dominated the Dominican market in guitar-based music: the extremely popular Mexican boleros and rancheras (Pedro Infante, Toña la Negra, María Luisa Landín, La Prieta Linda, Los Hermanos Michel, Los Tecolines, and others), Colombian/Ecuadorian vals campesino artists (Olimpo Cárdenas, Julio Jaramillo, and Bombilla Fuerte), important Cuban artists such as Celina y Reutilio and Los Compadres, and Puerto Rican jíbaro musicians such as Tommy Figueroa, El Jibarito de Lares, Paquetín Soto, and El Trío Vegabajeño. As Aracena himself said of his expanding catalogue, "Nos convertimos en un pulpo" (we became an octopus) (interview). By 1959 his Tienda la Guarachita occupied a large storefront on Santo Domingo's most fashionable shopping street, Calle el Conde.

Aracena attributes his success to several factors. First, he had good instincts for what music would become popular in the Dominican Republic; he claims that even early in his career other disc jockeys would ask him which records would be likely to please the public. Second, he effectively used radio to promote the records he sold in his store. Aracena always considered radio to be a medium for promoting records rather than as a form of entertainment. Throughout the 1950s, even after his record store became highly profitable, he continued to work as an announcer, always working for air time (rather than cash), which he used to play only records for which he had exclusive distribution rights. Third, he benefited from fortuitous events quite beyond his control. For example, stars such as Pedro Infante and María Luisa Landín, invited to perform on La Voz Dominicana's major week-long musical revue, the Semana Aniversaria, recorded on record labels distributed by Aracena.

Aracena also benefited from the wide popularity of Mexican films, especially musicals known as *comedias rancheras,* which spread the Mexican ranchera all over Latin America. Manuel Peña has pointed out that the link between the comedia ranchera film genre and the success of companies selling rancheras was no accident, but rather the result of a deliberate tactic to promote Mexican music internationally (Peña 1985: 70–71). As Dominican musician Luis Dias has observed, this strategy was very successful in the Dominican Republic: "At the time the movies were vital. Mexican films that were shown in the country were mostly musicals. People could see the Luis Aguilars, the Jorge Negretes singing on the screen, and people would go crazy, seeing artists from another country that was supposedly more developed. The style was copied, assimilated, and in fact was assimilated into bachata as well" (interview).

In the late 1950s Aracena left Onda Musical to direct another radio station, La Voz del Trópico, where in payment for his services he was given air time under the same conditions as before: complete control over the musical programming. He called his new show Canal Cero (Channel Zero). The show's name made reference to television, which had recently arrived in the Dominican Republic and had captured the imagination of the country. At the time, there were two television channels—Canal 4, belonging to Petán Trujillo, and Canal 7, belonging to Radhames Trujillo (although each had a front man: Pepe Bonilla for Canal 4, Salomón San for Canal 7). In a playful but astute reference to these television channels that were powerful symbols of modernity and power, Aracena referred to his show as "Canal Cero—donde no se ve nada y se oye todo" (Channel Zero—where nothing is seen but everything is heard) (interview). Again, Aracena used Canal Cero to promote the imported records he was distributing, almost all of which were guitar based. His financial interests in promoting these guitar-based musics—Mexican rancheras, Cuban son and guaracha, Puerto Rican jíbaro music, Colombian-Ecuadorian vals campesino, and boleros from all the above countries—shaped the musical preferences of Dominicans of rural origins for years to come.

In 1959 Aracena's record-selling business was threatened when the Trujillos became involved in establishing a record-pressing plant, Fábrica de Discos Dominicana, after which the importation of foreign records was forbidden. Aracena felt the effects almost immediately. He recalls that while a few permits to import records continued to be given out while the record factory got organized, the supply of records in the country began to run out. Aracena, always resourceful, fell back upon a recently introduced aspect of the entertainment business—pinball machines—which he placed in his now under-stocked record store on the Calle el

Conde. The pinball machines provided him with an alternative source of income while the import restrictions were in place; nevertheless, by the time imports were opened again after Trujillo's death, he had lost much of the capital he depended on for buying imported records. Even this latest business, however, felt the impact of the Trujillo family's greed. After Rafael Trujillo's death, his family began collecting all the movable wealth it could amass in preparation for their departure. Paper bills became scarce, and Aracena recalls that at one point even coins disappeared when Trujillo's son Ramfis began melting them into bullion. Consequently, Aracena had to import U.S. coins from Miami for his machines.

The Death and Legacy of Rafael Trujillo

As long as the country as a whole prospered, Dominicans tolerated Trujillo's abuses: there was so little opposition to his regime that he was able to take extended trips abroad without threats to his power (Bosch 1986b: 395). However, about 1955 the country's economic health had begun to decline, due partly to a fall in world sugar prices and partly to the enormous costs—over $30 million—of a sort of world's fair, inappropriately named the Feria de la Paz y la Confraternidad del Mundo Libre (Free world's fair of peace and fraternity) that Trujillo had constructed in the capital to glorify his regime. The opposition, some of it inside the country but most of it from exiles outside the country, began to make itself felt.[6] World opinion, already wary of Trujillo after a series of outrageous actions (such as the massacre of thousands of Haitians in 1937) became openly hostile as his repression of the opposition became more visible. In the United States and among the OAS (Organization of American States) countries the proverbial last straw came in 1960 when Trujillo sent henchmen to Venezuela to assassinate its president, Rómulo Bétancourt. Within the Dominican Republic itself, it was probably the brutal triple murder of the three Mirabal sisters that turned the tide against Trujillo. The Mirabal sisters, from a distinguished Cibaeñan family, were beautiful, well educated, and, along with their husbands, active in opposing the Trujillo regime. In 1960, as the sisters were traveling from their home in Tenares to visit their jailed husbands, they were ambushed and beaten to death by Trujillo's guards. The entire country, including the Catholic Church, was outraged at the crime, and the church thereafter began to take a more active part in the opposition.

On May 30, 1961, a group of conspirators (which included a few members of the military), armed with guns supplied by the CIA, ambushed and assassinated Trujillo as he drove to his estate in San Cristóbal, just outside the capital. The conspirators made several blunders and most of them were caught and executed, so the planned transition to a democratic government was not achieved. Trujillo's relatives remained in power, although they were pressured to leave by strikes and general discontent within the country, as well as from the United States and the OAS. The family accepted the inevitable and began gathering as much of the nation's wealth in transportable form as they could. By November 1961 the last of the Trujillos had left the country.

The influence of the Trujillo family had indelibly colored the development of the Dominican music industry, which for decades had responded more to the family's personal economic interests and eccentricities than to market forces. Nevertheless, given the Trujillos' interest in music, it is surprising that they did not become more deeply involved in the music industry. With their practically unlimited wealth, they could have established modern recording facilities in which to record the country's best musicians. They could have established a record-pressing plant within the country much earlier than they did. They could have promoted their musicians and their records internationally, earning handsome profits as well as boosting the prestige of the regime. They could have done this by monopolizing the entire music business, from recording to retail sales, as they did with every other enterprise they owned. But, inexplicably, they did not. I repeatedly asked Dominicans to speculate on why Petán or any other Trujillo did not take a keener interest in developing and exploiting the record business, which they surely knew could be lucrative, but no one was able to offer an explanation. Perhaps it was again, as Amaro said of Petán's insistence on live radio, "chifladuras del dueño."

Trujillo's influence on the Dominican popular music landscape, however, went far beyond the sort of direct interventions—largely visited upon urban people and resources—that have been described in this chapter. In the course of his thirty-one-year regime, Trujillo and his associates expropriated vast tracts of land (mostly for sugar plantations), pushing thousands of peasants into previously uncultivated lands. For example, between 1950 and 1960 the area of land cultivated in sugarcane effectively doubled, from 1,519,316 to 2,982,949 hectares; and of the sixteen *ingenios* (sugar plantations and mills) occupying these lands, Trujillo himself owned twelve (Maríñez 1984: 85). By the time of his death, Trujillo, his family, and associates owned 6 million *tareas* (1 tarea equals 628 square meters) of land (Duarte 1980: 142).

Peasants forced off the land later moved into the cities in search of jobs in the country's growing industrial sector (comprised largely of factories founded and owned by the Trujillos), setting in motion an irreversible decline of the country's rural character. Between 1950 and 1960, the rural population fell from 76 to 70 percent of the total population, while the urban population in the same time period grew from 24 to 31 percent

(Maríñez 1984: 86). In 1953 Trujillo tried to stop the exodus to the cities with a decree forbidding peasants to migrate to the cities and instructing those who had migrated since 1951 to return to their place of origin. The decree slowed but did not halt the migrations.

The consequences of rural land shortages caused by Trujillo's policies, however, would be felt for many years after his death. By 1980 over half the country's population was living in urban areas, a quarter of them in the city of Santo Domingo. The majority of the country's population, whether rural and urban, was poor, uneducated, and ill prepared to participate in the rapid modernization and expansion of the Dominican economy that occurred after the death of Trujillo in 1961. They retained their aesthetic preferences, however, for the broad range of guitar-based musics—from Mexico, Puerto Rico, Cuba, Colombia, and Ecuador—that had been so vigorously promoted by entrepreneurs such as Radhames Aracena. These were the social and musical conditions under which bachata was to emerge in the immediate post-Trujillo era.

Traditional guitar trios such as this one were popular in the Trujillo era, and served as models for later bachata ensembles.
By Editora Barranquilla

This photo of rural musicians playing merengue típico dates from the Trujillo era, but similar ensembles are still widely popular, especially in rural areas.
By Editora Barranquilla

Dominican guitarist Danda
Lockward was known
for his boleros.
By Deborah Pacini Hernandez,
from the collection
of Juan Lockward

Many early bachateros
imitated the vocal style of the
Puerto Rican singer
Jibarito de Lares.
By Ansonia Records

Mexican singer Pedro Infante's melodramatic style of singing boleros also influenced early bachateros.
By Editora Barranquilla

Colmados like this one have long provided residents of poor neighborhoods with a place to socialize and to listen to music.
By Deborah Pacini Hernandez

The dictator Rafael Trujillo loved to dance merengue.
By Revista de las Fuerzas Armadas

Petán Trujillo's interest in popular music had a chilling effect on the development
of recording in the Dominican Republic.
By Editora Taller

Petán Trujillo's radio station La Voz Dominicana.
By Editora Barranquilla

Chapter Three

T̲he Birth of Bachata

*W*ith the assassination of Trujillo in 1961 the Dominican Republic was suddenly released from the yoke of a thirty-one-year dictatorship. In the ensuing period, different sectors of Dominican society began to compete vigorously with each other for positions of control or advantage in the new order, ushering in a period of internal chaos that included a coup, civil war, and foreign occupation and profoundly altered the country's political, economic, demographic, and social configurations. The chaos subsided somewhat in 1966, as a government headed by Joaquín Balaguer—one of Trujillo's former officials—established a semblance of order by resorting to renewed internal repression. This chapter will discuss the changes that took place in the initial post-Trujillo era, focusing on those that influenced the profound transformations in Dominican popular music and the music industry that had emerged to market it.

Restoration and Loss of Democracy

Throughout his long regime, Trujillo's principal interest had been to increase his personal wealth rather than to oversee the growth of the nation as a whole. With his unlimited power and immense greed, Trujillo was able to transform the Dominican Republic into an almost private enterprise: when he died, he and his associates owned over one half of the country's total assets, and directly employed almost half the country's labor force and another 35 percent indirectly through the government bureaucracy, while he himself had become one of the wealthiest individuals in the world (Black 1986: 27).

After his death, the country was faced with the challenge of dismantling the distorted, self-serving political, economic, and military institutions that Trujillo had constructed to insure the perpetuation of his power, and replacing them with new ones more appropriate to a modern nation. This was not an easy task, given the existing political vacuum: an entire generation of Dominicans had grown up under the Trujillato (an eponym commonly used to refer to the regime) and had no experience in participatory government; moreover, there were few independent or state institutions that could serve to facilitate the transformation. For example, all of Trujillo's holdings passed to the control of the state—yet in effect there was no state, but rather an arena in which contending sectors of Dominican society (principally the land holding and industrial elite, foreign multinationals, peasants, and the working classes) struggled for possession and/or control of resources (Maríñez 1984). Unprepared for a smooth transition to democracy, the country suffered through a series of temporary governments until 1966, when Balaguer assumed power, thereby putting the country once again under Trujillo's shadow until 1978.

For two months after the departure of the Trujillos the country remained under the control of their associates: Balaguer acted as president, while the power behind him was held by one of Trujillo's military officers, Air Force Commander Pedro Rodríguez Echevarría. In December Balaguer and Echevarría, under pressure from the United States, created a Council of State, which included some members of an anti-Trujillista group, the Unión Cívica Nacional (UCN). When the UCN called for a general election, Echevarría responded by arresting its leaders. The public disorders that ensued motivated the United States to pressure the military to get rid of Echevarría. The reinstated Council of State, minus Echevarría and Balaguer, called for elections in December. In the elections, the UCN's candidate was challenged by Juan Bosch, a liberal intellectual and leader of the Partido Revolucionario Dominicano (PRD), an opposition party he had founded in 1939 while in exile.

Bosch won by a wide margin and took office in early 1963. He began his tenure by sponsoring a constitution instituting a series of reforms, such as the separation of church and state, guaranteed civil liberties, and the redistribution of Trujillo lands (then under state control) to peasants. These rather modest programs were perceived by some military and civilian conservatives as far too radical—not to mention that agrarian reform threatened their own interests in the vast tracts of Trujillo land that were up for grabs. In September 1963, under the banner of preventing "another Cuba," they carried out a coup against Bosch, who was sent into exile. A civilian junta known as the Triumvirate was set up, nominally headed by a local businessman, Donald Reid Cabral, but with full control of the government retained by the military. In the United States, the Kennedy administration refused to recognize the Triumvirate. But while President Kennedy personally supported Bosch's liberalizations, others in his administration supported the conservative/military factions. As soon as Lyndon Johnson assumed the presidency after Kennedy was assassinated, he promptly recognized the junta, and the United States adopted a hard line against those who continued to struggle for civil, economic, and political rights.

Discontent with the Triumvirate was strong, and opposing factions began to plot against it, although their agendas differed considerably: some desired the reinstatement of Bosch, others wanted new elections altogether, while the most conservative factions demanded military rule unhampered by the mask of a civilian junta. In April 1965 after Reid Cabral fired a military officer, the opposition moved against the Triumvirate. Immediately, however, the different factions began fighting among themselves for control of the government. Large numbers of the civilian population of Santo Domingo took to the streets in support of the more liberal elements in the military that backed a return to the constitutionally elected government. The conservative factions, known as the Loyalists, retreated to a military base just outside Santo Domingo, from which they launched attacks on the Constitutionalists, who had taken control of the center of the city. The Constitutionalists, many of whom were civilians fighting with makeshift weapons, were on the verge of defeating the Loyalists.

On April 28, 1965, however, the tide turned against the Constitutionalists. Lyndon Johnson sent 23,000 U.S. troops to the Dominican Republic, ostensibly to protect American lives, but in reality, the intention was to prevent the return of Juan Bosch. The fighting continued for several months, but in spite of the courageous resistance of the Constitutionalists that cost thousands of lives, they were unable to defeat the well-armed U.S. forces.[1] After a negotiated cease fire and settlement on August 31, an interim president was installed until elections could be held. In 1966 Juan Bosch returned from exile and ran against Joaquín Balaguer. The election process, marred by violence, electoral fraud, and the ominous presence of the U.S. Marines, resulted in victory for Balaguer (Black 1986).

While the struggle for control of the government and Trujillo's assets continued to take place principally in Santo Domingo, the demographic transformations that had begun in rural areas in the previous decade intensified. After Trujillo's death, with the restrictions on both internal and external migrations gone, peasants began moving into the cities, especially Santo Domingo. Some peasants were forced to migrate, as they had been in the previous decade, by the lack of adequate land for subsistence. Others moved in consequence of the political turmoil of the 1961–66 period. Most, however, were motivated by the hope of obtaining industrial jobs and of participating in what was believed to be a new era of modernity and prosperity. The attractions of the city were also relentlessly promoted on the media: radio and television reached distant corners of the country, providing rural people with seductive images, both aural and visual, of urban life. These images of modernity were reinforced by an influx of ideas, culture, and people from beyond the country's borders. Dominicans in exile returned; Dominicans who had not been able to travel during Trujillo's time left the country to visit (or to stay abroad); foreign travelers could more comfortably visit the country; and last but not least, the country was opened up for foreign investment, which brought in capital, personnel, new consumer products—and the powerful influence these foreign interests inevitably exercise upon local socio-economic structures.

Urbanization and the Informal Sector

In 1960, 70 percent of a total population of three million still lived in rural agricultural areas. The migrations that began after Trujillo's death and continued over the next twenty-five years swelled the urban population. Between 1960 and 1970 the population of Santo Domingo almost doubled, rising from 370,000 to 699,000 inhabitants (Maríñez 1984: 101). Santo Domingo, however, was unprepared to deal with this demographic explosion, and a proliferation of shantytowns sprang up around the margins of the city, their inhabitants, unable to find a wage-paying job, working instead in the informal sector.

The informal sector is comprised of those persons unable to find employment in the formal economy (i.e., in businesses such as construction or industry that are officially regulated, pay taxes, provide worker benefits, etc.) and is distinguished by the following characteristics: (1) recent arrivals in urban areas can access this sector easily; (2) raw materials tend to be national/local rather than imported; (3) informal activities are small-scale, operate within an unregulated marketplace, and depend primarily on manual labor; (4) workers in the informal sector have received no formal training for their activities. The wide range of activities within the informal sector includes domestic service, home services (food preparation, sewing, ironing, etc.), small-scale manufacture (such as shoemaking), small-scale commerce out of the home (for example, selling popsicles or cigarettes), and street vending (both ambulatory and fixed). The informal economy is often contrasted with the formal sector, suggesting a dual economic configuration. But this dualistic model has been criticized for not taking into account the active relationship between the two sectors (Safa 1982; Kleinekathoefer 1986). According to those who stress that the two economies are, in fact, integrated, the informal economy helps to subsidize the formal economy by providing cheap goods and labor for others in the informal economy, therefore serving to maintain a readily available, cheap labor pool (Safa 1982: 5–6). In short, workers in the informal sector are actively exploited rather than simply the victims of benign neglect. While the informal economy does provide more bene- fits to the formal sector than vice versa, it is important to remember that the informal sector also depends on the formal sector for materials, cash, and clients. The business of producing and distributing bachata, for ex- ample, exemplifies the sort of (unequal) reciprocity between activities be- longing to the informal sector (i.e., records were distributed via makeshift street stalls) but closely related to and dependent upon the formal sector (i.e., expensive equipment and raw materials were needed to manufacture records).

Those forced to work in the informal economy are sometimes re- ferred to as marginalized, not because they are isolated, disconnected, or numerically insignificant, but rather, because they have been actively excluded from participating in the mainstream of Dominican economic life. In her book *The Myth of Marginality*, Janice E. Perlman observed that " 'marginalization' is the consequence of a new model of development (or underdevelopment) that has as a basic characteristic the exclusion of vast sectors of the population from its main productive apparatus" (Perl- man 1976: 251). While those working in the Dominican informal economy were in fact marginalized, in the sense of being excluded from the offi- cially recognized economic system, they were by no means marginal in terms of the number of people earning their living within it: by the early 1980s almost half the population was working in the informal sector (Kleinekathoefer 1986: 10–11). These marginalized citizens, and the rural poor, were bachata's practitioners and patrons.

Intrinsically associated with the informal sector were the shanty- towns or *barrios marginados* (lit., marginalized neighborhoods) in which the unemployed and underemployed resided and worked. Shantytowns were first established on uncultivated land surrounding Santo Domingo in the 1950s, when campesinos displaced by Trujillo's expropriations were forced into the cities. Santo Domingo's older shantytowns such as Los Guandules and Gualey were located on lands that Trujillo had taken from large landowners in order to accommodate the growing numbers of migrants (*Un barrio estudia a sí mismo*, 1983). As the city grew, however, these barrios were surrounded and engulfed by new urban development projects that were incorporated within the city limits. Newer shantytowns such as Guaricano and Los Alcarrizos were built on undesirable lands located farther out of the city (e.g., Guaricano was next to the garbage dump); these lands had been claimed for settlement, legally or illegally, either by new migrants or by older migrants seeking more space. The living conditions in these areas were dreadful; residents obtained water and electricity by illegally tapping into existing lines whenever possible and compensated for lack of public transportation by moving in and out of the barrio on foot or in privately owned motor vehicles. The government largely ignored the shantytowns, refusing to improve or extend whatever water, electrical, garbage, and transportation services might have been put in place by residents themselves. In short, shantytowns were only tenuously connected to the rest of the city; whether a shantytown was old or new, whether it was located within or outside of city limits, it was spatially and infrastructurally marginalized from other parts of the city.

Michael Kleinekathoefer observed that people in the informal sector tended to identify themselves not just by occupation, but by the experience of shantytown life. He argued that the informal sector was more than an economic system; it was a cultural system as well: "Hidden behind the quantitative economic terms is a peculiar form of life. It is a dense network of social and economic relations, cultural patterns, and new forms of coexistence and survival that are attempts to overcome the situation of misery" (Kleinekathoefer 1986: 9–10, translation mine). For example, barrio language included rural pronunciation and grammatical patterns and a distinct urban vernacular lexicon and imagery; these could vary according to a person's region of origin and age, but they always identified the person as poor and uneducated. However, of the numerous characteristics defining the barrio culture that emerged in the 1970s, among the most important was the preference of shantytown dwellers for the guitar-based music that would later be called bachata.

The Music Industry in the Post-Trujillo Period

The music business, like most other components of the national economy, underwent major transformations in the 1960s. The most significant change was that the business, unfettered by interference from Trujillo or his family, was opened up to anyone with capital. A number of new recording facilities were established in Santo Domingo, allowing Dominican musicians to compete more successfully with foreign musics—whether from the United States or Latin America—in the national marketplace. Radio Caribe was the first to install a new recording studio in the immediate post-Trujillo years, although it burned down shortly after it was established (July Ruiz, interview). Soon afterwards, about 1962 or 1963, another recording studio, Estudio de Grabación Fabiola, was established by Fabio Inoa, who had previously worked as a technician at the Fábrica de Discos Dominicana (Arístides Incháustegui, interview). In 1964, Estudios Mozart was founded by the Blandino family. The owners of Fabiola and Mozart also became involved in other aspects of the record business—Fabiola purchased the Fábrica de Discos Dominicana, while Mozart owned a record store and a radio station (Radhames Aracena, interview). La Voz Dominicana continued to record at their facilities, but they did not keep up with either technology or musical currents, and they were left behind by their new and more vigorous competitors.

By the time the chaos that had characterized the immediate post-Trujillo period had subsided somewhat, a wider variety of musical genres and styles had become available to Dominican consumers. Recognizing the economic potential of consumers anxious to participate in international trends and able to operate freely within the country, foreign promoters vied with their Dominican counterparts—as well as with each other—for primacy on the airwaves and in the market. Given the considerable economic resources and experience of the foreign interests, the fledgling Dominican music industry was initially at a distinct disadvantage.

Rock and roll—which the Trujillo regime had frowned upon but not forbidden—began to dominate the airwaves, and recordings could easily be imported and purchased. Throughout the mid-1960s, *música norteamericana* (North American music) became the strongest competitor not only to Dominican merengue and guitar-based music, but to other foreign genres as well. Disc jockey Willie Rodríguez recalls his radio shows in the Santiago/La Vega area at the time: "My most popular programs were 'Willie with the youth,' on Radio Santa María, that played North American music, and 'Willie discotec,' on Radio Nacional in Santiago. . . . And why did I play North American music? I had a few variety programs, baladas, salsas, basically baladas and boleros, good shows, but the most popular of all in 1967 was the one with North American music" (Rodríguez 1986, translation mine).

As far as the local music industry was concerned, the principal beneficiary of the post-Trujillo economic, political, and cultural openness was unquestionably the merengue. New stylistic influences from outside the country were introduced by a new generation of young, energetic musicians and enthusiastically supported by the country's invigorated music industry; and as a result, a revitalized merengue began to evolve in directions that made it increasingly competitive with the international musical genres—although it did not really achieve hegemony until the 1970s.

Merengue had already been well established by Trujillo as the country's national dance music par excellence. Remarkably, merengue was able to transcend its unsolicited but long marriage to the Trujillo dictatorship and continued to be almost universally accepted as the country's quintessential national music. Merengues with lyrics glorifying or even mentioning Trujillo were forbidden in 1962, but merengue itself remained untainted by its relationship with the Trujillo regime. For example, even those musicians most closely associated with the regime, such as Luis Alberti, have continued to be loved and respected. (As recently as November 1986 Juan Demóstenes Cotes Morales, the country's secretary of interior and police, was fired by President Balaguer when it was revealed publicly that he had played merengues associated with the Trujillato at a private party. Yet while the public commentary expressed outrage at the personal behavior of Cotes for playing specific Trujillista merengues, the fact that the merengue genre as a whole had been so closely associated with the dictatorship was not even raised.)

Merengue in the Trujillo era had been relatively free of foreign influence. As Johnny Ventura, a successful merengue singer since the late 1950s, observed: "In the period before 1961, musical currents from the rest of the world were much less noticeable in the merengue, first of all because of the closed situation imposed by the tyranny of Trujillo, but also because at the same time the communication media were not as developed as in the last twenty years" (Ventura 1978: 28, translation mine). After Trujillo's death, however, the merengue was profoundly transformed and became, instead of a symbol of the power of the dictatorship, a symbol of the new openness and vitality of Dominican society.

The musician most responsible for modernizing and internationalizing the merengue was Johnny Ventura, who deliberately sought to distance himself from the Trujillo-era merengue: "When the dictator Trujillo died, many people will remember that we had a more or less traditional merengue, that soft and monotonous merengue that already was beginning to lag behind a people who were moving quickly towards their liberty and progress, most of all because of the opening of the country's frontiers to all modern currents, of politics, of ideas, of the high arts and the popular arts" (Ventura 1978: 23, translation mine). Ventura, whose youthful imagination had been stimulated by rock and roll in the late 1950s, introduced elements of rock into the merengue orquesta, combining fast, brassy music with spicy, satirical lyrics. He kept the horn sections used by earlier orquestas, although in the latter part of the 1960s, imitating salsa's pared-down ensemble, he reduced these to five instruments—two saxophones, two trumpets, and a trombone (Austerlitz 1986: 123).

Rock influences were evident in Ventura's performance style: rejecting the staid performance style of the Trujillo-era merengue orquestas, his ensemble, which he referred to as a "combo show," included energetic choreography and glittery costuming that transformed the merengue performance into a dynamic multi-media spectacle.[2] Cultural commentator and television host Yaqui Núñez del Risco observed that changes in Ventura's style also responded to the requirements of television, which demands a dynamic, visually complex image:

> There was a turning point in popular music in recent times—precisely when the musicians stood up from their chairs. Up until then, the orquestas, the big orquestas, even those of La Voz Dominicana, had still played while seated, sometimes to read the music; but sometimes even knowing the music they stayed seated, and the only one to stand was the singer, the soloist. . . . After this point, the orquesta emerged as a frontal spectacle; now they were preparing themselves to be important on television, because television is audiovisual. (Núñez del Risco 1986, translation mine)

Ventura's music served as a lighting rod for attacks by Dominicans, especially the older generation, who were deeply disturbed by the intrusion of foreign elements perceived as incompatible with a more nationalistically defined image of Dominican identity. Younger Dominicans, on the other hand, embraced Ventura's vision of merengue because it symbolized a country that was outward looking, modern, and progressive, one that could participate as an equal in the larger international arena:

> We can't forget how significant it has been to merengue as a popular music to have come into contact with the popular music of other countries, especially with the popular music of the developed and civilized countries. . . . While the original merengue remained the interpretive responsibility of folkloric groups, and even of museums of history and popular art, the merengue of the modern orquestas and conjuntos had to march shoulder to shoulder with the progress of popular music all over the world. (Ventura 1978: 26–27, translation mine)

In the immediate post-Trujillo era, then, the corollary of the struggle for control over the form and content of the country's new political and economic configuration was a struggle to determine the form and content of the country's cultural identity. As Rodríguez and Ventura's comments reveal, a younger generation wanted to openly and fully embrace the outside world and its modernity, while others wanted to maintain a national identity grounded in the country's traditional past.

Ventura's band also stimulated a major change in the perception and status of professional music within Dominican society. Music had long been considered a professional as well as a recreational and ritual activity; indeed, Trujillo himself participated in institutionalizing music as a full-time, paid profession. But music was still considered primarily as either an art or a cultural form rather than as a commodity that could be marketed like any other consumer product. The introduction of the notion of the musical ensemble as commodity in the Dominican Republic has been attributed to Ventura's business partner, William Liriano.

Liriano developed the idea of applying marketing principles and techniques to the merengue ensemble while studying economics at the Universidad Autónoma de Santo Domingo. Liriano and Ventura became equal partners in a corporation, Johnny Ventura y Asociados, that represented the "Johnny Ventura Combo Show": Ventura supplied the music, Liriano the promotional techniques. As Liriano recalls:

> The invention of marketing the popular orchestra and giving it economic dimensions within a productive apparatus was our invention, because to sell popular art you use the same marketing tools as to sell a fried plantain or a can of juice or a car. These tools for marketing any product are scientifically and technically established in light of a whole series of scientific instruments that oblige one to establish a marketing policy in which one has to segment, where one has to stratify the market, and where you must define the consumer profile of the consumer of the product you wish to sell. (Liriano 1986, translation mine)

Liriano understood that while he might encounter stiff competition from foreign music on the radio, the field was wide open in terms of live performances, which could be used to build a broad constituency for the band. Instead of waiting to be called upon, as had previously been the custom, Liriano aggressively sought out performance contracts for Ventura's band. For example, knowing that live music was an important component of the *fiestas patronales* (patron saints' festivals) of towns and villages all over the country, he compiled the dates of these occasions in order to offer the band's services at the appropriate times. Liriano also understood the importance of what he called "consumer profiles," leading him to pay close attention to regional cultural diversity. For example, observing that in some towns people preferred to hold or attend dances on Saturdays while others preferred Sundays, he was careful to schedule Ventura only on the day the dance was most likely to succeed.

But Liriano did not limit himself to merely responding to the musical tastes of various social groups; rather, he worked purposefully to segment musical tastes, and furthermore, to invest them with socio-cultural meanings that would facilitate the marketing of Ventura's "Combo Show." Eschewing appeals to broad-based characteristics such as cultural authenticity or nationalism, Liriano strove to link Ventura's merengue with a certain class of people and a certain lifestyle. To this end, he made full use of the power of symbols to communicate the sort of socio-economic images he was trying to associate with merengue. One such symbol, for example, was the big Ford Gran Torino he drove—called by his admirers a *nave estratosférica* (space ship)—intended to present an image of modernity, progress, and economic power. Similarly, he deliberately stayed in first-class hotels and lavishly wined and dined potentially lucrative customers, thus presenting his band as a class act that would fit well into elite venues. The strategy paid off: "I spent a thousand dollars in public relations, but I made 5,000,000 [pesos] more on a weekend contract I made for Johnny Ventura in Caracas." As Liriano himself said, "I sold myself as a commodity of ostentation" (Liriano 1986, translation mine).

This deliberate association of music style with social class represented a major change in how popular music was represented and marketed. During the dictatorship, the live music heard by Dominicans had been limited to that favored by the Trujillo family, while the recorded music available was predominantly foreign. As musician Luis Dias suggests, this had created a public with relatively homogeneous musical tastes: "In the post-Trujillo period musical taste did not correspond to social class. It was generic, from the seediest bar to the most high-class, everybody, because there were no taste options; the country was just emerging from a dictatorship. Taste was what the state had imposed. The options available were common to everybody" (interview).

Differences between rural and urban styles of music and between poor and elite musical contexts had, of course, existed previously. But Dias's points are that the variety of music known by and available to Dominicans was limited in comparison to what came in the following decade, and furthermore, that the associations between musical genres and social class had not yet developed as fully as they would later on. Miguel Holguín, commenting on the nature of radio during the Trujillo era, confirms Dias's contention that clear class associations with musical styles did not exist in that period: "Radio stations weren't as specialized as they are today; in those days there wasn't that economic separation there is today. All the stations played all sorts of music" (interview). Dominican peasants shared with the dictator and his wealthy associates an appreciation for the same genre of music—merengue. And while they could not dance to Luis Alberti's Orquesta Presidente Trujillo at the luxurious (Trujillo-owned) Hotel Jaragua, they listened to it perform live on La Voz Dominicana. Rural merengue conjuntos may not have played at the Hotel Jaragua, but they too performed on La Voz Dominicana, and there was no social stigma attached to their music. Similarly, Dominican guitarist/songwriter Juan Lockward (son of Danda Lockward) may have been the darling of the Trujillo coterie, but he was equally appreciated by ordinary Dominicans. As for foreign guitar-based musics such as the Cuban son or Mexican boleros that were heard on the radio, these were generally accepted by all Dominicans; for example, the Cuban son conjunto, the Trío Matamoros, was popular with Dominicans of all social classes. Liriano's attempts to segment and stratify merengue's audience, then, represented a major departure from musical practice in the Trujillo era.

Another significant innovation of the Johnny Ventura y Asociados corporation was introducing a new model of economic relations between band leader and band members. The previous custom had been to pay musicians by the performance, according to the instrument played (players of percussion instruments, the güira and tambora, typically received less than those who played European instruments such as piano and sax). In Ventura's band, members were put on salary—each band member receiving the same salary regardless of the instrument played—and at the end of the year some of the total profits were distributed equally among all the band members (Liriano 1986). Given Liriano's enthusiasm for the principles of capitalism, the idea of a cooperative-style band with profit-sharing salaried employees seems more likely to have been the product of Ventura's populist sentiments: as a staunch supporter of Bosch's progressive Partido Revolucionario Dominicano, he had composed songs commenting on the 1965 disturbances, and his band had played for the Constitutionalists in order to lift morale in the days shortly before their surrender to the U.S. troops. Liriano recalled that the cooperative arrangement worked well as long as there were profits to divide up among the musicians; when there were losses that had to be made up by the musicians out of their own pockets, the musicians rejected the cooperative arrangement (Liriano 1986). Interestingly, the trajectory of Johnny Ventura's band parallels the country's trajectory during this period: its initial outburst of energy and its willingness to assimilate outside influences; its political radicalization after the experience of coup, civil war, and invasion; its desire to explore new models of social and economic arrangements; and, after the failure of the experiment, its ultimate submission to a fully capitalist mode of production.

Early Bachata

At the same time that merengue, salsa, balada, and rock were being aggressively marketed to the working and middle classes within the Dominican Republic, thousands of rural migrants were flooding into Santo Domingo in search of employment and were establishing residence in shantytowns. Among the migrants were musicians aspiring to careers in popular music, now that they could record what and how they pleased in the city's new recording studios. Moreover, radio, freed from the chilling effects of the dictatorship, offered rural musicians new venues through which to promote records to the rapidly increasing number of migrants establishing themselves in the city, whose long-standing preferences for música de guitarra clearly offered them a competitive advantage. The first rural guitar musician to record in the immediate post-Trujillo era was José Manuel Calderón; born in San Pedro de Macorís in 1941, he later migrated to the capital. In August 1962 he recorded his first record, "Borracho de amor" (Drunk on love), with his backup group, Trío los Juveniles (composed of Andrés Rodríguez, first guitar, and Luis Pimentel, second guitar); he personally financed the production costs. In spite of the poor recording quality of Calderón's first record, he was able to persuade a radio announcer to play it on the air. The record was well received, and was followed shortly thereafter by "Quema esas cartas" (Burn those letters), "Te perdono" (I forgive you), and "Llanto a la luna" (Lament to the moon), all of which eventually became very successful (liner notes to LP *Este es José Manuel Calderón*).

Because prejudices against rural guitar-based music had not yet developed fully, Calderón was not stigmatized as a second-class musician, nor was his music pigeon-holed into a marginal position in the music business; on the contrary, on the basis of his vocal abilities he was able to sing with a variety of well-known ensembles:

> When Calderón started to sing—he is one of the oldest musicians of guitar music in our country—the music wasn't called bachata, because Calderón was among the most sought-out singers. He recorded many songs with Johnny Ventura, whose orchestra accompanied him, and with Pepe Delgado—I think he's Cuban—who always accompanied Roberto Ledesma. Yomo Toro I believe accompanied him with guitars. An orchestra that accompanied Bienvenido Granda also accompanied Calderón. And Calderón recorded with guitars, but then it wasn't called bachata. (Tony Díaz, interview)

The next singer to record after Calderón was Rafael Encarnación in 1963; however, he died in a motorcycle accident after having recorded only one LP. Luis Segura, who later came to be considered the father of bachata, began recording in 1964. Segura, of poor rural origins, had to finance his first single himself; later, seeking better possibilities for nationwide exposure, he signed with Radhames Aracena, for whom he recorded fifteen successful LPs with his Guarachita label, leaving the company only after his career was firmly established in the early 1980s. Segura's musical trajectory typifies the experience of bachata musicians: his origins in the countryside but his artistic development in the city; his self-taught musical skills; and his guitar-based repertoire drawn from several different Latin American countries:

> I was born in Valverde, Mao—that's a village in the Santiago plains— and I grew up in the capital. My career started when I was very young. I liked music a lot. I first started playing the güira with a little group. Then I started playing percussion. Then I shifted to the guitar. I started with a little guitar made of *yagua* (palm), the kind you made when you were a boy. At the time the popular groups were Los Panchos, Trío Matamoros, Los Compadres, Jíbarito de Lares, Julio Jaramillo was listened to a lot, Olimpo Cárdenas. Our conjunto was called

Los Inolvidables (The unforgettables). It was trio music—boleros. Then I came to the capital where I started making professional music. It was then that I recorded my first single. (Segura, interview)

Subsequently, a number of other rural guitar musicians began recording; all can be considered seminal figures in the emerging bachata genre: Ramón Cordero, Oscar Olmo, Fabio Sanabia ("el Policía"), Bernardo Ortiz, Mélida Rodríguez, and Cuco Valoy (the only one to later abandon guitar-based music and go into orquesta merengue). Like Segura's, their highly romantic music was modeled after that of foreign musicians whose records were popular at the time, such as the Mexican Los Panchos, Pedro Infante, and María Luisa Landín; Puerto Rican jíbaro musicians such as "el Jibarito de Lares," "el Gallito de Manatí," Tommy Figueroa, and Blanca Iris Villafañe; Ecuadorians such as Julio Jaramillo and Olimpo Cárdenas. They did not intend to introduce a new musical genre or style; they were simply trying to replicate the same sort of guitar-based popular music they had grown up listening to: "In the sixties [the music] was more or less slow, because it was a copy of the Jibarito de Lares, of Blanca Iris Villafañe, of people like that, of Julio Jaramillo—that way of playing the bolero" (Ramón Cordero, interview).[3]

Like the music it was modeled after, the Dominican music recorded by musicians of rural origins was highly romantic, and the lyrics were sung in a melodramatic vocal style. The following song, recorded about 1962 by José Manuel Calderón, is typical of these early bachatas:

Lágrimas de sangre
(Tears of blood)
Singer: José Manuel Calderón

Aun te llevo dentro	I still carry you inside
Tú me has hecho llorar	You've made me cry
Lágrimas de sangre	Tears of blood
Te sigo esperando	I'm still waiting for you
Te sigo queriendo	I'm still loving you
Igual que ayer	As much as yesterday
Tú ya no me quieres	You don't love me anymore
Pero eso no importa	But that doesn't matter
Y si tú me odias	If you hate me
Yo te quiero más	I'll love you more

The person most frequently associated with the emergence of bachata is Radhames Aracena, who successfully took advantage of the political, economic, and social chaos characterizing the post-Trujillo transition period to become the country's leading promoter of Dominican guitar music. Nevertheless, his influence on the genre did not begin until after 1965, when he started his own radio station, Radio Guarachita. Until that time, Aracena's programs on various Santo Domingo radio stations had been based on the foreign guitar music he distributed, and he initially refused to record or promote the local versions of guitar music because of what he considered their poor quality. The first person to regularly play the Dominican guitar-based records on the air was José Tabar Asilis, a Santo Domingo disc jockey on La Voz del Trópico, whose radio name was "Charlie Charlie." Unlike Aracena, Charlie Charlie was willing to give rural guitar musicians like Calderón a chance by playing their records on his show. Charlie Charlie told me he initially agreed to play the records because he felt sympathy for the young musicians; Aracena, on the other hand, claims that Charlie Charlie played the songs because the musicians paid him small sums of money to play them. Nevertheless, Aracena acknowledged that Charlie Charlie was the first to play on the air the music that would later be known as bachata: "Eso es el origen de la bachata aquí" (That's the origin of the bachata here) (Radhames Aracena, interview).

At about the same time, Cuco Valoy parted company with Radhames Aracena, for whom he had been recording with his guitar conjunto Los Ahijados (modeled after the Cuban son duo Los Compadres), to found his own radio station, Radio Tropical, on which he himself served as a disc jockey with the radio name "el Suki-suki sabrosón." Being of humble rural origins, Valoy recognized the potential market for guitar music among the poor residents of the city, so he began playing the records of local guitar musicians alongside other popular music such as merengues típicos, son, and imported romantic guitar music. Valoy himself experimented with recording romantic guitar-based music, putting out his own versions of what would later be called bachata under the name "El Pupi de Quisqueya." Valoy also began to finance other musicians too poor to pay for their own studio recording time at the Estudio de Grabación Fabiola, and released the records under his Tropical label. Among the musicians to record for Tropical were Oscar Olmo, Bernardo Ortiz, and the Duo Lidia y José; he also recorded rural son musicians such as Pablo Mendoza. Aracena recalled that Valoy, whose own radio show was "muy mal pronunciado" (very poorly pronounced), did not correct the musicians' pronunciation, thereby exposing their poor, rural backgrounds. The following passage from an interview with bachata guitarist Edilio Paredes illustrates the sort of musical and cultural background typical of bachateros:

> I was born in the countryside in Pimentel, San Felipe. Ramón (Cordero) and I were born in the same area. Ever since I was little I liked music—when I was a boy I started being interested. There was a colmado near my house and the son of the owner had a *tres*. I know I was little, because a desk is about this size, and he put the *tres* on the

desk and I played a merengue, standing up. One day a string broke
and they never let me play it again. But people noticed. I come from
a humble class, my mother raised me alone—it's important to say all
that. And once someone nearby bought a guitar and they never lent
it to me. Later the owners of the colmado moved to town. But the
same little *tres* was broken, it was destroyed. One guy said, of all that
group of kids around, the only one who can learn to play is that kid.
And he himself got the *tres* and took it to the carpenter and they fixed
it up; he bought strings and gave it to me. And I started like that.
After three months I played it, being a boy of about eleven. No one
taught me. But I listened to the Jibarito's songs, and I used him for a
guide and I learned. Later I played with an uncle of Ramón's—he
played the guitar and I played the *tres*. But after we'd been playing in
a few places, a few months later, he didn't want to play any more,
because I had surpassed him. . . . Once a musician, Tatico Henríquez
(a merengue accordionist), lived around there, visiting the countryside—he spent about fifteen months there. Someone killed a man in
a bar. So that day I went to take Tatico—there wasn't even a road, I
took him to the main road by horseback— . . . to his house in Nagua.
And as we were going, he said, I'm going to go to the capital. I said,
I think I'm going to go too. So we went together to the capital. I lived
in Gualey [one of the city's worst shantytowns]. There, I started right
away. I went to the Casa Alegre, a record store. That's where I started.
I went to Cuco Valoy's and I started there. (Paredes, interview)

As the decade progressed, opportunities continued to become available to rural guitar musicians. For example, another entrepreneur, Ramón
Pichardo, began financing recording costs for rural musicians and releasing the records under the San Ramón label. Pichardo's company was
short-lived, but he did discover some of the major talents in Dominican
country music: Mélida Rodríguez, the first female bachata singer, and Tatico Henríquez, considered to be one of the best típico accordionists of the
post-Trujillo generation. Another important broadcast venue opened up
in 1964 when Radio Santa María, a radio station directed at campesinos,
was founded in La Vega by the Catholic Church. This station was established primarily to transmit literacy programming, but it also broadcast
popular guitar and accordion music in order to attract listeners. Thus, by
the time Joaquín Balaguer assumed power in 1966, Dominican guitar-
based music had evolved from a predominantly live, recreational music
that largely imitated foreign guitar genres, to an autochthonous and, in
the marketplace, increasingly viable music genre.

Most of this domestically recorded guitar music was initially perceived as poorly recorded imitations of outdated music from elsewhere
in the Caribbean, and it attracted little attention from the mainstream
media, which were far more interested in the flashy new style of merengue and other fashionable international genres. Indeed, these recordings
were considered so similar to their musical antecedents that no one both-

ered to label or categorize the music: it was simply called bolero campesino, música de guitarra—or simply música popular. As Ramón Cordero
recalled: "No one called it amargue or bachata; it was just the popular
music of the time. So it's not like today when it has a name, called bachata
or amargue; in that time it didn't have a name. It was durable music; it
has always existed and has always been liked" (interview).

Empresas Guarachita: Negotiating Tradition and Modernity

While Radhames Aracena was not the first to give airplay to domestically
produced popular guitar music in the immediate post-Trujillo period, he
was unarguably responsible for disseminating bachata throughout the
country via the radio station he established in 1965, Radio Guarachita.
The influence of Radio Guarachita extended beyond the music industry
into the social realm: it helped to introduce people of rural origins to
patterns of urban life and provided a significant cultural link between
urban and rural contexts. Moreover, almost every bachata musician of
note recorded with Aracena's record label, Discos la Guarachita, at some
point in his or her career. Because of his importance, I will devote the
following section entirely to Radhames Aracena and his various Guarachita enterprises—although in doing so I occasionally transgress the chronological boundaries that otherwise characterize this chapter.

Radhames Aracena had entered the post-Trujillo era in financially
poor condition. His retail record business, Tienda de Discos la Guarachita, which depended on foreign records, had been severely hurt when
Trujillo restricted record imports after the Fábrica de Discos Dominicana
was established in 1959, leaving him with little capital to invest in new
stock when imports opened up again after 1961. In 1962 Aracena recognized and seized an opportunity to regain capital: a record store in Puerto
Rico was selling off its stock of RCA records at bargain basement prices;
many of the recordings were by long-popular bolero singers such as
María Luisa Landín and Fernando Valadés. Because the demand for old
favorites was still strong—especially from jukebox owners—he invested
his remaining cash in the sellout stock. (He recalled that because the soon-
to-depart Trujillo family was amassing all the bills they could carry, he
had to take suitcases full of coins to Puerto Rico in order to purchase the
records.) He sold the records he had bought for ten cents for two pesos
apiece and used some of the profits to begin recording again. But this
time, wanting to directly associate the music he recorded—mostly típico
merengues—with his record store, he named his label Discos Guarachita.

Meanwhile, Aracena had continued to serve as the program director
of La Voz del Trópico. Typically, he managed to use the current political

turmoil to his own advantage, as the following anecdote reveals. In 1962 a heated controversy was raging between those still loyal to the Trujillo regime and the anti-Trujillistas, some of whom were represented by the Unión Cívica Nacional. The Cívicos had a very popular radio show on La Voz del Trópico, which Aracena had deliberately scheduled between 7 and 8 P.M., just before his own show, Canal Cero, because he calculated that most people wouldn't change the radio dial immediately after the Cívicos' show; he thereby provided his already popular musical show with an even larger audience. Aracena used Canal Cero to promote the records he was producing under his Guarachita label as well as the foreign music he was importing for his shop.

Aracena, initially determined to record only refined, foreign-sounding versions of popular guitar genres, emphatically rejected the raw-sounding guitar music being recorded by other rural musicians and played by his competitors Charlie Charlie and Cuco Valoy. He recalls that about 1962 José Manuel Calderón requested that he play his recording "Lágrimas de Sangre" (Tears of blood) on Canal Cero. Aracena refused: "At the time my recording interests were influenced by foreign music. I heard that record, so badly played, so bad, and I told him, 'This record is very bad, awful, very poorly recorded, very poorly sung'" (interview). Aracena soon realized, however, that the music of Calderón and others like him was selling better than the music he was recording. He recalls: "I felt I couldn't go backwards, only forward . . . but I realized that it was a reality" (interview). Putting aside his aesthetic preferences in favor of his economic self-interests, Aracena began recording Dominican guitar musicians—although he tried to imitate the quality of sound that characterized the foreign records he imported, which he considered to be more sophisticated. "What I played was a refined bachata, in another style. The bachata that's played today, I didn't accept that kind of music then" (interview). Among the first musicians he recorded in this period were Los Hermanos Veloz, Inocencio Cruz, and Fabio Sanabia ("el Policía"). These recordings, Aracena recalled, did extremely well: Sanabia sold *montones de discos* (tons of records), and Inocencio Cruz was *de otra categoría* (in another class).

In 1963, Aracena quit Canal Cero because the new owner of La Voz del Trópico had demanded that he give airplay to records he was not distributing; he closed his last show promising his listeners that he would be back later with his own radio station, Radio Guarachita. Temporarily off the air, Aracena continued to sell records in his store while he designed the kind of radio programming he wanted for his new station. He listened carefully to the foreign radio stations that came in clearly at night, paying particular attention to popular Colombian radio networks such as Caracol, Todelar, and Coltejer, taking note of all aspects of the

Colombian programming—the station identification slogans, the jingles, everything: "The radio I heard sounded so nice, so dynamic, so different from what we had here. I wanted something like the Colombians, something lively, with all those cumbias and all those kinds of musics" (interview).

Hearing about some secondhand transmitting equipment for sale in Puerto Rico, he traveled there to purchase it and received permission from the Bosch government to import it free of taxes. This transmitting equipment, installed in late 1964, was the most powerful that existed in the country at the time—five kilowatts, compared to the one-kilowatt transmitters used by most of the country's eleven other radio stations. In order to attract attention and to build an audience for his new station, Aracena devised a clever scheme: he prepared about twenty tape reels of his favorite selections, old as well as new, from his stock of Colombian, Mexican, Cuban, Puerto Rican, and Dominican music, with absolutely no talking on the tapes, not even station identification. He began broadcasting the tapes between 6 and 8 A.M., and slowly lengthened the broadcasts over the next four months until the broadcasts were running from 8 A.M. to 8 P.M. Needless to say, the mysterious musical broadcasts generated considerable interest.

Aracena had chosen the radio band for Radio Guarachita with great care. He knew that Dominicans listened to foreign radio stations at night, so he selected a band that would not be interfered with by these stations. The band he chose, 690, was the clearest available, although it caused Aracena some trouble: it happened to be the same band used by Cuba's revolutionary Radio Rebelde, whose radio signals were not powerful enough to interfere with Radio Guarachita's broadcasts by day, but they came in clearly at night after Guarachita went off the air. Aracena recalls that the people who listened to the station throughout the day, particularly those living along the country's north coast, sometimes forgot to change the dial after Guarachita went off the air, and some were accused of communism because they were caught listening to Radio Rebelde. Furthermore, because some officials thought the all-day music was a tactic by Radio Rebelde to capture a Dominican audience before its evening broadcasts, Aracena was instructed by the country's communications minister to include station identification or lose his license.

Still, his sense of showmanship prompted him to avoid fully unveiling Radio Guarachita to the Dominican public until he had generated even more expectations. Responding minimally to the government's orders to identify the station, he announced only the station's name and call number, followed by a swishing sound like that of a flying saucer. There was still no disc jockey and not a single advertisement, even though advertisers were by then offering him large sums of money to promote their products on the new and already popular radio station. It was not until March 1965 that Radio Guarachita officially came on the air with the full complement of features usually associated with radio programming such as advertisements and identifiable disc jockeys, plus the kind of "extras" he had always included in his programming—jingles, contests, sound effects, and so on. The disc jockeys had been personally trained by Aracena himself to speak a Spanish free of any regionalisms that might identify the disc jockeys' origins, and he forbade them to use slang.[4]

Radio Guarachita's dramatic debut was disrupted shortly thereafter by the fighting that broke out in April 1965. The radio studio was located on Calle Palo Hincado in the center of Santo Domingo, which was held by the Constitutionalists; but the transmitter was across the Ozama Bridge in Alma Rosa, which was occupied by the Loyalists and shortly thereafter by the U.S. Marines. When the Loyalists and the Marines took over the center of the city, they removed some parts of Guarachita's facilities, temporarily incapacitating the radio station. Nevertheless, shortly after the election of Joaquín Balaguer in 1966, Radio Guarachita went back on the air.

The preceding account of the birth of Radio Guarachita is derived from an interview with Radhames Aracena himself. Other accounts suggest that Radio Guarachita's beginnings were somewhat more complex. One observer, for example, attributed Radio Guarachita's initial lack of advertising to Aracena's belief that he could support the station by promoting his record sales alone (Brea 1975: 82). Another pointed out that when Aracena established Radio Guarachita, he had the support and protection of Donald Reid Cabral, who served as transitional president of the country from late 1963, after Bosch was deposed, until the April 1965 revolution. Reid Cabral helped Aracena in several ways, not the least of which was helping him secure the relatively clear 690 band for Radio Guarachita, in hopes of later using the station to promote his own candidacy in the next presidential elections. Radio Guarachita would certainly have been an effective tool in Reid's presidential campaign not only because of its large urban audience, but because its transmissions reached the entire countryside (Miguel Holguín, interview).

As the 1960s progressed, three important socio-cultural changes began to influence the direction of Radio Guarachita. First, the country's social fabric was becoming increasingly segmented and stratified. Second, the various genres of popular music were similarly being stratified and associated with different socio-economic classes—U.S. and European rock with the elite, orquesta merengue and salsa with the working and middle classes, and the guitar music being recorded by the likes of José Manuel Calderón and Luis Segura with the poorest classes. Aracena realized that the sort of guitar music he had been importing and on which he had based his retail record business was being rejected by the urban middle classes in favor of orquesta merengue and other more modern international musics, but that the music of local musicians, which Charlie Charlie and Cuco Valoy were promoting, was being eagerly accepted by the city's growing population of poor rural migrants. Thus, when Radio Guarachita resumed broadcasting in 1966, Aracena—abandoning his initial plans for a "refined" Colombian-style radio station—committed Radio Guarachita to domestically produced guitar music, thereby targeting a particular segment of the Dominican population.

While Radio Guarachita was not the only Santo Domingo radio station that appealed to the recent migrants, its musical programming and marketing strategies were unique in that they were aimed not only at poor urban migrants but at the rural population as well. Guarachita appealed to people all over the country who were undergoing change, but who appreciated continuity, and who desired to preserve at least some aspects of the past—such as certain kinds of music—that they considered timeless and worthy of perpetuation. So, for example, its programs of old favorites tacitly reassured its audience that the old, the traditional, was still valid and valuable. In contrast, contemporary mainstream radio stations that played only the latest hits, whether domestic or foreign, implicitly made the claim that newer is better, and by extension, that the old was useless and should be discarded.

Radio Guarachita's programming also indicated that while Aracena realized his audience was overall poor and uneducated, it was not monolithic; that while the aesthetic preferences of his poor rural and urban listeners might be rooted in the same broad category of música de guitarra, the lifestyles and musical behavior of each group were not identical. Broadcasting began at 5 A.M. with old Mexican and Colombian favorites that appealed most to campesinos. The morning show that followed consisted of the guitar music—bachata—being produced by Guarachita. At the lunch hour, the station played instrumental music by musically homogenized and insipid non-Dominican groups such as Las Cuerdas que Lloran and Los Diplomáticos (both Colombian), which would be considered "in good taste." (Brea has suggested that this noon-hour show was programmed so that maids, who listened to the bachata show all morning while they were doing household chores, would not have to change the dial when the *patrones* (employers) returned home for lunch [1975].) After 2:30 P.M. the station again broadcast locally recorded guitar music until the early evening, when it broadcast more Mexican music (e.g., a half hour of Pedro Infante) and some merengue típicos. At night the programming was "by request": callers were put on the air to identify themselves and to request a record—which tended to be the same "hits" of the moment that were played on the daytime shows. On Sundays the programming would vary somewhat, concentrating more on old favorites, but including a live broadcast program on which visitors to the station's studios could send a greeting to friends or relatives. Without exception, the distribution rights of all the music played by Radio Guarachita—regardless of country of origin—were held by Aracena and the records sold at his record stores.

In addition to playing the familiar guitar music liked by people of rural origins, the station attracted loyal listeners by offering *servicios públicos*—free public-service announcements—one of Radio Guarachita's most distinctive features. In the 1960s the country's roads and mail service were poor, and telephones in the countryside were practically nonexistent, leaving people who had moved to the city with no quick way of communicating with relatives in the countryside when an emergency arose. In cases of sickness, death, or other personal problems, Radio Guarachita's listeners could request that a message be announced over the air, an almost certain way to reach relatives. Similarly, if a rural person arriving in the city could not locate relatives or friends, or if someone lost identity papers, Guarachita would broadcast a message. To people in trouble, whose family members were dispersed throughout the country, as well as those having difficulties coping with the urban environment, Radio Guarachita's servicios públicos gave listeners a sense that if a crisis occurred, at least one institution, Radio Guarachita, could help them solve the problem. Beyond their humanitarian purposes, however, the personal dramas underlying each servicio público also provided Guarachita's listeners with entertainment—part gossip and part soap opera—whose economic value was not likely to have been underestimated by consummate showman and entrepreneur Radhames Aracena.

Other features of Radio Guarachita reflected how Aracena used his understanding of his audience's culture and lifestyle. For example, the studio's location—within easy walking distance of both the working class shopping district and major bus stops—allowed Radio Guarachita's listeners to easily visit the studio without incurring extra expenses. Once inside, visitors could observe the broadcasting process, because the disc jockey's console was located not in a closed booth, but rather on a raised platform in a *radioteatro,* a small theater holding about one hundred chairs. The radioteatro was used for the station's live programs; for example, típico accordionist Tatico Henríquez played live merengue on a regularly scheduled Sunday afternoon program. The rest of the time, it was used to seat visitors wishing to see how a radio show was conducted, or who wanted to wait until their servicio público was announced on the air. Thus, Guarachita's technology was made available to the gaze of people of humble rural backgrounds, who regarded it with awe, admiration, and gratitude for being allowed access to it.

One of Radio Guarachita's live programs directed at people of rural origins was the Sunday afternoon *programa de saludos* (greeting show), in which visitors lined up to take a turn at the microphone to send greetings to friends and relatives. The *saludo* (greeting) is a form of ritual behavior typical of Dominican traditional culture and serves to communicate important social information—a person's knowledge of good manners, as well as his or her verbal skills. When rural Dominicans encounter one or more persons, they individually greet and shake hands with each and every individual in the group, establishing the greeter and the greeted as members of a group and serving as a symbol of belonging to it (Barreiro 1986). In public settings, saludos can provide individuals with the opportunity to display their rhetorical abilities through more elaborate verbal flourishes.[5] Guarachita's programa de saludos served as an important link between urban and rural listeners not only in a literal sense—through the message contained in each saludo—but also because it transformed a rural oral tradition in which greetings were personally delivered and received into a new kind of urban-centered, mass-mediated communicative event.

Radio Guarachita's radioteatro was also used for special live broadcast events such as contests. In 1987, for example, I witnessed the final drawing of a riddle contest, *concurso de la adivinanza*, in which a riddle had been read over the air and participants mailed in their answers. The entries, thousands of them, were placed in a large bin. On the day of the drawing, Aracena personally served as MC of the show, calling upon an audience member to draw individual letters, reading out the sender's name and address (always emphasizing the geographical location of the entry) before reading the participant's answer. The grand prize winner received 50 pesos (then worth about US$17), the runners-up somewhat less. Again, this radio event was not simply entertainment: Aracena told me he used these contests to gauge the size of the station's audience. According to his calculations, the contest I observed drew about 20,000 entries, mailed from all parts of the country. While this may seem a large number of entries for such a small prize (taking into consideration the effort and costs involved in writing and posting the letters), Aracena told me that this contest did not generate nearly as many letters as he had received before the proliferation of competing radio stations, when three and four times as many entries were common.

To people dispersed throughout the countryside and in urban shantytowns accustomed to frequent personal interactions with community members, Radio Guarachita offered membership in a large, imaginary family. Indeed, one of its slogans was: "We are a big family. There are more than a quarter of a million of us. We are the biggest and most powerful family. We are the Radio Guarachita family. We are a quarter of a million listeners always united" (cited in Brea 1975, translation mine). The physical accessibility of the radio station, its public service announcements, as well as its contests, call-in request and saludo programs, all served to create a sense of personal involvement: those who called, wrote, or visited the station to participate in contests and to send greetings or emergency messages had names, lived in identifiable places, and suffered from familiar problems. This Guarachita "family" existed in a protected and secure space undivided by political struggle and untroubled by the country's economic difficulties: until the mid-1980s the station's programming included no news shows or references to specific current events.[6]

Dominican sociologist Ramonina Brea, who published a detailed and perceptive analysis of Radio Guarachita's programming in 1975 (on which much of the program analysis in this section is based) observed that while Guarachita's audience may have been the poorest and least educated segment of the population, it was, nevertheless, the largest segment, and its constituents regularly consumed laundry soap, health aids, rum, cigarettes, and other manufactured products, and as such represented an important new market that advertisers could profitably target. Through its advertising strategies, she argued, Radio Guarachita played a significant role in integrating the rural population into the country's modern market economy. In spite of its references to traditional culture, then, Radio Guarachita's purpose was quite modern: to encourage its listeners to participate in the country's growing market economy as active consumers.

Brea observed that because most of Guarachita's audience was in transition between rural and urban contexts and values, the language and symbols used to communicate with them had to draw on both traditional and modern imagery. It was no accident, for example, that more than half of Radio Guarachita's advertising was for nonprescription medicines and health aids. Rural Dominicans had a long tradition of relying on folk medicine (see Davis 1987), which was perceived as an obstacle to the sale of manufactured remedies being produced in the cities. Because health products were not conceived of as luxury goods, the rural population could more easily be convinced to accept them than other products not considered essential. Guarachita's advertising strategies were intended to convince people of rural origins to purchase "modern" (i.e., more efficacious) manufactured products instead of relying on traditional practices when a health problem arose. Once people began to prefer the manufactured to the homemade product, all sorts of manufactured goods could be successfully promoted and would eventually displace preferences for the traditional and the homemade (Brea 1975: 83). These manufactured goods, of course, would include recorded music as well.

Brea also pointed to other techniques used in ads (most of which were produced personally by Aracena) and in the station's identification slogans and jingles that drew from familiar, traditional cultural features shared by Guarachita's audience. For example, the constant sound effects, such as a bell ringing between each servicio público, were designed to attract the attention of persons whose culture was primarily oral, and ads made use of frequent repetition in order to stimulate their memory. I would add to Brea's observations that Guarachita's advertising style drew upon patterns of rural narrative structure. For example, its ads were usually situational and chronological rather than relying on the rapid collage of images characteristic of ads trying to convey urban modernity: Guarachita's listeners were located within extended narratives in which they vicariously experienced a problem that could be solved by the use of the product being promoted. The following example of a Guarachita ad for Laboratorios Dr. Collado illustrates not only how Guarachita's ads used repetition and linear narratives, but also how they made explicit appeals to campesinos' sense of inadequacy in a new urban environment:

> —Didn't you know that Dr. Collado has a quality product that's called Reuma-
>   nol, that with only twenty drops you will become strong as a cannon?
> —Oh, I didn't know.
> —Well, start knowing it. Let's hear you say it.
> —Ruiminol . . . Roiminol. What did you say?
> —Reumanol.
> —Oh, yes. It's that I don't know how to pronounce it, I'm from the country, I
>   just got to town.
> —Reumanol, Reumanol. I cured myself with Reumanol.
> *(Cited in Brea 1975, translation mine)*

Brea also noted that a majority of the slogans on Radio Guarachita concerned time. For example, jingles referring to each particular day would be repeated throughout that day (e.g., "Today there's a lot of work to do, the week begins. Today is Monday, today is Monday"). This led her to hypothesize that Guarachita was trying to adjust campesinos' notions of time as a prerequisite for assimilation into a modern, urban lifestyle and economy:

> One of the characteristics that differentiates the peasant from those in urban areas consists of different perceptions of time and space. This difference is important inasmuch as the functioning of any economic system is based on this type of perception. A person in an urban area increasingly utilizes "objective" ways and instruments to perceive time and space, which permits a type of social organization that takes into account changes in time. It is not the same with the peasant in the countryside, whose notion of time is extremely vague, based on changes in nature: seasons, position of sun and moon. Thus Radio Guarachita indicates, specifies constantly, the time, the day, the date; but not in the same way that other stations do, but instead, the listen-

ers' attention is drawn to these temporal categories. . . . The effects of
these 71 percent of the slogans referring to time are extremely important in the process of transforming the mentality of the campesino
since it makes possible, to begin with, the transition from a traditional
rural area to a rural area in transition. (Brea 1975: 84, translation
mine)

The tension between the simultaneous appeals to the modern and
to the traditional resulted in a mixing of modes of discourse that reflected
the social and cultural transformations being experienced by the station's
audience. Thus, Brea continued while the ads and slogans were attempt-
ing to associate the products with newer concepts of modernity and scientific efficacy—for example, ads for health aids included frequent
repetition of words such as *doctor, modern,* and *laboratory*—they simultaneously offered "miraculous" cures, appealing to the strong beliefs in supernatural powers still held by rural people. Also, in the slogans
reminding the listeners what day it was, the intent may indeed have been
to remind people of rural origins about the importance of precise time
keeping; but the form of these messages was traditional, being based on
old adages or superstitions (some of which are known all over Latin
America), for example, "Hoy es martes, ni te cases ni te embarques"
(Today is Tuesday, neither marry nor travel) (Brea 1975; interview).

At the same time that Radio Guarachita tried to invoke traditional
features of rural culture, it also tried to represent itself with images of
progress and modernity, and it encouraged the deference that rural people felt towards the technological (and hence cultural) superiority of urbanites. For example, its station identification utilized a series of technical
terms beyond the understanding of most listeners which were clearly intended to inspire respect and awe:

Radio Guarachita, a station that transmits to towns all over the Dominican Republic for 19 hours a day, on the frequency of 690 kilocycles,
long wave, with its modern RCA transmitter convertible from 5,000
to 10,000 kilowatts of power with a multidirectional antenna of 360
degrees and 90 megacycles per second, modulated frequency. . . .[7]
The programming that we have offered was conceived in order to
take the most modern radio broadcasting to all sectors of the Dominican public, counting on the most advanced equipment, recordings,
and human resources. . . . Our only aspiration has been to be useful
to you through our public service announcements and to entertain
you with our musical programs. (Cited in Brea 1975: 88, translation
mine)

Guarachita's communicative link between rural and urban areas
thus provided for a two-way dialogue: on one hand, it introduced rural
people and recent rural migrants to the urban context, promoting certain
features of urban culture—including bachata—throughout the country-

side; on the other hand, it kept certain aspects of traditional rural culture alive in spite of the disapproval of mainstream Dominican culture, which instead looked outward toward a modern, homogeneous international culture rather than inward to its traditional rural interior.

As a result of Aracena's astute promotional and advertising strategies, Radio Guarachita developed into one of the most successful radio stations in the country. Radio Guarachita's financial success, however, did not depend exclusively on its advertisements for various consumer goods, but rather on its promotion of the bachata music that Aracena himself was producing. Aracena had purchased his first recording equipment (consisting of one microphone and an ordinary commercial tape recorder) in the late 1950s; he installed it in his office behind his store on Calle el Conde, where he had recorded merengue conjuntos during the Trujillo era. In the early 1960s, sensing the public demand for the guitar-based music of domestic musicians such as José Manuel Calderón and Rafael Encarnación, he began producing local guitar musicians himself. He also established a pressing factory, the Fábrica de Discos la Guarachita, in order to manufacture his own records within the country—although he also pressed records for other local producers. Not surprisingly, Aracena continued his practice of giving airplay only to the songs he himself produced or distributed in his retail store, thereby avoiding all intermediaries and maximizing his profits. In effect, Aracena was able to gain control over all aspects of his musical production—recording, pressing, broadcasting, and distribution, giving him a distinct advantage over his competitors promoting other types of music.

While Aracena was closely involved in all aspects of Empresas Guarachita, he participated most actively in recording. For example, he personally auditioned and advised each musician that aspired to record with Guarachita. Aracena's auditions and practice sessions, which I observed in 1987, reflected the highly personalistic and paternalistic nature of the larger Guarachita enterprise. Musicians interested in recording with Guarachita gathered regularly on Saturday mornings at Aracena's house in El Paraíso, an upper-middle-class residential neighborhood in Santo Domingo, where the recording studio was located. Arriving early, they waited outside the house, under the carport, until Aracena was ready to receive them. The carport was directly adjacent to the house, so the musicians could peer through the security bars and the glass doors that ran the entire length of the house into Aracena's modern and relatively luxurious (by U.S. standards) dining and living rooms, where the family moved around having breakfast, talking on the phone, and so on. Unconcerned that some musicians had been outside for hours, Aracena made them wait until he was ready. When they were finally asked to come in, the musicians had to pass through Aracena's personal domestic space in order to reach the studio, which was located on second floor of the house and did not have a separate entrance.

Before entering the house, however, they were told to remove their shoes at the door, even though Aracena, his family, and the domestic servants were wearing their shoes. Dominicans are very particular about their shoes because they can indicate a person's social class: less than spotless shoes reveal that the wearer resides in a poor barrio or rural area, where the lack of sidewalks or paved streets make it impossible for those who have to walk to keep their shoes clean. By making the musicians take off their shoes before entering his house—whether or not they were dirty—Aracena transformed the shoes into symbols of pollution and of their low social standing, locating the musicians at the bottom of an implicit but well-understood social hierarchy and effectively establishing a social distance between himself and the musicians that otherwise might have been reduced by their presence in his domestic space.

Aracena's recording "studio" merited the name only because it contained recording equipment, not because it had been designed with special architectural or acoustic features such as control booths, sound-proofing, and so on. It was an ordinary room with cement walls and tile floor that had been minimally adapted for recording: sound absorption was provided by shelves of records and tapes that covered most of the walls, and there were a few small rugs on the floor. Aracena did not perceive the room's lack of acoustic improvements as a disadvantage; on the contrary, he told me that the somewhat hollow, echo-like quality of records recorded in his studio distinguished Guarachita's records from those recorded in the city's more modern studios, which produced a more muffled, dry sound.

Once in the studio, each musician was given a chance to sing his composition, and Aracena listened attentively. If Aracena liked the song, he would record it on a small cassette deck and later personally transcribe the lyrics, typing them out on an antiquated typewriter. During the transcription process, he corrected the grammar and would then instruct the musician to learn the changes, thereby eliminating the sort of regionalisms or grammatical errors that might glaringly link the musician or music with any one geographic area or social class. Some musicians resented Aracena's changes to their compositions; but others recognized the value of Aracena's care in correcting the grammar and pronunciation of their lyrics, and they perceived him as a teacher, or at least as someone who made an effort to compensate for their lack of schooling. As one bachatero, Solterito del Sur, said:

> Before, bachata songs were sung without sophisticating, properly grammaticizing the lyrics that one was singing. But recently all the

singers first make a copy [of the lyrics] and then they study them to
grammaticize the lyrics properly, where an *r* goes, an *s*, how to spell
the words of the song. And after we study the copy, we go to record.
Until we can grammaticize the words well, we don't record. He cor-
rects us right then and there. Because there are other bachateros who
record for other record labels that perhaps don't correct them [the
lyrics]. And we are compared to them; because of them we all suffer.
(Interview)

In spite of the care Aracena took with the song lyrics, his producing
style was in general highly informal and spontaneous. Leonardo Paniagua, recalling the beginning of his career, said he was in Aracena's studio
playing maracas for another singer when Aracena, frustrated with the
singer's mistakes, asked Paniagua to try singing something. Without Paniagua knowing it, Aracena kept the tape recorder on, and when Paniagua
was finished, announced that it was perfect. He released the song and
thereby launched Paniagua's long and successful career.

Aracena did not employ specialized recording technicians: he personally set up the microphones and made necessary adjustments in recording levels in an adjoining room where the recording equipment was
located. His equipment had the capacity for four-channel recording, although he did not record the musicians separately: each song was recorded by the entire ensemble simultaneously, although he sometimes
made subsequent corrections. Also located in the small adjoining room
was a mastering lathe on which he himself produced acetate masters. The
acetate masters for producing stampers were taken to Aracena's pressing
factory, the Fábrica de Discos la Guarachita, located nearby on Avenida
Kennedy, where the records were pressed by workmen on manually op-
erated machines. The graphic design, photography, and printing for labels and record jackets were also done on the premises in an adjoining
section; again, Aracena himself often took the photographs used on
album covers. After the records were packaged, copies would be sent to
Radio Guarachita for promotion on the air, and the rest were sent to Aracena's three Guarachita record stores for distribution: the largest store on
the first floor of the building in which the broadcasting studio was
housed (until 1989); another located nearby in the heart of the city's principal working-class shopping district; and another in Santiago, the country's second largest city and the capital of the important Cibao region.
From these stores, Guarachita's products were sold wholesale to record
vendors for distribution throughout the country as well as retail to individual consumers.

Aracena promoted a public image of this conglomerate, Empresas
Guarachita (Guarachita Enterprises), as a family business. His wife, Doña
Zuni (after whom he named one of his labels, Zuni), managed Guarachi-

ta's accounts—no small feat for an enterprise of that size. His office was in his home, and he did not have a personal secretary. Compared to other media owners and executives, he was unusually accessible. His radio advertisement for the record factory's facilities, for example, gave one of his home telephone numbers. (On the several occasions I called that number, the domestic servants, Doña Zuni, or he himself answered the telephone—a very different style from that of merengue record producers, whose desire to convey an image of modernity and efficiency demanded an overzealous secretary to maintain a distance between themselves and callers.) At the height of his success, Aracena continued to "micromanage" his business: for example, personally selecting and training potential disc jockeys, writing the station's jingles and slogans, and overseeing, as I discussed above, almost every aspect of record production. Clearly, Guarachita did not fall within the sort of pattern one would expect of a modern, highly successful capitalist enterprise.

Empresas Guarachita, however, was no mom-and-pop enterprise. In spite of its "folksy" image, it was tightly controlled and nothing was left to improvisation. For example, Radio Guarachita's disc jockeys were required to use playlists, even for the call-in request programs; only requests for records on the playlist were honored. The disc jockeys, however, kept a record of what songs were being requested so that Aracena could gauge their relative popularity. However popular a song might become, however, Aracena made it a policy never to divulge any figures or statistics on record sales. I was told by someone in the music industry that when a Guarachita musician won an award, he refused to attend the ceremonies because he did not wish to reveal the number of records sold. Because Empresas Guarachita was a highly profitable and almost self-contained operation, Aracena did not need to seek the sort of positive publicity—and its snowball effects—that news of extraordinary record sales can generate.

The reasons for Aracena's refusal to reveal sales figures are related to the darker side of Aracena's business practices. While he was willing to bestow considerable personal attention on preparing and recording musicians' songs and promoting them on the station, his concern for the musicians did not extend beyond the boundaries of his own economic interests. Indeed, Aracena's highly personal yet hierarchical style of dealing with his musicians is characteristic of traditional Dominican paternalistic patron-client relationships, in which social and economic subordinates are flagrantly exploited, but their loyalty is maintained through personal favors. Musicians were paid only a one-time pittance for each recording, and they received no royalties, no matter how many thousands of records sold—hence his reticence to divulge sales figures. One successful musician under contract to Guarachita told me that his backup musicians each received only three and a half pesos for a single and only twenty-three pesos for an LP of twelve songs. Almost all the musicians I interviewed in the course of my fieldwork, all of whom had recorded for Guarachita at one time or another, were unanimous that Aracena was utterly unscrupulous in exploiting them. Nevertheless, musicians pragmatically recognized the indisputable value of Radio Guarachita in giving them national public exposure. As Luis Segura said of Aracena:

> He never paid well. He took everything for himself. He has always played that music, which has been the life of Guarachita. It was with this genre of music that he became rich. Guarachita was the first, I would say number one, in audience, in record sales, and in everything, because that was what was most listened to. I have hardly made anything from record sales because the producers here don't pay. They are exploiters. José Luis (another producer) pays a little more, but he doesn't have the strength that Radhames has, because Radhames has the station, which is the most important base. (Interview)

Radhames Aracena was not the only producer of bachata in the 1960s, but he was certainly the most important one, launching the careers of dozens of bachata musicians and disseminating bachata throughout the country. Yet while domestically produced guitar-based music did indeed gain a strong foothold among the country's poorest and most dispossessed citizens, it did not fare well in the mainstream musical marketplace, which was increasingly dominated by orquesta merengue and its well-financed promoters.

The parallel—if structurally unequal—growth of bachata and merengue during the 1960s clearly reflected the needs of different sectors of the population undergoing change through modernization at different rates. Orquesta merengue served as an agent of socialization, guiding the country's new middle classes into a more sophisticated and consumer-oriented world and serving as an icon of the country's increasingly cosmopolitan national identity. Bachata's appeal, in contrast, rested on its ability to introduce its listeners, principally peasants and shantytown dwellers of rural origins who had little chance of participating in the glitzy world represented by modern merengue orquestas, to urban values they needed to understand—and adopt—in order to survive on the margins of modern, urban Dominican society. The community they were part of was defined not by national citizenship but by low social class and, for the urban poor, by shantytown residence and cultural patterns.

By the end of the decade, issues of national identity that had been incontestable during the Trujillo era moved to the center of the Dominican political and cultural arena. Subsequently, struggling within and against the constraints of the authoritarian regime of Joaquín Balaguer (1966–78), the country sought to redefine its national identity under conditions of rapid economic growth and increasing socio-cultural diversity. In this struggle, which will be described in the following chapter, popular music became a key arena in which issues of power, representation, and identity were tested and contested.

Chapter Four

Power, Representation, and Identity

"What they are looking for with the word *bachata* is to keep it beneath the saxophone. To keep the guitar beneath the saxophone. It can't be. The two instruments are equal." In this statement made by bachatero Leonardo Paniagua, musical instruments—the guitar and the saxophone—symbolize the struggle between musical genres—bachata and merengue—in which the former is forcibly subordinated to the latter. But Paniagua's image also symbolizes class struggle, with the guitar representing the poor and the saxophone representing the elite—and again, with the former being subordinated to the latter. Paniagua was by no means inventing or exaggerating the musical and class struggles that characterized the Dominican Republic in the late 1960s and 1970s. In fact, the period between 1966 and 1978—the twelve years in which Joaquín Balaguer served as president of the country—was characterized by intense conflicts on all levels of Dominican life—political, economic, and cultural—that were directly articulated in music and indirectly reflected in various aspects of the music business. These conflicts resulted in what Dominican musician Luis Dias called *la lucha sonora*, which translates somewhat awkwardly as "the sonic struggle." On a political level, songs of protest and resistance in several genres of popular music expressed opposition to Balaguer's government, whose policies were perceived to be inimical to the interests of the majority. On an economic level, different genres of music that represented the interests and values of distinct social and economic groups, competed vigorously with each other in an open marketplace. There was, moreover, an international component to the economic struggle, as merengue, which was promoted as the music that best represented the country's national identity, had to compete with foreign musics in both the domestic and international market. Culturally, public debates arose concerning the role of music in constructing and representing both past and future configurations of the country's national identity. This chapter will explore how these struggles to reconstruct the economic and political landscape and to redefine the national identity manifested themselves materially and symbolically in the complex and multidimensional interactions between different sectors of society seeking control of the country's cultural resources.

While ordinarily one should avoid personifying musical genres— after all, music can only be made and promoted by human beings—for purposes of narrative simplicity, in this chapter I will refer to competition among musics rather than among their producers or promoters. In the struggles I will describe below, bachata was a relatively low-profile contender compared to other more powerful musics such as salsa and merengue—although its role was by no means insignificant.

The Political and Economic Setting

One year after the bloody revolution of April 1965 and the occupation by U.S. Marines, national elections were held under the watchful eye of the United States. All the major parties participated in the elections, which were won by Joaquín Balaguer, a man who had served as both vice-president and president during the Trujillo regime, and who was considered by some to have been the intellectual mastermind of the dictatorship. Balaguer's opponents charged that he had won by fraud, encouraged and condoned by the United States. Others offered a more benign explanation for Balaguer's victory, claiming that Dominicans were simply tired of the turmoil, and though Balaguer may not have been the best solution, he offered the stability and order necessary for economic progress to take place. Balaguer's government did turn out to be stable as far as its institutions and policies were concerned, because he was able to hold on to power for twelve years without interruption. Nevertheless, while order did prevail in some respects, it was not achieved through peaceful consensus. Enormous resentment toward the Balaguer government was felt by large sectors of the population who were dismayed that a former Trujillo official could again be in control and, worse, that he reinstituted Trujillo's repressive tactics against those who opposed his policies. Indeed, among his first official acts were strengthening military and police powers and amending Bosch's 1963 constitution that guaranteed civil rights.

The thrust of Balaguer's economic policies was to "modernize" the country, for which two changes were considered necessary: land reform and industrialization. Land reform was an abysmal failure, because most of the better Trujillo lands had already been usurped by the military and turned into cane plantations for the country's principal cash export, sugar. Lacking adequate land, impoverished peasants were forced to move into the cities in search of subsistence: between 1960 and 1970, the population of Santo Domingo almost doubled, rising from 370,000 to 669,000 inhabitants (Maríñez 1984: 101). Thousands of other migrants departed, traveling to the U.S. mainland, Puerto Rico, or Venezuela in search of better paying jobs.

Industrialization was to be achieved by encouraging foreign investment and by offering both foreign and domestic entrepreneurs a series of incentives designed to guarantee attractive profits. These incentives included import tax exemptions on raw materials and machinery, generous government loans, income tax breaks, and most important, a cheap work force (Duarte 1986: 181). This work force, swelled by the thousands of peasants migrating into urban areas, was deliberately kept cheap by freezing salaries—in spite of the rapidly rising cost of living—and kept docile by actively suppressing union activity.

The unions were not the only targets of Balaguer's repression: all political organizations of the left were persecuted by Balaguer's military and police, who responded to any sort of opposition with vigorous force. The worst violence occurred in the first years of Balaguer's regime, when the popular struggle against his policies was most active and the government's determination to disarticulate these organizations most brutal: over 1000 Dominicans were assassinated for political reasons (and many more imprisoned and tortured) between 1966 and 1971 (Black 1986: 48). As Pablo Maríñez observed, "[Balaguer's] first six years of government were dedicated entirely to the most ferocious repression known in Dominican history, exceeding several fold that of Trujillo's tyranny" (Maríñez 1984: 118–19, translation mine).

Thanks to the favorable conditions for industry and commerce secured by Balaguer, the country did in fact experience economic growth, and the Dominican Republic was considered (by the United States) to be an economic miracle, a showcase for the benefits of free market democracy. But, as Jan K. Black observed, this "was an era of selective prosperity. . . . While GNP growth rates and per capita income rose, the standard of living of the majority dipped even lower. Unemployment was chronic, at a level higher than 30 percent. Illiteracy and infant mortality remained high, and malnutrition was widespread" (Black 1986: 44). As the Dominican elite and the upper middle classes got wealthier, the poor got poorer: "Average wages were lower, at least in real terms, and in some cases in monetary terms as well, by the end of the 1970s than they had been at the end of the 1960s'' (Black 1986: 97).

In addition to causing increased economic hardship for the majority of Dominicans, Balaguer's policies resulted in increased stratification of an already stratified society, exacerbating divisions within the lower class itself. The migrant population of Santo Domingo had not been homogeneous to begin with. The first wave of migrants to arrive in the 1950s and early 1960s had been comprised primarily of peasants whose parents had owned at least some land and who had received some education. Those who migrated later, in the late 1960s and 1970s, tended to be the more impoverished peasants, people whose families did not own land, who had worked as paid agricultural laborers, and who were less educated than their predecessors (Duarte 1986: 152–60).[1] The earlier migrants were more successful than later migrants in getting the better paid, more stable jobs in industry and construction as they opened up and thus were able to make the adjustment to urban life more easily. The later arrivals, on the other hand, were mostly limited to seeking subsistence in the informal economy and to residence in the shantytowns. In the 1970s, social and cultural cleavages between the steadily working poor and those limited to subsistence activities in the informal sector began to manifest themselves in their musical preferences.

Competition in the Musical Marketplace

The Dominican economy, like that of other third-world countries, contained only limited resources, such as investment capital and media access, indispensable for success in the marketplace. Thus, the success of one music (and its promoters) depended on successfully excluding or limiting other musics' access to these resources. While the struggle for access to resources was fundamentally economic, it also exhibited ideological dimensions, because ideology could serve to legitimate the inclusion or exclusion of one musical genre. During the Balaguer era, several musics competed in the commercial musical arena. Among the domestic contenders were orquesta merengue, merengue típico, Dominican *nueva canción* (new song—a domestic variant of a Pan-Latin American form of protest music), and bachata. The principal foreign contenders were salsa, balada, and U.S./U.K. rock. Of the domestic musics, orquesta merengue, whose status as the national dance music and the favorite of the elite had been firmly established by Trujillo, was clearly in the best position because it enjoyed easiest access to both investment capital and media coverage. Merengue típico and bachata (which were very closely related contextually if not musically) had each been consolidated as viable commercial genres, although their dissemination relied on the informal music economy because they lacked access to the mainstream music industry and media. Nueva canción was also marginalized to a certain extent, not because its practitioners were socially or economically marginal according to the definition of marginality I outlined in the preceding chapter, but by choice, because they challenged the values of mainstream society and assumed a defiantly militant political stance against the Balaguer government.

Of the foreign musics, the country's attraction for U.S./U.K. rock that had been so appealing in the immediate post-Trujillo era began to decline in the latter part of the 1960s, partly in reaction to anti-U.S. sentiment in the aftermath of the 1965 invasion and the U.S. support of the Balaguer regime, and partly as a result of increased competition from other Latin American musics, balada and salsa. Nevertheless, U.S. top-40 rock, financially backed by powerful international record companies and considered by many young Dominicans to represent the latest in musical modernity, retained an important niche in the Dominican music market.

By far the most visible musical competition in the 1970s was between merengue and salsa. Salsa was an unmistakable product of the modern Pan-Caribbean experience: salsa musicians were mostly Puerto Rican, its rhythms were principally Cuban, and its social context was primarily the Latino barrios of New York City (see Rondón 1980, Baron 1977, Singer 1983, Duany 1984, Boggs 1992). Emerging in the mid-to-late 1960s, salsa was aggressively promoted all over Latin America by the New York–based Fania record company. Salsa reached its peak of popularity (and, most aficionados agree, of musical creativity) in the early 1970s, although it continued to dominate the Latin music industry throughout the decade.

The relationship between salsa and merengue was multidimensional and complex. Salsa, like merengue, appealed to Dominicans because it was considered to be great dance music—energetic, creative, and thoroughly Caribbean. Unlike rock or balada, salsa is a close relative of merengue, both of which share several Spanish Caribbean features, among them African-derived rhythms, highly danceable improvisational sections (*montuno* in salsa, *jaleo* in merengue), and spicy, satirical lyrics drawing heavily on Spanish Caribbean vernacular language and imagery. Furthermore, one of the most important contributors to the early development of salsa was the Dominican Johnny Pacheco, which meant that Dominicans could claim at least some measure of paternity for salsa. Another important point of contact between salsa and its Dominican consumers was the Dominican Republic's long-standing and active tradition of son music, salsa's principal musical root. Finally, salsa's grounding in the culture of New York Latino barrios and its hard-edged urban lyrics were easily understood by Dominicans who were similarly experiencing the difficulties of modern urban life, whether in Santo Domingo or as migrants in New York City.

Nevertheless, even though salsa became immensely popular in the Dominican Republic in the 1970s, it was not essentially Dominican, a point repeatedly stressed by those promoting orquesta merengue when trying to convince their compatriots to dance to merengue instead of salsa. Initially salsa had more powerful backers able to finance massive public-relations and promotion campaigns and, moreover—given the Dominican Republic's payola-driven broadcast system—able to purchase radio and television exposure as well. As disc jockey Willie Rodríguez recalls:

> Many people ignore that merengue in 1974–75 did not achieve a maximum national or international projection. Many people are unaware that Fania took it upon itself to boycott the merengue, not only in New York, Puerto Rico, and in other countries, but in our own Dominican Republic. Around these years Fania, in a market whose maximum sales were 4000 copies, had an office on El Conde, with a flamboyant director sent from Argentina and with the willing support of a Dominican record producer, because unfortunately there are always Dominicans who will lend themselves to this type of thing. History repeats itself, and you will see how it does: Fania enters, shuts down merengue, takes one of the principal figures of the new generation of merengue, Wilfrido Vargas, includes him in its ensemble. . . . At that time Fania was interested in maintaining in the market the image that salsa was the representative Latin rhythm. They had to maintain that position, merengue couldn't be Latin. Which is what is happening today, merengue is winning, but this couldn't have happened in 1974. (Rodríguez 1986: 17, translation mine)

Rodríguez's language reveals that the competition between salsa and merengue was neither unconscious nor coincidental. It also confirms my contention that while the *lucha sonora* in the 1970s was in large part about controlling the marketplace, it was also a struggle over the meanings associated with different popular musics, particularly as they related to questions of national identity—which shifted situationally. Confronted with rock, Dominicans perceived salsa as an expression of a shared Pan-Caribbean identity. But confronted with merengue, salsa became foreign and hostile, and the competition fed upon latent conflicts between Puerto Ricans and Dominicans.

While this volume is not the place for a lengthy analysis of Dominican–Puerto Rican relations, I will point to a few factors suggesting that this conflict went beyond simple economic desires to control a record market. The Dominican Republic and Puerto Rico are close neighbors, not only geographically and culturally, but historically as well, both having experienced—to varying degrees—the humiliation of U.S. occupation and its overwhelming cultural and economic domination. Nevertheless, their economic well-being and their positions vis-à-vis the United States were quite different. On the one hand, Dominicans could point with pride to their country's independent status; on the other, there was a certain envy of the economic privileges Puerto Ricans enjoyed as a result of their commonwealth status. Both countries had lost large segments of their population to migration to the United States. Puerto Ricans had begun their migrations earlier and enjoyed access not only to the industrial jobs that were available in the 1950s but to the full gamut of social services as well. When Dominicans began migrating, first in the 1960s but in much larger numbers in the 1970s, New York's shrinking industrial base no longer provided enough jobs; furthermore, many Dominicans were illegal immigrants and had no social supports outside those offered informally by the Dominican community itself. In New York—as well as in Puerto Rico itself, to which Dominicans began migrating as a first step toward reaching the U.S. mainland—Puerto Ricans and Dominicans had to compete with each other for scarce jobs, housing, social services, and political influence (Cabezas 1987). In the Dominican Republic, common wisdom had it that Dominicans, in spite of being handicapped by lack of documents and social services, worked harder than Puerto Ricans to succeed; and Puerto Ricans, they believed, resented them for this and wanted to keep Dominicans out.

As salsa became increasingly commercialized in the course of the 1970s, it became more homogenized, less original and creative. By the end of the decade, merengue, by then financially better supported and technically more sophisticated, began to replace salsa as the dance music of preference not only in the Dominican Republic, but in Puerto Rico and among Latinos in New York as well. Lucrative contracts in clubs that had once been enjoyed only by salsa ensembles began to be given to merengue orquestas. To some Dominicans, merengue's triumph in the international marketplace was sweet revenge, and the musicians who had achieved the victory were perceived as warriors and heroes. As Willie Rodríguez said of Dominican merengueros: "They are the guerrillas of music, who go to Puerto Rico and place a bomb in the places where they play" (Rodríguez 1986: 21, translation mine).

Puerto Rican musicians protested merengue's challenge through the media, musicians' unions, and in one case, by urging the U.S. Immigration and Naturalization Service not to give visas to Dominican musicians. When the U.S. government moved the office that gave visas from Puerto Rico to Vermont, an article in a Santo Domingo newspaper related the story in the following terms:

> They got theirs, the little group of resentful musicians who protested the presence of Dominican orchestras in our neighboring island. They

got what they wanted, but now they've been left with no pan to fry in, because the Immigration and Naturalization Service took away their power to give visas. From now on those who want a visa to work in Puerto Rico have to go to Vermont to get it, far away from there. The musicians, resentful, frustrated, had been constantly pressuring the INS not to give visas to merengue orquestas. . . . In their rush to boycott the Dominican orquestas these musicians, very few, to be sure, went so far as to propagate fantastic lies such that hundreds of Dominican orquestas were traveling constantly to Puerto Rico. . . . Now the protests will be because they lost their frying pan. They won't be able to apply pressure so that only the musical groups and artists that they feel are qualified should be allowed to enter. What's more, they've already begun to protest. They are even insulting musicians who are here. (*Tarde Alegre*, November 25, 1986, translation mine)

The Pan–Latin American balada, the other important musical contender in the Dominican musical marketplace, had emerged in the late 1960s, drawing partly from the Cuban bolero but also from a music from Spain known as *nueva canción*—which, in spite of its political content in its early years, was not identical to the Latin American music of the same name (Enrique Fernández, personal communication). By the 1970s, however, balada's increasing obsession with sentimental themes had made it more akin to the romantic Cuban bolero than to the politically and socially conscious Spanish nueva canción. Unlike the guitar-based romantic Cuban bolero, balada was characterized by highly sophisticated arrangements and production values, which endowed it with a modern veneer that the traditional bolero lacked. While balada was popular throughout the Spanish-speaking world, it was not associated with any particular country; it was a form of transnational music culture, defined by Roger Wallis and Krister Malm as "the result of a combination of features from several kinds of music. This combination is the result of a socio-economic process whereby the lowest musical common denominator for the biggest possible market is identified. . . . It is a product that has not originated within any special ethnic group" (Wallis and Malm 1984: 300).

Balada's transnational character was largely responsible for its enormous success: its romantic lyrics were not specific to any time, place, or social group, promotion strategies did not need to be modified for individual countries, and marketing costs could be spread throughout the continent. The *baladistas* (balada singers) themselves came from all over Latin America—Mexico, Venezuela, Argentina, Puerto Rico, and Brazil all boasted major figures—as well as from Spain. The Spaniard Julio Iglesias (the only baladista to achieve fame in the United States) was but one of dozens of balada superstars who enjoyed devoted followers all over Latin America and Spain. Balada's audience also cut across class lines: it was most popular within the middle and upper classes, but also attracted those from lower classes who identified with or aspired to middle-class status. These social groups were (and have remained) balada's largest constituency in the Dominican Republic.

In spite of the fact that balada, like salsa, was also non-Dominican and was similarly promoted heavily in the country by multinational record companies, it was not perceived as a threat to merengue because they were functionally different and were not competing for the same economic niche: salsa was dance music, while balada was romantic music. Balada was, however—in terms of its function as a romantic music—the principal competitor to the romantic, largely bolero-based music produced by Dominican musicians of rural origins. Here, the competition for audience share was fundamentally unequal. From bachata's perspective the balada—slick, sophisticated, prestigious, well financed, international—was an opponent it could not compete with, particularly since it was perceived as the romantic music of choice for anyone, no matter how poor, with middle-class aspirations. In contrast, the rough-edged bachata presented no threat to balada's position as the preferred form of romantic music among the moneyed classes.

Although bachata had an apparent disadvantage in competing with the other musics contending for hegemony in the Dominican musical arena, the growing numbers of migrants moving into the cities in the 1970s increased the size of its audience. As a result, a number of independent producers emerged to challenge Radhames Aracena's dominance of the bachata business by offering financial backing to poor musicians who either would not or could not record with Guarachita. The more notable of the new labels to appear in the late 1960s and 1970s were José Luis's Discos José Luis (1966), Ramón Antonio Alejo's ("Mamita's") Discos Negra (ca. 1967), Maximino Sánchez's Discos Unidad (ca. 1972), Rafael Mañón's RM Records (1977), and Manuel Meregildo's Discos Marisol. Additionally, there were countless other producers who released but one or two records before abandoning the enterprise.

Most bachata producers and distributors, it should be noted, worked simultaneously with merengue típico, the traditional accordion-based style of merengue that had been overshadowed on the national stage by the orquestas but had continued as an active tradition in rural areas—especially in the region of its birth, the Cibao. Aracena, for example, recorded and/or promoted the music of well-known típico musicians such as the Trío Reynoso, Tatico Henríquez, Guandulito, and others on Radio Guarachita. Another bachata producer, José Luis (based in Santiago, capital of the Cibao), owed as much of his success to his típico musicians as to his bachata musicians. While merengue típico had always enjoyed more social cachet than bachata and was not actively banned from record stores for reasons of social disreputability as bachata was, it was benignly ignored by urbanites because it was considered too rural. Since bachata and merengue típico shared the same constituency—people of rural origins—the same informal networks used for disseminating bachata served to disseminate típico records as well.

It is important to mention here another producer of this period who began his career working with bachata. Bienvenido Rodríguez began as a traveling salesman of bachatas and merengue típicos, but later he was able to acquire a tiny record store on Avenida Duarte and to finance the production of bachata and merengue típico records. In 1967 he acquired a small label, Montilla, which he renamed Karen after his daughter. An astute businessman, Rodríguez realized that modern merengue had more economic potential than the socially unacceptable bachata and stopped producing bachata, instead signing up-and-coming merengue orquestas and other musicians with mainstream appeal. Based on his success with these groups, in the early 1970s he was able to obtain the lucrative distributorship for the New York-based Fania Records, the hemisphere's most important producer of salsa. (He was the Dominican "traitor" referred to in the passage by Willie Rodríguez cited above.) By the 1980s Karen had become the Dominican Republic's largest and most successful record label, producing a number of the country's top musicians, including Juan Luis Guerra and 4:40's *Bachata rosa* (Tejeda 1993: 129–30).

Bachata producers were, like the musicians they promoted, of humble origins and poorly educated. Most of them had started out as record vendors and, as they accumulated a little capital, had moved into small-scale producing. Because they could not obtain access to Radio Guarachita or any urban mainstream media, they depended on provincial radio stations and on barras and colmados to play the records; and because they could not distribute their records via the larger urban record stores, they relied on a rapidly expanding informal music economy that was growing up alongside the mainstream music business.

The bachata business that emerged in the 1970s evolved in an irregular and casual manner typical of the informal sector, and there was little inclination to replicate the conventions of the official music business in terms of contracts and copyrights. For example, there were no extended contracts between producers and musicians: producers simply bought a song outright. In other cases, when the musicians themselves financed a production, they sold to producers not the rights to songs, but the rights to distribute in a particular format. Thus, for example, one producer could have the rights to a bachatero's single, while another might have the rights to the same song on an LP. (Later, when bachatas began to be released as cassettes, a third producer might have the rights to distribution in that format; and when bachata began to be marketed in the United States to Dominican immigrants, a fourth person might have the rights to distribute there.) Because producers paid very little, musicians were little inclined to remain loyal, and as a result, many musicians recorded for several producers at a time—sometimes even recording more than one version of the same song for different producers. Piracy and plagiarism were common practices and no efforts were made to dissimulate: if one musician had a hit song, another bachatero might unabashedly release his own version. Radhames Aracena was among the worst offenders: his musicians recorded versions of other bachateros' hit songs, which he was able to promote nationally with the tremendous advantage of Radio Guarachita. For example, immediately after Tony Santos' song "Amarilis" became a hit, Guarachita released the same song sung by Solterito del Sur.

The vast majority of bachata recordings were released as 45 RPM singles; only well-established bachateros with a few hits to their credit released LPs. The records themselves reflected the freewheeling nature of the bachata business during this period; some 45 RPM singles, for example, had a song by one musician on one side and a song by a different musician on the flip side. On other records, musicians were sometimes identified by their nicknames or pseudonyms; for example, the singer on one record was identified as "el niño bonito de mamá" ("Mama's pretty boy"), and I later learned it was by Blas Durán. The most unusual record I encountered was a single, one of whose sides was at 45 RPM speed, with the flip side at 33 RPM.

Cassettes were introduced in the 1970s but did not overtake vinyl until the late 1980s, reflecting the low buying power of typical bachata enthusiasts; cassettes and LPs were often beyond their means, because the price of a cassette or LP ran from about nine to twelve pesos, as opposed to three pesos for a single. Cassette technology, however, had more potential for reducing costs than did the long-playing record, which often contained unwanted songs—a feature that encouraged a rather small-scale form of piracy: record store owners and radio disc jockeys often prepared cassette compilations of hit songs and sold them to the public. Pirate compilation tapes were not limited to bachata, however: cassettes of current hits in all genres—orquesta and típico merengue and balada—were also widely available, even in Santo Domingo's major downtown record stores.

All bachata, regardless of format, was sold to the public via the thousands of sidewalk record stalls strategically located in working-class shopping districts and near bus stops in cities and towns throughout the country. Sidewalk record stalls were not permanent structures (they were usually dismantled every night), but nevertheless they were recognized as legitimate, if unofficial, businesses: in Santo Domingo, at least, owners paid the municipality a small monthly fee for permission to use the sidewalk. These were not permanent rights, however, because the stalls could be ordered to move at any moment.

Sidewalk record stalls served as important links between the informal and the formal economy, serving as an efficient transfer of cash from the informal sector back into the formal sector. In addition to bachata, vendors sold mainstream-oriented music produced and distributed by major Dominican and international record companies, particularly the latest merengues and baladas (or pirate versions of these), which they carried in order to offer their customers a variety of music. Their profit margin, however, was lower than with the cheaper bachata records; moreover, purchases of merengue and salsa records from the principal distributors were in cash only. Bachata records, on the other hand, could be purchased from traveling salesmen (usually self-employed entrepreneurs) on credit or consignment or sometimes by exchanging in kind; for example, a vendor could swap records he or she already had in stock for something else carried by a traveling salesman (César Plácido, interview). As a result, the economic survival of those depending on the marginal profits that could be earned through sidewalk record vending rested primarily on selling bachata.

The point of greatest intersection between the bachata economy and the formal economy was at the production stage, because both recording studios and pressing plants utilized expensive imported equipment and supplies (e.g., vinyl, magnetic tape, etc.) owned by those with large amounts of capital, and which required the most cash up front. After these initial stages, bachata remained dependent on extended informal networks composed of musicians, producers, traveling record salesmen, owners of makeshift street stalls, rural disc jockeys, and owners of colmados and barras. Unlike the merengue business, then, which was thoroughly integrated into the formal economy via the country's officially registered and regulated mass media and retail outlets, the informal bachata economy as a whole was far more autonomous. Most of those who made a living from bachata did not pay taxes or keep records, and their businesses were not located in permanent structures. The bachata economy did articulate with but was not controlled by the larger formal economy of which it was a part. In fact, the informal bachata economy empowered those excluded from the formal, hegemonic music system to participate in the business of music.

Bachata in the 1970s

While two of bachata's most promising musicians, Rafael Encarnación and Mélida Rodríguez, both died after releasing only a dozen or so songs, the rest of the guitar musicians who first recorded in the 1960s, such as

Luis Segura, José Manuel Calderón, Bernardo Ortiz, and Oscar Olmo, continued releasing records in the 1970s. They were joined by a growing group of new musicians attracted by the success of their predecessors; these newcomers included Marino Pérez, Aridia Ventura, Bolívar Peralta, Lilo Acosta, Leonardo Paniagua, Blas Durán, as well as many others who never became well known. Almost all these musicians, it should be noted, either started or consolidated their careers with Radhames Aracena.

With the entrance of so many new musicians and producers into the music business in the 1970s, popular guitar music started to change. The sort of "uncultivated" language that Radhames Aracena tried to expunge from the guitar-based music he recorded was appearing more frequently on recordings. Indeed, raw, street-level language was becoming one of the most distinctive features of Dominican popular guitar music, clearly setting it apart from its more refined antecedent genre, the bolero. Moreover, the acute economic suffering and social dislocations experienced by the poorest sectors of Dominican society were reflected—in all their harshness—in bachata, whose song texts exhibited the deepening imprint of shantytown life on the consciousness of bachata musicians and their audience. Darker sentiments and moods—sometimes despairing or violent, sometimes nakedly carnal or debauched—increasingly colored bachata song texts, many of which began exhibiting what Andrés Rivera Payano called "características mejicanadas" (Mexicanized characteristics), because their preoccupation with drinking and womanizing were more akin to Mexican rancheras and corridos than to the quintessentially romantic bolero (Rivera Payano 1983: 42). Unlike the balada singer, who might have made discrete references to sipping a glass of wine, bachata singers in the 1980s celebrated—indeed flaunted—their drinking, and many songs glorified womanizing or expressed contempt for women. Teodoro Reyes' song, "Homenaje a los borrachones," an unabashed paean to drunkards and prostitutes, exemplifies bachata musicians' refusal to accept the values of a social class that exploited and scorned them.

Homenaje a los borrachones
(Homage to drunks)
Singer: Teodoro Reyes

Traigo homenaje a todos los borrachones	I pay homage to all the drunks
Los que beben por tercio, por litro o por galones	Those who drink by pints, by liters, or by gallons
Tonto es él que no bebe	Foolish is he who doesn't drink
Nada más para que diga	Just so he can say
Que es bueno con su mujer	He's good to his woman
De veinte pesos que se ganan en el día	Of twenty pesos they earn in a day
Dejan cinco en la casa y quince para la bebida	They leave five at home and fifteen for drinks

Y las hembras de la barra	And the barmaids
Que a ellas nunca se les olvida	May they never be forgotten
Que vivan todos los hombres borrachones	Long live all the drunken men
Y que vivan las mujeres de la barra	And long live the barmaids
Yo no veo las razones	I don't see the reasons
De que las estén criticando	That some people criticize them
Y diciendo que son malas	And say they are bad
¡Ay 'manito! Que vivan todas las mujeres de la barra	Brother, long live the barmaids
Y todos los hombres borrachones	And all the drunken men

These songs only fueled mainstream society's criticism of bachata as a vulgar music appropriate only for bars and brothels. Bachata's increasingly prominent signs of poverty and low-class status did not pass unnoticed by the rapidly expanding Dominican popular music industry, particularly those disturbed by the fact that among the lower classes bachata was consistently preferred to musics such as salsa, balada, and orquesta merengue that the industry was promoting.

Compared to the formidable salsa, it was relatively easy for orquesta merengue to knock its other rival, bachata, out of the national arena. Readers might think I am extending the analogy of musical competition and confrontation too far, but bachata musicians themselves analyzed their situation in these terms. Bachatero Blas Durán, for example, recalled that early bachata musicians were most consistently excluded from the media precisely when orquesta merengue began to establish its hegemony: "I remember it was when the merengue started to change, and salsa started coming, or what they called *guaguancó* and now is salsa. Ever since the arrival of the merengue with trumpets, saxophone, and piano, they started to marginalize the guitar. . . . There are many interests involved, owners of record labels who wish that the guitar would disappear" (interview).

Another strategy used to eliminate guitar music from the musical marketplace was to stigmatize it with a pejorative name. Until the 1970s romantic guitar music like that made by Luis Segura had been referred to as música popular, música de guitarra, or bolero campesino. As the competition between music producers and promoters for audience share intensified, however, the term *música popular* for the rough-sounding guitar music recorded by musicians of rural origins was considered unacceptable by better-financed promoters of other musics, particularly merengue, who were trying to claim the term *popular* for their music. The word *bolero*, on the other hand, bestowed too much respectability on the unpolished guitar music. Ignoring the assertions by guitar musicians themselves that their songs were boleros or, more generically, popular guitar music, various derogatory terms to refer to the undesirable music gained currency in the media. The term *música de guardia*, which had originated in the Trujillo period (see Chapter 1), was revived, not just for the more *machista* songs, but to refer to—and denigrate—all popular guitar music. Another equally disparaging term, *música cachivache* (lit., knick-knack, i.e., trivial or insignificant), appeared. Blas Durán noted the effect of these terms: "By 1970, or before '70, in '69, '68, they were starting to give a name to guitar music. They first called it cachivache, later música de guardia. [Before that] they played it on all radio stations. Today they won't play it" (interview).

Bachata guitarist Edilio Paredes recalled the first time a radio announcer referred to his own music as cachivache:

> In San Francisco de Macorís they called it low, they made it lower. But I know who started to give it that name, so-called cachivache. [The disc jockey] was playing one of my records on the station, and he was saying, "And now, the next cachivache. . . ." And I said to the DJ, "Give me that record; you can't play that record here. . . . My records are not cachivaches. This is not garbage, it is not rubbish; this is a song that cost me money, that cost me effort to compose. People accept it, but you come to tell me that it is a so-called cachivache. Take that 'garbage' off; give it back to me!" I had a problem with him. (Interview)

But the term that really stuck to guitar music was *bachata*. Musicians may not have disliked the word *bachata* itself, but they clearly understood and resented the intent with which it was used. As Paredes said, "It bugged me quite a bit, because I know what bachata is. I know the word *bachata* and the meaning it has of an informal party; a get-together is a bachata. But here it was given a low meaning, something quite different" (interview).

Leonardo Paniagua similarly felt that the problem was not with the word itself but the way it was used to deliberately deprecate the musicians and their audience: "If it were only to identify it [the music], I would agree with the name, because it has to be called something. If it were to identify it or to distinguish it from the merengue or the balada, let's call it bachata, but without discrimination, without it being inferior to the merengue or inferior to the balada" (interview).

In the 1970s, then, the uncouth music made by upstarts from the countryside was forced into a subordinate position from which it could not threaten the agendas of promoters of other musics: it was marked with the term *bachata*, which was stripped of its original value-neutral connotation as an informal backyard party and transformed into a term of disrespect and denigration by being loaded with a set of undesirable associations including rural backwardness and vulgarity. Ramón Cordero remembered the feelings of humiliation and indignation he felt when people began insulting guitar music and musicians: "There was a time when if you went out with a guitar they screamed 'Los Panchos!' at you, and after Paniagua became very popular they would call out, 'Adios, Paniagua!' You could see it was a form of blackmail [*sic*]. One happened to be a certain way and one felt bad about it. Because everyone who earns a living in whatever way, it's a job, it doesn't matter. No matter what it is, it's a job, and one is earning an honest living. We are workers" (interview).

The elite and middle classes were not the only ones to denigrate the newly denominated bachata. The poor residents of the city's slums and shantytowns who had migrated earlier, who had better access to permanent employment, and who were more fully assimilated into urban life tended to prefer the orquesta merengue, since they identified themselves with the classes above them and with the urbanity and progress associated with modern merengue. The poorer, more recently arrived migrants, on the other hand, who preferred the guitar and accordion music they were more familiar with, made up the bulk of bachata's audience. While the two groups frequently shared the same residential spaces, the way they identified themselves, socially as well as musically, was quite different. For example, in 1987 residents I interviewed in Zurza, an older shantytown located within the city limits, claimed to prefer merengue and balada, while the residents of the newer barrio Guaricano preferred bachata and stated so without embarrassment. Clearly, to those with aspirations of upward social mobility, bachata was considered a sign of rural backwardness, and they refused to associate themselves with it. As Ramón Cordero said, "In the barrios . . . a little complex exists that says, 'I don't want the girl to realize that I like this type of music,' because they think if you are a bachatero it somehow lowers you a few notches" (interview).

Edilio Paredes was more explicit in condemning people who rejected their rural roots and who unquestionably accepted the social stigma attached to the music: "Before, there was a situation in which [guitar] music was heard a lot, but then it was put down and it was only played by guards and people from the country. Campesinos liked that type of music. I think that here (in Santo Domingo) there is no one who is not a campesino. Everybody here is a campesino. But the ones who live [in the countryside], who still don't have this complex, they like their music. Here most people had a complex: 'No, that music is too low, it's guard's music.' And that's how it was" (interview).

The economic effects of bachata's increasing social and economic marginalization were not missed by bachateros themselves, although their responses varied. Some, such as Cuco Valoy and Bienvenido Rodríguez, abandoned guitar music altogether and dedicated themselves to merengue, which was clearly on the ascent. Ramón Cordero, who also played accordion, sought to increase his audience by releasing merengue típico recordings as well as bachatas. Others tried—with limited success—to disassociate themselves from bachata altogether and to identify their music as variations of internationally accepted genres such as bolero and balada. Leonardo Paniagua, who began recording for Guarachita in 1972, was the first to deliberately target that segment of his audience who either aspired to or considered themselves members of a higher social class. In order to project a more refined, international image, he recorded cover versions of boleros and baladas already popularized by famous international composers or musical groups: his first recorded song was by the Brazilian singer Roberto Carlos, and his first major hit, "Chiquitita," was a version of a song popularized by the Swedish pop group ABBA. Paniagua also experimented with various musical idioms and styles—he once recorded a mariachi album in Mexico, and occasionally he added violins and piano to his recordings. As he himself said proudly of his cover versions, "You take the original record and compare it with the second, and they sound the same" (interview). Ultimately, however, nothing Paniagua or any other bachata musician could say or do was able to change the social stigma that had been imposed on their music.

The Struggle in Song Text: Music and Politics in the Balaguer Years

Surrounding the economically motivated competition between musical genres taking place in the late 1960s and 1970s were larger social struggles occurring between different social classes and political ideologies, which were reflected in music, particularly in song texts. The most visible, consistent, and militant vehicle of political protest during this period was the Dominican nueva canción movement, which made a significant impact on the Dominican popular music landscape throughout the decade. Years later, in the 1990s, a number of musicians who began their careers in the nueva canción movement were responsible for introducing bachata into the mainstream; for that reason, it is important to take note of the musical and philosophical soil out of which they emerged.

The term *nueva canción* originally referred specifically to the Chilean folk/protest music that emerged in the late 1960s and flourished in the progressive political climate characterizing the years Salvador Allende served as Chile's first elected Marxist president (1970–73). Chilean nueva canción was inspired locally by singer-songwriter Violeta Parra's pioneering reinterpretations of Chilean folk music, as well as by her Argentine contemporary Atahualpa Yupanqui's similar work with his country's folk music. Cuban musicians such as Sylvio Rodríguez and Pablo Milanés—

whose less folk-rooted music, originally known as *canción protesta* and later as *nueva trova*, expressed the ideals of the Cuban Revolution—also served as models for other politically conscious musicians throughout Latin America who in the 1970s were seeking to employ their own folk traditions as vehicles for commentary on local conditions. Nueva canción had a clear sense of mission and purpose, part of which was to establish new, progressive patterns of music making and consumption that would befit a new society that the songwriters envisioned would follow revolutionary change, making nueva canción more an ideological position than a musical genre:

> The movement as a whole can be characterized as a fusion of traditional folkloric musical forms with sociopolitical ("protest") lyrics. Rather than seeking to create escapist entertainment, this music is intended to express current reality and social problems in a meaningful style. New Song musicians share a commitment to honest expression and absolute opposition to what they term the typical "disposable consumer songs" of most commercial music. (Morris 1984: 1–2)

The Dominican nueva canción movement, like its Latin American counterparts, was emphatically opposed to international commercial musics such as U.S. rock, balada, and salsa, all of which it identified with cultural imperialism and the evils of capitalism. Instead, this movement's goal was to find autochthonous modes of expression that would clearly distinguish it from commercial musics. Largely eschewing electric instruments, they relied heavily on acoustic guitars, although they also made use of European instruments such as flutes that were not part of Dominican folk traditions.

In 1974 an international nueva canción festival was held in Santo Domingo, organized jointly by Rafael "Cholo" Brenes, the leader of the first Dominican nueva canción group called Expresión Joven (Young Expression), and the Central de Trabajadores Dominicanos, the nation's largest and most radical workers' union. This concert, called Siete Días con el Pueblo (Seven Days with the People), stimulated an intensifying struggle concerning the role of music in the country's political, social, and cultural development. In addition to providing a showcase for the Pan-Latin American nueva canción movement, the concert was intended to bring attention to—and to denounce—the repressive Balaguer regime and to aid in politicizing workers. It was the largest nueva canción event of its kind to take place in Latin America and included major performers such as Sylvio Rodríguez and Noel Nicolás of Cuba, Mercedes Sosa and Bernardo Palermo of Argentina, El Topo and Danny Rivera of Puerto Rico, and Víctor Manuel of Spain (Víctor Camilo, interview). The Dominican Republic was represented by the two nueva canción–inspired groups

Expresión Joven and Convite. Convite (which, like the Haitian term *com-bite*, is an African-derived word for communal work) was not a musical ensemble in the usual sense of the word, but rather a loosely structured group of musicians, folklorists, and social scientists with a common de-sire to rediscover and reexamine the country's autochthonous musical traditions, particularly those with clear African roots, which had been most persistently ignored by folklorists and cultural observers since the Trujillo era (Convite 1976). Popular music was represented by Cuco Valoy and Johnny Ventura: the Valoy and son duo, Los Ahijados, played sones with political content, including one that had been forbidden by the gov-ernment; Ventura closed the concert with a merengue that had become well known because its refrain—"¡los indios!"—had been adopted by those opposed to Balaguer to refer to the police. "¡Los indios!" was called out whenever the police arrived at a demonstration (Sonia Silvestre, inter-view). The seven-day concert, held in the city's sports arena, drew over 40,000 people a night; as Luis Dias observed, "Eso no se lo olvida el pueblo dominicano" (the Dominican people will never forget that).

The success of the Siete Días con el Pueblo concert encouraged other young Dominican nueva canción musicians to expand popular music's capacity to effect social change. In 1974 a middle-class entrepreneur named Freddy Ginebra established a small avant-garde theater called Casa de Teatro, and a year later singer-songwriters Sonia Silvestre and Víctor Víctor (members of a nueva canción group called Nueva Forma) established a cafe-theater called La Junta. Both venues were conceived specifically to provide a stage for art that was "al servicio del pueblo: en favor de las mayorías, en aliento a los irredimidos" (in the service of the people, in favor of the majority, in support of the unredeemed) (Tejeda 1993: 67–69). These venues were by no means commercially successful (La Junta closed not long after opening) nor did they attract mainstream audiences, but they undeniably became key sites for artistic and political expression by a young, radical generation of musicians and intellectuals, a number of whom, years later, used the weight of their influence to break down the prejudices against bachata.

In spite of its populist inclinations, nueva canción needs to be distin-guished from other popular musics whose practitioners also wrote lyrics that were politically motivated, though less confrontational and less fre-quent. Dominican nueva canción was certainly not elite music; yet neither was it "popular" in the sense of having a broad base among the primarily poor and uneducated majority. Most of its principal proponents were fully urbanized and well-educated intellectuals who, because of their class and educational backgrounds, were able to obtain access—however limited—for their music in the media, either through personal connec-tions or through political organizations; for example, Víctor Víctor and

Luis Tomás Oviedo had a weekly television show entitled "Nosotros a las ocho" (We at eight), on which their nueva canción colleagues appeared as musical guests. Moreover, even though nueva canción music was supposed to be enjoyed by its audience, its primary purpose—unlike that of other forms of popular music—was not to entertain but to teach or to inspire political action. Most nueva canción compositions were political, although songs about love and other aspects of daily life were included in repertoires if they advanced nueva canción's progressive mission; songs celebrating carousing and womanizing were decidedly inappropriate. Practitioners of more grass-roots-oriented popular music, on the other hand—whether merengue, son, salsa, or bachata—tended to be far more interested in exploring the experience (or absence) of pleasure, and they cared little whether their songs might be considered vulgar, demeaning, or insulting.

There was a strong tradition of social commentary in Dominican popular music, although it had been co-opted and distorted for over thirty years by Trujillo (see Chapter 2). Although immediately after his death popular music's ability to freely address a wide range of topics was restored, the legacy of thirty years of fear and repression resulted in a preference for using humor and double entendres, rather than explicit statements of opposition, to express social criticism. To give one example, the lyrics of Cuco Valoy's merengue song "No me empuje" (Don't push me) employed richly nuanced vocabulary in telling its story, which, complemented by the visual imagery of the cover for the LP recording of the same name, created a humorous but incisive commentary on Dominican racism and police brutality during the 1965 civil war. Valoy's song was based on a supposedly true story of a black Dominican (who had once lived in the United States) ordered by some soldiers to put out a street fire during a street disturbance. The man tried pretending he was a black American, speaking to the soldiers in English, but they refused to believe him and unceremoniously hauled him off to jail for resisting their orders. As Valoy's song told the story, however, the black man was a U.S. Peace Corps worker who was mistaken for a Dominican and abused by the military in spite of his protests. The record cover showed a very black Cuco Valoy being grabbed by a white *guardia*, while the band members— pictured as bystanders—guffaw at the man's attempts to extricate himself by claiming he is a gringo.

While Valoy's humorous account of police brutality and racism was typical of the kind of social commentary expressed in popular genres such as merengue, bachata, and son, most bachatas produced in the Balaguer era concentrated more on emotional problems than on political ones. Nevertheless, in the shantytowns and in rural areas, musicians were not untouched by the social turmoil and political radicalism characterizing the Balaguer years, and a small number of bachatas addressing political, economic, and social concerns did appear. Those that did, however, were produced without any of the social or economic support enjoyed by nueva canción musicians and were, as a result, less mediated expressions of popular protest than were nueva canción compositions.

It is important to note that whereas most romantic bachatas were based on the bolero, most of the political bachatas produced during the 1970s were performed in other genres such as merengue—either accordion or guitar based—son, or guaracha. The reasons for this are clear: the traditionally more topical merengue, son, and guaracha lent themselves more easily to themes of social commentary than the romantic bolero. Nevertheless, these songs were unequivocally bachatas because they were played with acoustic instruments, they were made by and for poor people of rural origins, they used vernacular language and imagery, and they were circulated within the informal economy—i.e., via street stalls and colmados rather than established record stores and the mainstream media.

Textually, some of the political bachatas produced in the Balaguer period exhibited a similar consciousness of class struggle as that found in nueva canción; for example, in terms of its political analysis, the following bachata song could have been part of a nueva canción repertoire.

Hay que seguir protestando
(We must keep protesting)
Singer: Ramón Torres

El que sea dominicano	He who is Dominican
Y de noble corazón	And is of noble heart
Al ver lo que aquí sucede	Upon seeing what's happening
Debe sentir gran dolor	Should feel great pain
Las aguas del mar Caribe	The waters of the Caribbean
Poblada de tiburón	Teeming with sharks
Se quedan con nuestra gente	Take our people
Que con desesperación	Who in desperation
Tratan de ir a otra tierra	Try to go to other lands
Huyendo a la situación	Fleeing the situation
Unos van a Puerto Rico	Some go to Puerto Rico
Otros van a Venezuela	Others go to Venezuela
Unos mueren en el mar	Some die at sea
Y otros mueren en la selva	Others die in the jungle
Cómo existe la miseria	How much misery exists
En tierra dominicana	On Dominican soil
Hay quien se está haciendo rico	There are some getting rich
Traficando vida humana	Trafficking in human life
Es que aquí a la clase baja	It's that here the low class
Esperanza no nos queda	We have no hope left
El obrero masacrado	The worker massacred

Y el campesino sin tierra	And the peasant without land
¿Quiénes serán los culpables?	Who's to blame?
Todos se lavan las manos	Everyone washes their hands
Pero seguimos perdiendo	But we keep losing
Más y más dominicanos	More and more Dominicans
No sé dónde llegaremos	I don't know where we'll end up
Si esto sigue como va	If this keeps up like this
El rico echando p'alante	The rich keep going forward
Y el pobre echando p'atrás	And the poor pushed backwards
Hay cantantes que le cantan	There are singers who sing
Al amor y la belleza	To love and beauty
Y se olvidan de su pueblo	And they forget their people
Que está hundido en la pobreza	Who are sunken in poverty
Pero yo le digo al pueblo	But I say to the people
Que luche y no se detenga	To struggle and not to stop
Que hay que seguir protestando	We have to keep on protesting
Aunque nos corten la lengua	Though they cut out our tongues
Esa gente que ha servido	Those people who have served
De alimento a tiburones	As food for sharks
Yo les tengo un homenaje	I have a tribute to them
Por muchísimas razones	For many reasons
Son los héroes de nuestra patria	They are national heroes
Pues conmueven corazones	Because they move our hearts

Other bachata texts, however, were constructed with the unequivocal language and imagery of the very poor. One extraordinary example is Los Macopejes' "El concón." *Concón* is the partially burned rice that is always left at the bottom of the *paila*, the pot used to cook rice. While many people do like the crunchy concón, the image refers to the fact that concón is formed because it is closest to the heat of the fire and remains in the pot after the soft rice has been spooned out onto people's plates. As such, it became a metaphor for the poor, the segment of society closest to the fire of unremitting hard work and economic hardship, which never developed as well as those on top.

El concón
Singers: Los Macopejes

Por una paila de concón	For a pot of concón
Que yo me la voy a comer	That I'm going to eat
Por una paila de concón	For a pot of concón
Que me brinden a mí	That's offered to me
Estoy dispuesto hasta a morir	I'm ready to die for it
Y para defenderlo	I'll fight anyone to the death
Me mato con cualquiera	In order to defend it
Ese craquiticraquiti	That crunch-crunch
A mí me hace feliz	Makes me happy
Por eso a mí no me importa	That's why I don't care
Morir de una hartura	If I die from overeating

Por eso no me importa
Morir cantando así
Quiero verte junto a un fogón de piedra
Caloroza con la paila y cucharón
Para luego yo correr con mi higuera
Y decirte negra tráeme mi concón
Tú me lo vas a echar todo muchachita
Estoy seguro cuando tú y yo nos casemos
No soy como alguna gente
Que privando en su cabina
Dicen que ellos tienen ese conconcito a
  menos

That's why I don't care
If I die singing like this
I want to see you next to a stone hearth
Warm, and with the pot and ladle
And later I will run with my gourd
And say negra, bring me my concón
You're going to give it all to me little girl
I'm sure that when you and I are married
I'm not like other people
Who, wasting away in their hut
Say that they scorn
That little concón

Hablado: Señores y señoras, vamos a hacer
un comentario relacionado con el concón.
Ese noble y sufrido concón, que en vez de
quedarse arriba y granearse como los
demás compañeros, se queda abajo, se
queda abajo cogiendo candela. Más
respeto con el concón, menos hambre, más
entretenimiento, justicia, Señor Concón,
digo Señor Presidente.

Spoken: Ladies and gentlemen, we are
going to make a commentary about
concón. That noble and suffering
concón, instead of staying above and
filling out like its other companions,
stays below, stays below taking the heat.
More respect for the concón, less
hunger, more entertainment, justice, Mr.
Concón, I mean Mr. President.

Dame mi concón, dame mi concón
Por candela he de valuarte
Y digno de admiración
Porque el hecho que se fabrica
Ese famoso concón
Tú me lo vas a echar todo
Y cuando ya nos casemos
Porque yo sí no le tengo
Ese conconcito a menos
Cuando tú me sirves el lonche
A la hora de las doce
No me des el concón ahora
Guárdamelo pa' la noche
Y con esto me despido
Y le diré la verdad
Concón en plato de higuera
Representa la amistad
Quiero a los prietos, pero el concón
¡Cosa tan seria!

Give me my concón, give me my concón
Because of this heat I value you
Worthy of admiration
Because of the way its made
That famous concón
You are going to give it all to me
When we are married
Because at least I don't despise
That little concón
When you serve me lunch
At the noon hour
Don't give me the concón now
Give it to me at night
And with this I'll say good-bye
And I'll tell you the truth
Concón on a gourd plate
Represents friendship
I love prietos (dark people), but concón
That's something serious!

In this text the Macopejes seem to have deliberately concealed the political commentary with unconnected nonpolitical references such as the singer asking his woman, negra, to give him his concón at night instead of at noon, or calling for more entertainment. Presenting the song with humor and double entendres was most likely Los Macopejes' effort to protect themselves from the consequences of publicly invoking class solidarity and openly criticizing the government's treatment of the poor.

Unlike protest singers belonging to the middle classes, bachateros could expect little protection from the wrath of the authorities—and it must be remembered that policemen might very likely have heard these songs.

While the textual content of these bachatas was clearly political, they differed from nueva canción composition in both their musical style and production values. With the exception of Convite, Dominican nueva canción as a whole looked abroad for its musical references, establishing solidarity with the political song movement in other Latin American countries by imitating their musical styles and using instruments, such as *zampoñas* and *quenas* (Andean wind instruments), which were not indigenous to the country. For example, the following song by Expresión Joven imitated the music of Argentina and Chile rather than Dominican styles.

Abra las rejas, Señor Gobierno
(Open the bars, Mister Government)
Singers: Expresión Joven

Pasos perdidos recorriendo el pasillo	Lost footsteps roaming the hallway
Que conduce a la soledad de una celda	That leads to the solitude of a cell
Rejas que se abren, se cierran	Iron bars that open, close
Y con ellas, hombres sepultados en vida	And with them, men entombed in life
Todavía se pretende encarcelar las ideas	They still seek to incarcerate ideas
Señor Gobierno, a las ideas	Ideas, Mister Government,
Nunca pretenda meterlas presas	Never try to imprison them
En esos muros, tras esas rejas	In those walls, behind those bars
Ya no están ellas	They are no longer here
Y es que no es cierto, Señor Gobierno,	It's not true, Mister Government,
Que alguna idea pueda estar presa	That an idea can be imprisoned

As this song indicates, the imagery in nueva canción texts was sophisticated and the language was grammatically correct and free of regionalisms, while the musical arrangements were complex, all of which gave nueva canción music a middle-class—if not elite—veneer that bachata and other grass-roots musics did not have. Political bachatas, on the other hand, reflected only the styles within the composers' traditional repertoire. Furthermore, Dominican political bachatas were intended to be fully integrated into the musicians' larger, entertainment-oriented repertoire: no attempt was made to set them apart in any way from nonpolitical bachatas. A bachata-son with political commentary by Los Neutrales, for example, sounded exactly like their bachata-sones without political content. The similarity in sound between political and nonpolitical bachatas was reinforced by the fact that all bachatas, whether political or romantic, were recorded with the same rudimentary production values. Nueva canción music, on the other hand, was recorded by well-educated, formally trained, and technologically knowledgeable musicians who were able to ensure that their recordings had a clean and sophisticated sound.

Despite the fact that bachata's performers and listeners were the poorest and most dispossessed citizens of the country—the very population being championed by the nueva canción movement—bachata received little attention from Dominican nueva canción groups. There were several reasons for this omission. For one, bachata was a relatively new form of popular expression that still closely resembled its antecedent genres such as the bolero or guaracha, which were not considered part of the Dominican Republic's folk tradition. Second, bachata's increasing preoccupation with drinking and its machista attitudes towards women were precisely the sort of socio-cultural patterns nueva canción was trying to combat. Finally, for those nueva canción musicians who were trying to revalidate the country's long-rejected African musical heritage, the guitar-based bachata whose percussive elements were subordinate to its melodic ones may have been too closely associated with Hispanic musical traditions to merit their attention. Whatever the reasons, bachata was not perceived as having the same kind of cultural authenticity and legitimacy that other traditional folk genres had, and as a result, no attempts were made to support bachata musicians in their efforts to gain equitable access to the Dominican music system—which, given nueva canción musicians' access to the media, should have been possible.

The Cultural Struggle: Race, Class, Region, and Tradition

In addition to the economic competition among domestic and international musics and the political struggles by different sectors of society to achieve political participation, a public discourse emerged concerning the shape and content of the country's national identity. The dialogue addressed not only the country's historical past but, more importantly, the configuration of the national persona that the country was in the process of reconstructing in the aftermath of the Trujillo dictatorship. Some Dominicans, especially the middle classes and the young, wanted the country to look beyond its borders, away from its painful past, and to fully embrace the outside world and its modernity in order to become a full-fledged, active member of the international community. These groups considered that while rural traditions should be respectfully acknowledged, the countryside was backward, and rural people needed to be integrated into modern Dominican life in order for the country to progress. Others, particularly those of rural origins and those who were older, preferred to look inward, considering the country's traditional roots a source of inspiration and strength; often, however, their ideas included idealized views of a rural past uncontaminated by conflict or modern intrusions. Yet others, especially those who had been politically radicalized by the tumultuous events of the immediate post-Trujillo period, wanted to reexamine the country's past and create a progressive new identity that would selectively draw upon some traditions while rejecting any traditions associated with the hierarchical and repressive structures of the past.

Of the Dominican musicians active in the 1970s, the nueva canción-inspired group Convite made the most profound contribution to the debate on the relationship between the country's music and its national identity. Convite acknowledged the existence of two distinct categories of culture: folklore and popular culture. Popular culture, like folklore, was considered to be associated with *el pueblo* (the people)—although this was sometimes problematic, because popular culture was often closely associated with the economic mechanisms of the capitalist system. As a result, they formulated a distinction between "authentic" and "degenerate" popular culture. A member of Convite, sociologist Dagoberto Tejeda, positioned Convite in opposition to "degenerate" popular culture, asserting that "not everything that the people produce belongs to popular culture. . . . An explicit official cultural policy of castration and penetration so conditioned the artistic field . . . that popular song was converted into a deforming and deformed commercial expression, which was not challenged until the birth in the country of an incipient nueva canción movement and the efforts of popular democratic organization and the action of progressive intellectuals" (Tejeda 1978, translation mine).

While they rejected commercial music, Convite recognized that some orquesta merengue musicians were genuine folk heroes. It established working relationships with popular merengueros such as Johnny Ventura and Wilfrido Vargas, who had identified with the opposition to Balaguer.

Convite's methodology was based on a combination of ethnographic fieldwork and participant observation: "It started by living with the people and, in an investigative task sustained by the scientific method, reclaimed rhythms, instruments, melodies, techniques, symbols, images, language, logic, etc., in order to use them as expression" (Tejeda 1978, translation mine). This statement indicates that while Convite was indeed interested in exploring the roots of Dominican folklore, it did not consider its mission simply to "rescue" folklore and to reproduce or preserve it faithfully; rather, the idea was to use their findings to produce a new kind of music, in accordance with the nueva canción philosophy. One of Convite's most polemical positions was their insistence on recognizing and emphasizing—for the first time in decades—the country's long unacknowledged African heritage. In doing so, they challenged the beliefs of the country's ruling elites who for decades had insisted that the country's culture was of Hispanic origins, with perhaps some Amerindian influence—but definitely *not* African.

Convite carried out important ethnomusicological fieldwork throughout the 1970s. Although most members of Convite resided in Santo Domingo, they took field trips into the countryside to collect instruments and to record traditional music. Back in the city, they arranged and performed music based on their findings, but their music was shaped by the group's stated intention to provide a more progressive vision of Dominican folk culture. Because many of Convite's members were urban intellectuals or musicians with prior connections to the music business, Convite enjoyed limited access to the media in publicizing their activities: at the height of their influence they made weekly television appearances, presented monthly lectures and performances at Casa de Teatro, and made several recordings. Convite's militant stance toward the Balaguer government was not received well by the authorities. On at least one occasion the members of Convite were arrested for singing a *salve* (a traditional music associated with popular Catholicism) with lyrics about Mamá Tingó, a peasant woman killed defending her land from expropriation (Dagoberto Tejeda, interview).

Together, Convite and other members of the Dominican nueva canción movement, supported by a radicalized generation of folklorists, sociologists, anthropologists, and ethnomusicologists, ignited public dialogues on the content and representation of the country's national identity. The most important question they raised, Where did merengue come from? symbolically asked the deeper and thornier question, Where did we Dominicans come from? The ensuing debate served as a convenient excuse for a necessary national dialogue about the country's African heritage and its legacy of racism, and it provided cultural observers of all socio-political persuasions with the opportunity to acknowledge—or to reject—the country's African heritage. Inevitably, accepting the reality of their African past required Dominicans to revise their view of their own history and to radically reconfigure the Iberocentric national persona they had constructed for themselves and had presented to the international community. This was a task few Dominicans wanted to undertake.

The subject of race in the Dominican Republic is extremely complex and has been the subject of a number of books (e.g., Tolentino Dipp 1992) and articles (e.g., Ferrán 1985); nevertheless I will make a few general observations in order to put this discussion in context. Keeping in mind that the Dominican standard of whiteness is more inclusive than in the United States—where anyone with even a hint of black ancestry is excluded from the "white" category—statistics show that 73 percent of the Dominican population is mulatto, 11 percent are black, and only 16 percent are categorized as white (Black 1986: 55). In spite of the number of people of African descent, the country has a long history of either actively rejecting or passively ignoring its unequivocally obvious African heritage. This attitude has often been linked to the historical consequences of a twenty-two-year occupation by Haiti that made the Dominican Republic the only country in Latin America to be subjugated by blacks. The Haitian occupiers implemented a number of policies that directly benefited the Dominican population; for example, they abolished slavery and distributed land to peasants. Nevertheless, the Santo Domingo elite chafed at being ruled by people of color whose culture and language, moreover, were different from their own.

As a result, the country's Independence Day, February 27, does not commemorate independence from the centuries-long Spanish colonial rule, but rather from the twenty-two-year occupation by Haiti. In the aftermath of the Haitian occupation, Dominicans conflated their hatred for Haitians with a generalized rejection of blackness and anything associated with African culture. Trujillo exacerbated these attitudes during his long regime by enacting policies—such as the prohibition of folk traditions with clear African or Haitian antecedents and his ultimate racist policy, the 1937 order to massacre all Haitians residing in the country—that made it impossible, even had there been an inclination to do so, for scholars or anyone else to affirm in positive ways the country's legacies from African culture (Davis 1987). In the post-Trujillo period, Dominican racism persisted unabated and indeed may have worsened as an influx of Haitian cane cutters was perceived as threatening to "darken" (i.e., corrupt) the country's presumably superior white blood. Joaquín Balaguer, himself a firm believer in these negative views of Haitians and their African-derived culture, published in 1983 a ferociously racist book about Haiti, *La isla al revés: Haiti y el destino dominicano* (The island upside down: Haiti and Dominican destiny).

In the Dominican Republic, no black consciousness or *negritud* movements stressing racial uplift and pride developed as they did in other Caribbean countries such as Haiti, Cuba, Puerto Rico, Trinidad, or Jamaica; such a movement might have contested these derogatory attitudes toward the country's African heritage, toward Haiti, and toward blackness in general. To see how generalized and insidious these prejudices are, one need only observe the absence of positive representations of Afro-Caribbeans, Africans, and African Americans in official public spaces. With the exception of one statue of the maroon leader Lemba outside Santo Domingo's anthropological museum, the Museo del Hombre, there are no monuments to outstanding individuals associated with black liberation or pride, whether from the Americas or from Africa itself. Moreover, while many of Santo Domingo's major streets and avenues are named either after Dominican patriots and statesmen (such as Duarte and

Mella) or after white international statesmen (such Abraham Lincoln, Winston Churchill, John F. Kennedy, and George Washington), not one street name commemorates a black leader.

On the contrary, the profoundly racist elite and middle classes clung to the carefully cultivated and long-cherished notion that the country's population and culture was Spanish and Indian—in spite of the incontestable fact that the island's indigenous population was virtually exterminated shortly after the Spanish invasion. Displaying an extraordinary capacity to ignore the historical reality of their African heritage, citizens of unequivocal African descent are referred to (and refer to themselves) as *indios* (Indians) rather than as *negros*, the latter term being reserved only for Haitians. This cultural myth has been perpetuated in a variety of ways: for example, the *cédula* (national identification card) uses the term *indio*, or sometimes more specifically *indio claro* (light Indian) or *indio oscuro* (dark Indian) for people of color; the same holds true in newspaper accounts, which routinely describe dark people as indio or as *de color indio*. Dominican sociologist Franco Ferrán employed the terms *negrofobia* (i.e., phobia of blackness) and *blancofilia* (i.e., love of whiteness) to describe this deep antipathy to anything considered tainted by blackness and its corollary, the clear preference for whiteness (Ferrán 1985).

Given this history of anti-black sentiment, the assertions by Convite and other progressive intellectuals that Dominican culture and music had strong African roots were rejected outright by many Dominicans, who cloaked their deeply ingrained racist attitudes in the guise of nationalism, defending the fatherland from the threat of Haitian incursions, as in Balaguer's book *La isla al revés*. To these Dominicans, the claim that merengue had African origins was tantamount to treason. In 1976, folklorist Fradique Lizardo (far from a radical figure even by today's more conservative standards) was severely criticized by musician Luis Senior for making assertions in this regard: "I was horrified to read the declaration of this man in the magazine ¡*Ahora!* in which he said that our merengue comes from Africa. This outlandish statement is unpatriotic" (Ysalguez 1976a, translation mine). The following response to Fradique Lizardo's assertions illustrates the tone of the debate:

> There is one detail that should not be ignored, because Africa in this case is synonymous with Haiti: it is not true that after the Dominicans proclaimed independence in 1844, the patriotism of the brave *criollo* was going to permit them, only eleven years after achieving the liberation of the territory and proclaiming the Dominican Republic, to attend parties with dance musics of African origins. Africa, camouflaged as French and with the indigenous name of Haiti, had dominated the Spanish part of the island for twenty-two years, but with the ideal of Duarte and the courage and decision of Mella [Dominican heroes of the war to expel Haitians from the territory] and their

companion . . . [they] achieved independence, overthrowing the oppressive yoke and creating the Dominican Republic on February 27,
1844. It is not true that at the time (1855) when French Africans were
fighting against the Spanish, and later Haitians against Dominicans
that Dominicans would dance a dance that according to Fradique had
origins in Africa. (Ysalguez 1976b, translation mine)

These adamant and vitriolic refusals to even acknowledge African influences on Dominican music contrast sharply with the views of neighbor-
ing Haiti, where any music that incorporated traditional (i.e., African)
elements was valued by being considered more "authentic" than music
that did not (Averill 1989: 207).

In fact, the controversy over African influences in merengue had a
long history, although in the past it was not articulated explicitly in racial
terms. Mid-nineteenth-century urban newspaper editorials, masking the
negative Eurocentric attitudes of the urban elite toward the strong African influences that characterized rural Dominican culture, demonstrated
horror at the appearance of the rural merengue in the salons of polite
society. In the latter part of the century, when the accordion replaced the
guitar as lead instrument in merengue ensembles, the complaints concerning the inability of the accordion to achieve the full range of chords
and tones available to the guitar may similarly be seen as expressions
of concern that merengue's melodic (i.e., Hispanic) elements would be
subordinated to the accordion's more percussive (i.e., African) style.

The debates on how merengue was linked to the configuration of
the nation's cultural identity culminated in two conferences held in Santo
Domingo in the latter years of the Balaguer regime. The first, organized
by Convite in 1976, was a "recital forum" entitled Origin and Evolution of
the Merengue; its intent was to "deepen and explain fundamental aspects
concerning merengue that are not yet coherent in the explanations on the
origins and evolution of merengue . . . because of the profound denatural-
izations that in this respect are being created in the name of 'progress'
and 'commercialization' " (Convite 1976, translation mine). The conference was designed to expose the then current tendencies of commercial
merengue, which Convite feared was absorbing too many outside influences, particularly from salsa. In this conference merengue's African roots
were mentioned but not particularly emphasized; the threat to merengue
and to the national character it symbolized was perceived to come from
abroad.

Two years later, however, race had become a major issue in the process of defining the national identity. The 1978 conference was entitled
Encuentro con el Merengue (Encounter with the Merengue), and included
presentations by folklorist Fradique Lizardo, musician Johnny Ventura,
and sociologists Manuel Rueda and Dagoberto Tejeda of Convite. In his

presentation, Dagoberto Tejeda insisted on the importance of acknowledging merengue's African roots and asserted that Convite's investigations were contributing to the "rescue and diffusion of the Dominican musical patrimony" by exposing this deliberately neglected reality. This militant position was clearly an attempt to force those concerned with national/cultural identity to look inward and backward, and to squarely face the issues of race and racism in the country.

In the debates concerning the content of the nation's cultural identity, issues of African influences were related but by no means identical to larger issues of authenticity, that is, what was to be considered "traditional" and hence part of the country's official conception of its past. In the Balaguer years, the Dominican Republic's clear desire to assume the trappings of progress and modernity conflicted with a deep concern for preserving the authenticity of its national cultural identity. As a result, many viewed any innovations as threatening to the integrity of the national character. Folklorist Fradique Lizardo, for example, took the position that any attempt to modify or recodify traditional elements negated their authenticity, and at the 1978 conference he viciously attacked his fellow speaker Tejeda and Convite for their reinterpretations of rural music because, he claimed, they caused "caos y desconcierto" (chaos and confusion) by deforming "authentic" musical traditions. Lizardo—who himself had been attacked for acknowledging merengue's African roots— was prepared to accept African influences on traditional Dominican culture but believed that contemporary innovations based on traditional culture, regardless of their sources or motivations, threatened the integrity of the original traditions.

I would suggest that such cultural conservatism may have been a product of the country's rather turbulent, irregular, and sometimes humiliating path toward nationhood: it was a Spanish colony until 1795, under French control until 1808, and returned to Spanish colonial status until 1821. It received its independence from Spain in 1821, but without having fought in the independence struggle. Shortly thereafter, it was occupied by Haiti, from 1822 to 1844. Later, the country had the ignominious distinction of being the only country in Latin America to request annexation both to Spain (in 1861) and to the United States (unsuccessfully, in 1865). While independent until the present, it has been occupied twice by the United States (1916–24 and 1965). Given this rather unorthodox process of nation building, it is not altogether surprising that continuity became a very important quality in Dominicans' construction of their national self-image—whereas in other countries whose sense of nationhood was less vulnerable, the boundaries of the national cultural identity have been more flexible.

Dominicans' preference for continuity can be observed, for example, in the persistence of the term *merengue* itself: the music referred to by that name has been around for over 150 years and has undergone repeated and profound transformations in sound, instrumentation, and social context. At most, the term *merengue* has been modified by the word *típico* to distinguish the accordion-based ensembles from the big band orquestas; but essentially, the name has remained the same. Cubans, on the other hand, whose sense of cultural identity is perhaps more secure, routinely give each new variation in rhythm that catches on a new name—witness the enormous variety of names for closely related musics and rhythms—without feeling that the integrity of their musical traditions are compromised by the innovations. Similarly, in Haiti, even minor musical variations were given different names (e.g., *konpa-dirèk* and *kadans rampa* were almost identical rhythmically but had different names for marketing purposes [Averill 1993: 71]). Given this deeply ingrained conservatism, Convite's efforts to put forward a more flexible concept of cultural authenticity did not sit well with Lizardo and other Dominicans like him, whose notions of authenticity remained firmly tied to an ideal of proximity to an unchanging rural past uncontaminated by the messiness of contemporary life.

As the 1970s came to a close, traditional merengue had become an icon of the country's agrarian past, while modern merengue, even while under attack for incorporating foreign elements, represented its modernity and progress. Bachata, on the other hand, continued to be perceived simply as a poorly rendered interpretive style of non-Dominican genres such as bolero, son, guaracha, and ranchera that did not possess any primary attributes associated with traditional Dominican culture. As a result, no one bothered to make the same sort of claims for its authenticity and cultural legitimacy that were being made for merengue and other musics such as salve, thereby excluding bachata from any platforms in which folk and/or national culture were discussed or promoted. This resistance to accepting bachata's cultural validity contrasted markedly with attitudes in Puerto Rico, where rural farmers known as *jíbaros* were considered quintessential symbols of the Puerto Rican national character, and the guitar music associated with them, *música jíbara*—whether recorded or live, whether played in the traditional manner or modernized with electronic instruments—was accepted with pride. Similarly, in the United States the importance of rap music within the historical continuum of African American music traditions has never been contested in spite of radical departures from its antecedent musical forms.

In fact, these highly conservative concepts of tradition and authenticity were shared by bachata's rural audiences themselves: in conversations I had with rural people in which I specifically asked them whether they considered bachata to be a part of their folklore, the answer was always no. Thus, in spite of bachata's deep roots in traditional rural musical practices, it was not perceived as representing continuity from older traditions, because its diffusion via commercial recordings, the urban contexts in which these recordings were produced, and the urban concerns articulated in bachata lyrics were perceived as deviating too far from traditional patterns of music making. As a result, bachata was also excluded from rural traditional rituals or sacred celebrations at which other recreational musics (e.g., merengue or any of its variants or other genres such as *mangulina* or *carabiné*) were played and danced between or following the ritual moments. Informal bachata ensembles might have congregated, I was told, outside the premises of a traditional ritual/celebration, but they were never invited inside.

Furthermore, issues of race never entered discussions about bachata, in spite of the fact that the people who made and listened to bachata were not only the poorest Dominicans, but generally the darkest ones as well: public discourse about bachata, its musicians, or its audience revolved around indicators of class, not race. For example, the music was called crude, the musicians uneducated, its fans country bumpkins, but possible African musical influences were simply not an issue. Most likely this was because bachata's origins in romantic guitar music traditions seemed to point so clearly to Spanish rather than African antecedents, and because of the subordination of its percussion to melody and lyrics: the bongos and maracas or güiro marking the basic four-four time never displayed the sort of rhythmic complexity and virtuosity most people associated with African music. It was not until the 1990s—after bachata was accepted as an authentic voice of the Dominican masses—that bachata was recognized as displaying African influences in its rhythmic groove and vocal style.

The African descent of bachata practitioners and audience, however, could be clearly discerned in the racially specific language of their song texts. In bachata lyrics singers frequently referred to color—their own or that of their mates—reflecting their keen awareness of racial categories. For example, the commonly used terms *negro/a, prieto/a, moreno/a*—all terms for black or dark men or women—clearly situated the singers, their mates, and, by extension, their audience within an Afro-Dominican social context (see song texts by Luis Emilio Félix and Sijo Osoria in Chapter 6). In the following bachata, Bolívar Peralta mentions four racial categories (in their feminine forms): *blanca/rubia* (white/blond), *india* (Indian, person of color), *morena* (brown, dark), and *negra* (black)—although the words most clearly denoting blackness, *negra* and *morena*, are used interchangeably. These verses explicitly articulate the idea that dark women are preferable to indias and blondes because they better understand their men—who, by implication, are also dark.

Espero por mi morena
(I'm waiting for my dark woman)
Singer: Bolívar Peralta

Yo fui dueño de una rubia	I once owned (had) a blond
Que la quise por demás	That I loved too much
Y también tuve una india	And I also had a dark woman
Era linda de verdad	She was really beautiful
Las blancas huelen a rosas	White women smell of roses
Las indias saben a miel	Dark women taste like honey
Pero esas benditas negras	But those blessed black women
Son buenísimas² también	Are really good too
Espero por mi morena	I'm waiting for my morena
Que me sabe comprender	She knows how to understand me

It is important to note that even among the light-skinned middle classes, terms such as *morena* and *negra* are sometimes used as terms of endearment in casual situations. Nevertheless, references to skin color were seldom if ever found in the lyrics of other romantic musics that projected a more refined image, such as bolero or balada, neither of which were likely to mention the dark color of the singer or his/her beloved. Bachata lyrics, like Peralta's above, occasionally referred to whiteness or to Caucasian features; but most commonly, the casual use of the terms for blackness implicitly expressed bachateros' acceptance and affirmation of their color, thereby challenging the Dominicans' preference for avoiding the unpleasantness of racial self-awareness. This, of course, only served to make bachata more unpalatable to those who were—or aspired to be considered—white and middle class.

The End of an Era: The Defeat of Balaguer

In spite of the steady domestic opposition to his repressive regime and to its conservative cultural values, Joaquín Balaguer managed to manipulate the electoral system and to remain in power for twelve years. By the mid-1970s, however, the middle socio-economic sectors, hurt by the energy crisis, began to join the ranks of those desiring a change of government. At the same time, international opinion of Balaguer's government became more negative, and U.S. President Jimmy Carter began to emphasize human rights over anticommunism as a criteria for U.S. support. The Partido Revolucionario Dominicano (PRD), still the strongest opposition party, nominated a wealthy rancher, Antonio Guzmán (instead of the party's charismatic leader Francisco Peña Gómez, handicapped by being quite black), to challenge Balaguer in the 1978 elections.

As the elections approached, it appeared as if Joaquín Balaguer might indeed be defeated—if they were allowed to proceed without fraud. The entire country was galvanized by the possibility of ousting the hated Balaguer, and bachateros, still under the influence of the political militancy that characterized the 1970s, joined the fray. Blas Durán's bachata-merengue "Ojo pela'o" (played not with an accordion or guitar, but with a piano) commented on the situation through the narrative device of urging a baseball umpire or *ampalla* (Guzmán) to keep an eye out for dirty players (Balaguer). In this song, Durán expressed his low opinion of Balaguer's character via metaphor rather than direct commentary, and he used highly vernacular language (e.g., the popular proverb "Póngase más chivo que un chivo" [loose translation, Be foxier than the fox]) and imagery (e.g., the baseball game) to communicate with his audience.

Ojo pela'o
(Keep an eye peeled)
Singer: Blas Durán

A mi ampallita querido	My dear ampalla
Vuelvo de nuevo a cantarle	I'm going to sing to you again
Para que abra bien los ojos	So keep your eyes open
Y no confíe en nadie	And don't trust anyone
Ojo pela'o, compay ampalla	Keep an eye peeled, ampalla
Tenga cuida'o que aquí hay gente mala	Be careful, there are bad people here
Hablado: Tenga cuida'o mi ampalla, que el otro día vi a algunos pichers que tenían reunión en la cumbre con el pelotero aquel. ¡Póngase más chivo que un chivo! hmmmm . . . ¡cuida'o!	Spoken: Be careful ampalla, because the other day I saw some pitchers who had a meeting on the mound with that baseball player. Be foxier than a fox! hmmmm, careful!
Ojo pela'o, compay ampalla	Keep an eye peeled, ampalla
Tenga cuida'o que aquí hay gente mala	Be careful, there are bad people here
Hablado: Recuérdese de un ampalla que había en el '63, que se durmió en los laureles y le dieron un knockout que todavía no ha podí'o levantar cabeza. ¡Hay que tener el ojo abierto con el enemigo! hmmmm	Spoken: Remember that ampalla in 1963 [Juan Bosch], who slept on his laurels, and they gave him such a knockout he hasn't been able to lift his head since. You have to keep an eye out for the enemy! hmmmm
Ojo pela'o, compay ampalla	Keep an eye peeled, ampalla
Tenga cuida'o que aquí hay gente mala	Be careful, there are bad people here
Hablado: Sáqueme esa gente de allí, que esa gente lo que están es dañando el juego. Póngase duro, que si a usted le pasa algo, se seca la grama. ¡Usté 'stá apoyado por nosotros, los fanáticos! ja ja ja	Spoken: Get those people out of here, those people are the ones who are spoiling the game. Be tough, because if something happens to you the grass will dry out. You are supported by us, the fanatics! ha ha ha

Después de tanto luchar	After fighting so hard
No nos vamos a dejar tumbar	Let's not let ourselves lose
Póngase duro, mi ampalla	Get tough, my ampalla
Con los malos jugadores	With dirty players
Vamos a demostrarles a ellos	We're going to show them
Que somos los campeones	That we are the champions
Abra los ojos, mi ampalla	Open your eyes, ampalla
Y levante bien la frente	And lift your forehead high
Qu'el camarón que se duerme	Because the sleeping shrimp
Se lo lleva la corriente	Gets taken by the current
Hablado: ¡Abra los ojos! ¡Aquí no se puede	Spoken: Open your eyes! Here you can't
sei [sic] muy bueno! Y para que se lleve	be too good! And so that you'll listen to
de mi consejo, le voy a rezar una letanía.	my advice, I'm going to pray a litany. Be
¡Cuídese bien de un bolazo!	careful of a dead ball!
Asegúrese mejor	Watch yourself better
Póngase duro, mi ampalla	Be tough, my ampalla
Con todo el conspirador	With all conspirators
Sáqueme ese hombre del juego	Take that man out of the game
Que ese hombre es un impostor	Because that man is an impostor
Todo el que no juega limpio	Anyone who doesn't play a clean game
Sáquelo del béisbol	Take him out of baseball

This bachata and others like it caught the spirit of the day, and to the dismay of Balaguer's Reformista party, the PRD drew a substantial majority of the vote. As Balaguer's defeat became apparent, it was clear that a PRD victory was not going to be tolerated by the Reformistas. The military silenced the media and occupied the election board's offices. There was an outburst of public indignation within the country, and the United States applied strong pressure to Balaguer and the military not to tamper with the election results. Finally, almost two months later, the announcement of the PRD victory was made public.

Balaguer's defeat inspired widespread joy among the population, which was expressed in a number of bachata songs, such as the following merengue de guitarra by Blas Durán (under the pseudonym El Solitario [The loner]), celebrating not the electoral victory itself, but rather the end of military repression and abuse.

Llegó la paz
(Peace has arrived)
Singer: El Solitario

Hablado: ¡Felicidad, compañero, y paz para	Spoken: Congratulations, compañero,
nuestro pueblo! ¡Pueblo unido para que	and peace for our people! Unified
ayudemos a nuestro presidente!	people so that we can help our
	president!

Coro: Llegó la paz, llegó la paz
A mi pueblo llegó la paz
A los que quieren seguir
Maltrando mi Quisqueya
Así no se logra nada
Con el pueblo no se juega
Nosotros seremos libres
No importa que hayan barreras
Teníamos veinte años
Pasando mucho martirio
Pero todo va a cambiar
Con los hombres ya elegidos
Y así vamos a decir
Que viva Santo Domingo
Que se acaben los relajos
Que tienen con nuestro pueblo
Todo el mundo a trabajar
Y dejemos los enredos
Que con tanta mala fe
No adelanta ningún pueblo
Eso no es así, compay
Yo no creo en ese fallo
Aquí van a aprobar leyes
Los que de verdad ganaron
Si el pueblo no lo eligió
No tiene ningún respaldo

Chorus: Peace has come, peace has come
Peace has come to my people
To those who want to continue
Mistreating my Quisqueya[3]
That way you don't get anything
Don't play with the people
We will be free
It doesn't matter that there are barriers
We've had twenty years
Of much suffering
But everything will change
With the men just elected
And this way we're going to say
Long live Santo Domingo
Let the foolishness
With our people stop
Everybody to work
Leave behind the entanglements
Because with bad faith
No people can progress
That's not the way, friend
I don't believe in that mistake
Here they are going to approve laws
Those who truly won
If the people didn't elect him
He's got no support

Hablado: ¡No hagan líos, señores, que eso es malo! ¡Recuérdense que Dios les está mirando, y unos van a'lante, y otros van atrás! ¡Echa pa'llá con ese garrote, que no quiero que me dé un golpe! ¡Cuidado con un golpe!

Spoken: Don't make problems, gentlemen, that is bad! Remember that God is watching, and some go forward and others go backwards! Get out of here with that cudgel, I don't want it to hit me! Watch out for a blow!

Vamos a acabar la mentira
La miseria y la maldad
Que este pueblo está cansado
Ya no puede sufrir más
Abajo los de mala fe
Y que reine la verdad
Este gobierno es de todos
No es sólo de dos o tres
Porque los que mandarán
Son hombres de buena fe
Que quieren bien para todos
Y no para dos o tres
Todo el pueblo está contento
Con el nuevo presidente
Porque ya vamos a tener
Las tres papas bien calientes
Ya no va a ser como ayer

We are going to end the lies
Misery and wickedness
Because the people are tired
And can't suffer any more
Down with those of bad faith
And may truth reign
This government is everybody's
And not just for two or three
Because those who will rule
Are men of good faith
They want to do good for all
And not just for two or three
All the people are happy
With the new president
Because now we're going to have
All three potatoes, nice and hot
It's not going to be like yesterday

Que na'más comía otra gente	That only other people ate
Teníamos doce años	We had twelve years
Pasando mucho martirio	Suffering much martyrdom
Pero todo va cambiar	But everything will change
Por hombres ya elegidos	By the men already elected
Y así vamos a decir	And this way we're going to say
Que viva Santo Domingo	Long live Santo Domingo
¡Que viva Santo Domingo de Guzmán!	Long live Guzmán's Santo Domingo
Llegó la paz, llegó la paz	Peace has come, peace has come
Llegó la paz a mi pueblo	Peace has come to my people, peace has
Llegoó la paz	come

In contrast to Durán's optimism, other bachateros expressed a far more cynical view of presidential politics, which were (correctly) perceived as little more than a spoils system. The following bachata's principal metaphor for political incumbency was a milk-filled teat, to which only the winners had access. This merengue de guitarra took the form of a dialogue between two individuals struggling over a teat: one (the winning PRD) insisting it was his turn and the other (the losing Reformistas) refusing to give it up.

La teta
(The teat)
Singer: Augusto Santos

Cámbieme la cosa, hermano	Change the thing for me, brother
Porque el cambio está de moda	Because change is in fashion
Llegó la oportunidad	The opportunity is here
De cambiarlo todo ahora	To change everything now
Présteme, hermano, la silla	Lend me the chair, brother
Quiero sentarme un ratito	I want to sit for a while
Es el cambio que la ordena	Change requires it
Siéntese usted en el banquito	You sit on the bench
Y me monto en el carro	I'll ride in the car
Y la cama está vieja	The bed is old
No camina la guagua	The bus doesn't run
Se rompió la cadena	The chain is broken
Eres aguayú	You are selfish and you want
Y lo quieres todo pa' ti	Everything for yourself
Pero el cambio dice ahora	But change says that now
Que hay un poquito pa' mí	There's a little bit for me
En otro tiempo, hermano	At another time, brother
Tú te adueñabas de to'	You took everything
Pero el cambio dice ahora	But change now says
Que ya ese tiempo pasó	That that time has passed
La película no es buena	The movie is no good
El actor no está en na'	The actor is nowhere
La mujer no me gusta	I don't like the woman
Hablemos de la teta	Let's talk about the teat
De ésa de la vaca	That one, the cow's

(Voz 1): Dame mi teta
(Voz 2): No se la doy
(1) Que me dé mi teta   (2): No se la doy

(1): Mi tetica tan buena   (2): No se la doy

(1): Ay mi tetota   (2): ¡Aguajero!
(1): Pásame mi teta   (2): No se la doy

(1): No me quite mi teta   (2): ¡Atrevido!

(1): Me la tiene que dar   (2): No se la doy

(1): Dame mi teta   (2): ¡Traicionero!
(1): Que me dé mi teta   (2): ¡No se la doy!

(1): Dame mi teta   (2): Que no se la doy
(1): Sigo pensando en mi teta
(2): ¡Atrevido!
(1): Ay, ¡oye el grito de Jeremías!
(2): ¡Qué Jeremías ni qué Jeremías! ¡Esa es mi herencia! Nadie me la va a quitar. ¡Mi teta es mi teta!

(Voice 1): Give me my teat
(Voice 2): I won't give it to you
(1): I say give me my teat   (2): I won't give it to you
(1): My good little teat   (2): I won't give it to you
(1): Ay, my big fat teat   (2): Bullshitter!
(1): Pass me my teat   (2): I won't give it to you
(1): Don't take away my teat
(2): Impertinent!
(1): You have to give it to me   (2): I won't give it to you
(1): Give me my teat   (2): Traitor!
(1): I say give me my teat   (2): I won't give it to you!
(1): Give me my teat   (2): I won't
(1): I'm still thinking about my teat
(2): Impertinent!
(1): Ay, listen to the cry of Jeremiah!
(2): Jeremiah, what a Jeremiah! That is my inheritance. Nobody is going to take it from me. My teat is my teat!

Lamentably, this song was prophetic: far from establishing a democratic government more responsive to the needs of the people, the PRD grabbed the teat of political power and began to suck as greedily and self-interestedly as its Reformista predecessors. The next chapter analyzes how severe social disruption and worsening pauperization wrought by PRD corruption were reflected in changes in bachata, particularly in how it articulated the genre's most essential concerns—emotional relationships between men and women.

Rafael Encarnación.
By Kubaney Records

Luis Segura in the 1960s.
By Discos Guarachita

Mélida Rodríguez.
By Gemini Records

Radhames Aracena auditioning a bachata musician in 1987.
By Deborah Pacini Hernandez

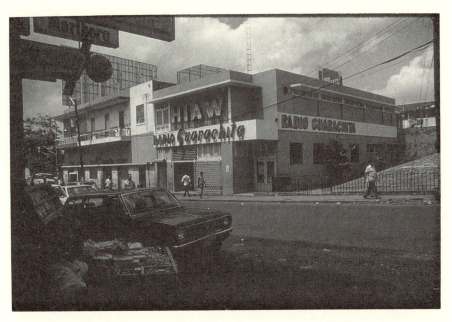

Exterior view of Radio Guarachita's downtown facilities.
By Deborah Pacini Hernandez

Nueva canción musicians Sonia Silvestre and Víctor Víctor in 1974 announcing a
concert by their group Nueva Forma.
By El Nacional

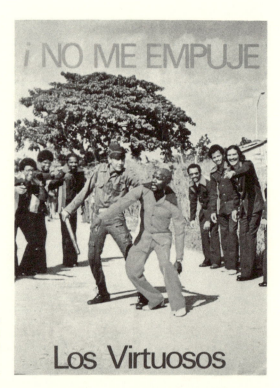

Cuco Valoy's merengue LP *No me empuje* commented simultaneously on racism and police brutality.
By Kubaney Records

Zurza, one of Santo Domingo's older shantytowns.
By Deborah Pacini Hernandez

Socializing in crowded shantytowns often takes place on the street.
By Deborah Pacini Hernandez

In shantytowns, bachata can be danced to in small bars that distinguish
themselves from brothels by calling themselves cafeterías.
By Deborah Pacini Hernandez

Many women survive by working in the informal sector selling food on the street.
By Deborah Pacini Hernandez

Bachata producer Mamita personally delivered his 45 RPM records to vendors.
By Deborah Pacini Hernandez

In the 1970s and 1980s major urban record stores such as
this one refused to sell bachata.
By Deborah Pacini Hernandez

Until 1990, bachata 45 RPM records circulated only via small street stalls.
By Deborah Pacini Hernandez

Leonardo Paniagua, from the
record containing his
1979 hit song "Chiquitita."
By Discos Guarachita

Bolívar Peralta.
By RM Records

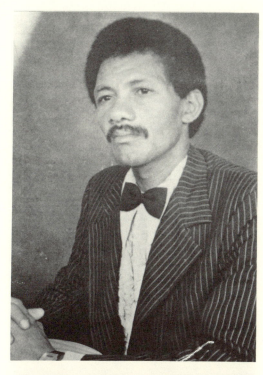

Marino Pérez.
By RM Records

Ramón Cabrera, "El Chivo
sin ley."
By RM Records

"La Verduga"

Aridia Ventura.
By Discos Guarachita

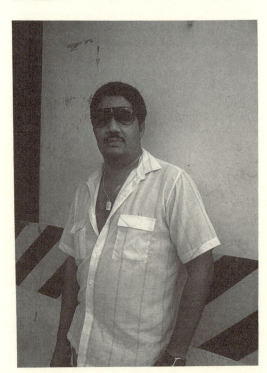

Bachata producer José Luis.
By Deborah Pacini Hernandez

Chapter Five

_L_ove, Sex, and Gender

_R_omantic music in the Dominican Republic—as elsewhere in the Hispanic world—has never been intended to be neutral, merely providing suitable background sound for courtship; instead, the power of song is used to construct and deconstruct emotions and emotional states. Romantic music serves as a surrogate voice for people who feel incapable of articulating their emotions and publicly expressing private feelings, and it helps them to negotiate their relationships, whether in the early stages of courtship, in the fullness of a mutually satisfying relationship, or in the painful and bitter moments of separation and solitude. In the Dominican Republic, there has been a long tradition of men actively using songs in courtship: giving a serenade, singing along with a romantic song while dancing with a woman, giving a woman a record with particularly appropriate lyrics, or sitting in a bar and playing a relevant song on the jukebox over and over again in order to reinforce feelings that may be expressed later in person. Similarly, if a relationship does not develop as desired, or if it falls apart, music about these aspects of a relationship is used to cope with the resulting feelings.

Love and the drama of courtship is without question the most common subject of popular songs all over the world; on this level, then, there was nothing particularly unique about bachata. What was noteworthy, however, was that bachata was transformed from a musical genre defined by its concern with romantic love into one concerned primarily with sexuality, and moreover, a specific kind of sexuality: casual sex with no pretense to longevity or legitimacy, often mediated by money, and whose principal social context was the bar/brothel. Bachata songs in the 1980s still related to the emotional domain, but the nature of male-female relationships was being conceptualized differently from that in the 1960s. In this chapter, I argue that these changes reflected deteriorating social and economic conditions that characterized the late 1970s and 1980s, which devastated the traditional family and community structures of bachata's practitioners and patrons.

Corruption and Economic Crisis in the PRD Years (1978–86)

In 1978, the almost universal repudiation of Balaguer's policies and political machinations resulted in the landslide election of the PRD's Antonio Guzmán, who took office with enormous popular support. It soon became apparent, however, that Guzmán was not the reformer the country had hoped for. He appointed friends and family to high government offices, and he added thousands of employees to the public payroll in order to solidify his base of support, swelling the bureaucracy by over 50 percent. When the increased government expenditures coupled with declining revenues inevitably created budget deficits, social programs were the first to be cut. Making matters worse, the international oil crisis raised the cost of food and other basic necessities, badly hurting the country's poor majority. Guzmán was not permitted by law to seek a second presidential term, but before leaving, his family and associates brazenly began emptying the government coffers. Humiliated by the public revelations of his family's misdeeds, Guzmán committed suicide just before relinquishing office (Moya Pons 1992: 557–58).

In spite of Guzmán's corruption and suicide, the PRD's Salvador Jorge Blanco won the 1982 elections on promises to run a clean government; he inherited, however, an almost bankrupt bureaucracy. In 1983, unable to improve the country's economy, he turned to the International Monetary Fund (IMF) for help. The IMF package placed onerous austerity measures on the country, the most painful of which were the elimination of government subsidies or price supports for essential items, such as petroleum and medicine, and the devaluation of the Dominican peso. Both measures caused sharp price increases for locally produced as well as imported goods, many of which were primary necessities, while wages were deliberately kept low. Moreover, inflation cut into workers' salaries: between 1984 and 1990 the real hourly minimum wage declined by 62 percent, while in the same period the cost of a family food basket more than doubled (Safa 1995). Debt servicing caused even more cuts in government services such as health and education.

At the same time, ill-conceived government economic policies coupled with cuts in the U.S. sugar quotas devastated the agricultural sector, which had long been the backbone of the country's economy, while favoring the rapid expansion of a new economic sector—export manufacturing. Thousands of displaced rural workers left the countryside to seek work in the new factories established in free trade zones in or around urban areas. The new jobs created in the free trade zones, however, could not compensate for those lost in the agricultural sector, and unemployment rates for the country as a whole increased, reaching 29 percent in 1986, with another 40 percent "underemployed." By the end of the decade, 59 percent of a population that only two decades earlier had been primarily agricultural now lived in urban areas (Safa 1995). Conditions in the urban shantytowns, where most of the migrants ended up, were dismal, because of the lack of basic services such as water and sewage and also because of intense crowding. Three of Santo Domingo's barrios, for example, had more than 50,000 people per square kilometer, and most others had around 30,000—compared to between 5000 and 14,000 for the city's upper- and middle-class neighborhoods (Gómez Carrasco 1984: 5).

Not everybody suffered from the economic crisis, however. Businessmen and politicians in favor with the government were able to obtain loans from the $467 million borrowed from the IMF to invest in their businesses. The military continued to enjoy generous wages and benefits, and an ever-increasing bureaucracy added more and more loyal party followers to the government payroll. Bankers and financiers made instant fortunes playing in the money market. Those with access to the IMF money flowing through the economy were able to buy the foreign luxury goods such as automobiles and appliances that flooded into the country after import restrictions were lifted. What was worse, in spite of Jorge Blanco's campaign promises to eliminate corruption, he and his associates gorged themselves shamelessly from the IMF trough, cynically taking advantage of the country's desperate economic situation to enrich themselves with the money borrowed at such a high cost to ordinary citizens.

As a result of the PRD's betrayal, the political activism and idealism that had characterized the opposition to Joaquín Balaguer's government throughout the turbulent decade of the 1970s turned into a potent concoction of cynicism, anger, and resentment that poisoned the social environment. So bankrupt was the PRD that in 1986 Joaquín Balaguer, by then almost eighty and virtually blind, won the presidential election and resumed power. No one had any illusions about Balaguer, but at least he was no hypocrite.

Changing Gender Roles

The economic crisis that ensued in the wake of Antonio Guzmán's failed economic policies and Salvador Jorge Blanco's draconian 1983 IMF package placed tremendous stresses on traditional Dominican family and community structure. Men found it increasingly difficult to fulfill their traditional roles as primary breadwinners, and women were forced to move into the workplace to supplement family income (Safa 1995). Families were dispersed when able-bodied members were forced to migrate in search of work; those who could went to the United States, but the less fortunate ended up in the shantytowns surrounding the country's already overcrowded cities. Of the new arrivals in the city, more than half were women; a 1983 study found that 56 percent of the migrants to Santo Domingo and 57 percent of those to Santiago were women (Duarte 1986: 188). Women were expelled from rural areas at greater rates because they were less central to the rural agricultural economy and because they were able to find employment more easily in the rapidly expanding export manufacturing sector or in the informal sector. Statistics illustrate the dramatic changes in male and female participation in the labor force: in 1960 only 9 percent of the country's total labor force was comprised of women; in 1980 it was up to 28 percent and by 1991 it had risen to 38 percent. Men's labor force numbers in that same period actually declined, from almost 80 percent to 72 percent (Safa 1995).

The most common option for recent female migrants was to work as domestic servants in the homes of the Dominican bourgeoisie; 26 percent of the economically active women in Santo Domingo worked as domestics (Duarte 1986: 198). Domestic service was not only poorly paid (less than half the country's minimum wage), it also severely limited a woman's free time and ability to socialize—but it offered the security of food and lodging to women arriving in the city for the first time. Once adjusted to urban life, however, many women rejected domestic service and sought other forms of employment. The lucky ones found work in factories or the public sector, but most women, only semiliterate and unskilled, needed to turn to other means of support within the informal sector, such as selling prepared food on the street or taking in washing and ironing; others were forced to turn to prostitution.[1] In 1983, over half of those underemployed in the informal economy were women (Duarte 1986: 205).

The fact that women were working more and contributing more to household maintenance at the same time that men were working and earning less had profound consequences on men's traditional role as primary breadwinners and on traditional patterns of marriage. Helen Safa notes that in a study published in 1991, almost a third of the unions between Dominican men and women were consensual rather than legal. Among women working in export manufacturing, the number of consensual unions was twice as high as legal marriages, suggesting an inverse relationship between the degree of economic independence and the stability of marriage. Because consensual unions were also linked to lower educational levels and lower socio-economic status (Safa 1995), it is possible to extrapolate that in shantytowns, where most women were poorly educated and unemployed, consensual unions were even more common than among the better educated, salaried women working in export manufacturing.

Safa notes that "women in consensual unions often assume greater responsibility for the household and are less economically dependent on men than legally married women" (Safa 1995). Still, she observed, ideologically many of these women still subscribed to traditional patriarchal values wherein men should support the family, suggesting that these women would have preferred a stable union in which the man shared more of the financial responsibility (Safa 1995). Isis Duarte observed, "The woman is obligated to work because the man (father, brother, husband, or other family member) does not have regular employment or works independently. This irregularity of income leads to a situation in which, although the man may be present in the home, it is the woman who provides the family food" (Duarte 1986: 246–47, translation mine). Whether by choice or by necessity, then, women were more frequently becoming heads of their households: in 1984 nearly one-quarter of all Dominican households were headed by women rather than men (Safa 1995).

Women who were not dependent on men were more prone to challenge their partners/husbands over household decisions, and more likely to leave them if differences could not be reconciled: "When male breadwinning inadequacy becomes chronic and women become co-breadwinners on a permanent basis, men are no longer able to maintain their superior and authoritarian position vis-à-vis their wives" (Constantina Safilios-Rothschild, cited in Safa 1995). Clara Báez noted the consequences of this change: "In the Dominican Republic a women's social movement has been emerging that is breaking with traditional customs that confined them to the domestic sphere, which demands a voice and participation in public life equal to that of men, and which is threatening to upset the old hierarchic order in all aspects of social life" (Báez 1985: 43, translation mine).

Women, no longer tied to a stable home, family, and kinship and community networks, experienced far more sexual and social flexibility than they had in rural areas. On the other hand, they lost the social supports they had enjoyed in rural areas, and they were required to struggle, just like men, to define and maintain a space for themselves within the social and economic context of the overcrowded and impoverished shantytowns. With men becoming increasingly dependent on women for support and no longer being able to control women's movements, the relationships between men and women became more conflictive. In these circumstances, sex ceased to be solely a physical/emotional activity; it could also be related to a man's very economic survival. Moreover, the emotions of love and pain and the physicality of sex and loneliness assumed social meanings as well: the inability to attract and keep a woman undermined a man's social competence and identity as provider and authority figure.

Finally, it is important to note that in the shantytowns recreational activity, which had always included music, dancing, and drinking, shifted from domestic to public spaces such as colmados or barras. Colmados and barras had long been loci of social interaction and musical activity for both men and women (see Chapter 2); barras, however, were more male-oriented spaces, and many of them were associated with brothels; as such, they were off limits to women with more traditional values.[2] Men, less connected to stable job and home, tended to spend more time in bars and brothels, where sex could be easily purchased without any strings attached, and where alcohol became a favored way to combat the hopelessness and depression of urban life. Alcohol consumption rose dramatically: in 1983 the Dominican Republic's per capita consumption of alcohol was second only to Yugoslavia's (Arvelo 1983), and a 1987 article reported that Dominicans spent more than 30 percent of their annual income on alcoholic beverages and cigarettes—more than on any other product except food (*Master* 1, no. 1, 1987).

As a result of these socio-economic changes, interactions between men and women, which in rural areas had taken place in family and community settings and according to traditional patriarchal values, became more anonymous, conflictive, and increasingly mediated by money. These transformations in male-female relationships and the conflicts they generated were clearly evident in the lyrics of bachata songs, a number of which I will reproduce below in their entirety so that readers can appreciate how these concerns were conceptualized and articulated.

Changing Lyrics

When the first bachata songs were recorded in the early 1960s, they were still unequivocally part of the broad, Pan-Hispanic tradition of romantic song described in Chapter 1: usually modeled after the quintessentially romantic bolero, they tended to be highly emotional expressions of lost or unrequited love. As the social and economic transformations described above unfolded, bachata songs began to address a wider range of possible relationships between men and women, suggesting that extended romantic courtship and a lifetime of cohabitation were no longer expected or desired. On the contrary, these songs implied that unions were likely to be short-lived and often mediated by money. Whereas in early bachatas a man might lament that a woman had left him, in bachatas of the late 1970s and 1980s, he was more likely to express anger, disillusion, and often an implacable hostility not only toward the individual woman but toward all women as a group. There were, to be sure, still many unequivocally romantic love songs, and in fact, some singers such as Luis Segura and Leonardo Paniagua specialized in such songs. But a growing proportion of bachata production in the 1980s communicated, either explicitly or symbolically, the growing social and economic as well as emotional tensions between men and women. If song texts serve to deal publicly with private emotions, then these songs revealed conflictive and indeed disturbing changes in gender relations.

In the late 1970s and 1980s bachata's most common theme had gone beyond the problems of love desired or lost, encompassing a broader range of emotions and experiences concerning male-female relationships that included: (1) sexual appetite and lust; (2) *engaño* (deception) by a woman; (3) abandonment, despair, and isolation; (4) the bar—as the location for male camaraderie or as the place to find a woman with whom to have sexual relations; (5) drinking—as a prelude to finding a woman, as therapy for heartbreak or anger, or simply as a pleasurable recreational activity in itself. What was *not* mentioned in the songs tells us as much as what *was* mentioned: marriage, family, children, commitment, jobs, home; while there were, of course, occasional exceptions, the absence of these themes reflected men's lack of a relationship with—or responsibility to—the domestic domain. In contrast to this situation, work, wives, and long-term relationships are not unusual themes in numerous popular music forms similarly associated with lower socio-economic classes such as U.S. blues and country music (country more than blues, however). Ruben George Oliven's 1988 study of Brazilian popular music of the 1930s and 1940s provides another comparative case, which points out that women and work are seen as threatening to the freedom of the vagrant's life exalted in the songs. Nevertheless, work and women, who are associated with family and stability, were at least part of the thematic landscape within which the Brazilian singers situated themselves as bohemians. With few exceptions, work and family were seldom mentioned in bachata.

Furthermore, there was little sense of place in bachata songs—rarely was a specific place name mentioned or invoked, in marked contrast to other Caribbean musical genres, particularly those associated with performers and listeners of rural origins, in which place names are constantly invoked for affective purposes. The people and events in bachata songs did not seem to have an identifiable location—except the bar, which, I suggest, was a metaphor for the urban shantytown itself. Neither was there a sense of movement, of going anywhere: there was no imagery of journey or travel, unlike other musics, such as Brazilian popular or U.S. country music, in which the road and trucks figure prominently. People were not being pulled or pushed anywhere—neither away from nor toward home or work. Life, as expressed in bachata songs, was spatially and socially rootless, fragmentary and lacking coherency—and in that sense, these songs were thoroughly modern.

The following song by Rafael Encarnación was typical of bachatas from the 1960s: its tempo was appropriately slow, the singer's voice was plaintive, almost sobbing, as if to suggest great emotional sensitivity, and the dialogue was addressed directly to the beloved woman. Its lyrics, even while expressing the heartbreak of abandonment, nevertheless vowed eternal love; it was pain without anger. The implied relationship was not situated in any particular space or time—it could be taking place in an urban or a rural setting, in a home, a party, or a serenade, in the past, present, or future: Encarnación's love existed in a timeless emotional space defined only by the presence of feelings of love.

Muero contigo
(I die with you)
Singer: Rafael Encarnación

Ay mi vida	Oh my darling
Tú tienes toda la culpa	Everything is your fault
Tú has logrado comprender	You have come to understand
Pero sé que me quieres	But I know you love me
Escucha, mi amor	Listen, my love
Las notas de esta canción	To the notes of this song
Los recuerdos más queridos de mis sueños	The most precious memories of my dreams
Vas conmigo	You are going with me
Comprende, tú sabes que te quiero	Understand, you know I love you
Todo a ti	Only you
No me niegues la esperanza de volverte a besar	Don't deny me the hope of kissing you again
Mi vida	My love
Tú, tú pretendes ver	You, you pretend to see
Que mi destino y tu amor se han separado	That my destiny and yours have been separated
Por rutas diferentes	By different paths
No puede ser	It can't be
Comprende, tú sabes que te quiero	Understand, you know that I love you
Sólo a ti	Only you
No puedo ya vivir sin tu querer	I can't live without your love
Ay mi vida	Oh my darling
Cómo he sufrido tu ausencia	How I've suffered your absence
Tu desdén, tu indiferencia	Your disdain, your indifference
Si ese dolor es por ti yo te perdono	If that pain is for you I forgive you
Muero contigo	I die with you

In subsequent decades, the narrative space constructed in bachata evolved from an intimate one occupied by only the two people involved in an emotional relationship (into which a listener to the song could insert him/herself) to a wider, more inclusive public space occupied by a group of people—the male companions of the singer: fewer songs were directed to the woman herself and more of them to the man's drinking companions. I analyzed dozens of bachata songs from the 1960s and found that most of them referred to the female subject of the song directly, in the second person familiar, *tú*. By the 1980s only about half the songs referred to the female subject directly: the other half were directed at other men and referred to the woman indirectly, in the third person, *ella*. In others, the singer shifted halfway through the song from the third person to the second person, or vice versa, again de-emphasizing a primary two-way relationship between the singer and a woman. The use of the third person not only distanced the woman from the singer, but objectified her as well: she became the problematic "other." These later bachata songs, then, were not so much imaginary dialogues between a man and a woman, but a dialogue between men *about* women. The following is a typical example of such bachatas:

A ésa me la llevo yo
(I'm taking that one)
Singer: Marino Pérez

Me cansé de llamar	I got tired of calling
Y ella no me hizo caso	But she paid me no mind
Pensé que estaba celosa	I thought she was jealous
O por otro hombre	Or because of another man
Me estaba olvidando	She was forgetting me
Ahora me doy cuenta	Now I realize
Que se está llevando	That she was being swayed
De gente que quiere	By people who want
Vernos separados	To see us separated
¿Por qué? me digo, mi amigo	Why, I ask myself, my friend?
Voces masculinos: No la quiera más, no la quiera más	Male voices: Don't love her anymore, don't love her anymore
No puedo . . .	I can't . . .
Voces masculinos: Aprenda a olvidar, aprenda a olvidar, aprenda a olvidar	Male voices: Learn to forget, learn to forget, learn to forget
¿Y cómo?	But how?
Voces masculinos: No la busques más, no la busques más, no la busques más	Male voices: Don't see her anymore, don't look for her anymore, don't see her anymore

No aguanto	I can't take it
Que me arranca el corazón de pleno	It's ripping my heart out
Pero a ésa no la olvido yo	I can't forget this one
Hablado: Dios mío, si no encuentro a esa	Spoken: Dear God, if I don't find that
mujer en esta noche soy capaz de matarme	woman tonight I'm capable of killing
al amanecer, ¡que Dios me perdone!	myself at dawn, may God forgive me!

During the same period a close relationship developed between bachata and the barra. Songs about eternal love and family were inappropriate in these contexts; instead, the songs tended to refer to the problems of transient relationships mediated not by traditional values of romantic love, but by the harsh social and economic realities of the urban shantytown. But most important, the bar and bachata songs about the bar became structural features of a male social space in which men, not women, were the providers of emotional support. Women's place in the barra context was to provide sexuality, not reliable companionship, and in fact they were perceived as forces of social disorder and emotional pain rather than of social stability and emotional warmth. The following songs by Bolívar Peralta illustrate this point.

Espero por mi morena
(I'm waiting for my dark woman)
Singer: Bolívar Peralta

Desde temprano yo estoy	I've been here a long time
Sentado aquí en esta mesa	Sitting at this table
Dígame usted, por favor	Tell me, please
Si no ha visto a mi morena	If you've seen my morena
Y no prequnte, señor	And don't ask, sir
Qué hago yo en este lugar	What I'm doing in this place
Ando en busca de mi hembra	I'm looking for my female
Y no la voy a dejar	And I'm not going to leave her
Porque hasta que ella no venga	Because until she really doesn't come back
No me canso de—	I won't tire of [ ]
Que venga, que venga	I want her to come, to come
Mi morena otra vez . . .	My morena, to come again . . .
Espero por mi morena	I'm waiting for my morena
Que me sabe comprender	She knows how to understand me
Ya te dije que yo estoy	I already told you I've been
Bebiendo desde temprano	Drinking for some time
Ando en busca de mi amor	I'm looking for my love
Y aquí la estoy esperando	And I'm waiting for her here
Y si la tiene escondida	And if he is hiding her
Anda buscándose un lío	He's looking for a problem
Porque es la que me domina	Because she's the one who dominates me
Cuando yo estoy más prendí'o	When I'm most turned on

Hablado: ¡Morena mía, corre!	Spoken: Morena, run, a fire is burning,
¡Quema prendí'o, que es un ingenio!	it's the sugar mill![3]

Que me sirva ella
(I want her to serve me)
Singer: Bolívar Peralta

La de mi tormenta	The one who torments me
Por la que yo brindo	The one I'm toasting
En un momento	In a while
La llevo conmigo	I'll take her with me
Señor cantinero	Mister barman
Mande la botella	Send me a bottle
Y yo lo que quiero	But what I want
Que me sirva ella	Is for her to serve me
Que me sirva ella	I want her to serve me
Y al temblar sus manos	And as her hands tremble
Cierto que me quieres	It's true that you love me
Tú me estás acabando	You are finishing me off
Sientes las caricias	You feel the caresses
De un amor sediento	Of a thirsty love
Y sus nervios tiemblan	And her nerves tremble
Con el pensamiento	With the thought
Te miro nerviosa	You seem nervous
Pero te comprendo	But I understand you
Porque una cosita	Because that little thing
Sé que estás sintiendo	I know you're feeling it
Con el pensamiento	With your thoughts
Se imagina todo	You can imagine everything
Y yo la contemplo	And I think about her
Cuando estemos solos	When we are alone

Contrasting these songs to the one by Encarnación cited above, we can see that while they concerned the singer's ardent desire for a woman, most of the lyrics were directed not to the woman herself, but to implied third persons. Furthermore, unlike the intimate relationship invoked by Encarnación, which existed in a nonspecific, ethereal realm, the listener to these songs was situated in a more public narrative space whose location was quite mundane, clear, and explicit—and masculine: Peralta is in a bar, where the woman he desires works as a bar girl (i.e., prostitute). And what Peralta wants from her is not undying love but rather the satisfaction of his sexual needs. Peralta's voice, although still plaintive, has none of the soft sensitivity of Encarnación's and instead is more demanding, like a child's. "Espero por mi morena" also refers to the social tension intrinsic to relationships with bar girls and prostitutes, whose sexuality, available to all men, becomes a potentially disruptive element in the male environment.

In this sort of bachata song, men were not merely talking to each other about their emotional problems; they were teaching each other as well. Bachata, like other forms of popular music, had cognitive as well as recreational functions, serving as a sort of audio-textbook that instructed young men about women and what to expect from them emotionally and sexually.[4] Composers of popular bachata songs tended to be men with enough urban experience to express the complex relationship between rural expectations and urban constraints. Those who listened to bachata, whether they were long-time shantytown residents, recent arrivals, or campesinos who had not yet left the countryside, learned how to negotiate gender relationships in the urban shantytown context. Bachata's didactic functions could be implicit in songs about emotional pain and disruption, but sometimes were quite explicit. In the following song the singer informs his listeners that when women come to the city traditional female behavior is replaced by disruptive new customs: they begin to act independently, betray their husbands, abandon the home, and threaten friendships between men.

Aquí la mujer se daña
(Women go bad here)
Singer: Manuel Chalas

Voy a hablar de la mujer	I'm going to tell you about the woman
Que viene a la capital	Who comes to the capital
A los tres días se pone	After three days she gets
Que no se puede aguantar	So you can't put up with her
Y se tira a caminar	And she starts to walk
A la calle sin compaña	In the streets alone
Y hasta con otro te engaña	And she even deceives you
Quizás con tu propio amigo	Perhaps with your own friend
Y por eso es que te digo	And that's why I'm telling you
Que aquí la mujer se daña	That women here go bad
Oye, hermano mío	Listen, my brother
Aquí la mujer se daña	Women go bad here
Si te hace falta el calor	If you miss the warmth
De tu linda mujercita	Of your beautiful woman
No, no vendas tu casita	Don't, don't sell your house
Pa' traerla a la capital	To bring her to the capital
Que aunque sea la más formal	Because even if she's well behaved
Aquí coge mala maña	Here she'll take on bad ways
Y hasta con otro te engaña	She'll deceive you with another
Quizás con tu propio amigo	Maybe even your own friend
Y por eso es que te digo	And that's why I'm telling you

Que aquí la mujer se daña	That women go bad here
Oye, Miguelito	Listen, Miguelito
Aquí la mujer se daña	Women go bad here
Yo tengo un amigo mío	I have a friend
Que vino y buscó trabajo	Who came to look for work
Cuando la mujer se trajo	When he brought his woman
Se le fue a los cuatro días	She left him after four days
Como una que yo tenía	Like one that I had
Que bajé de la montaña	I brought her down from the mountain
Y que cortaba la caña	Where she used to cut cane
Para mi mayor testigo	And I'm a witness
Y por eso es que te digo	That's why I'm telling you
Que aquí la mujer se daña	That women go bad here
Lo sé, lo sé, lo sé, lo sé	I know, I know, I know, I know
Lo digo con experiencia	I say it from experience
Aquí la mujer se daña	Women go bad here

The following song is equally explicit. Here, the singer taunts another man, calling him a *pariguayo*, a Dominican slang word that technically refers to an inexperienced fool, but which implicitly suggests the naive and unsophisticated rural manner of a country bumpkin. The male voices at the end of each verse calling out "Pariguayo!" challenge the social competency—and hence the very masculinity—of any man who trusts a woman, and urge any listeners with these or similar delusions to wise up as soon as possible.

Pariguayo
Singer: Toribio Jiménez

Esa mujer que tú tienes	That woman you have
Te dice, "Lloro por ti"	Says, "I cry for you"
Esa es mentira de un peso	That's a big lie
Y tú, como un pariguayo al fin	And you, like a bumpkin after all
Pariguayo, aprende a vivir	Pariguayo, learn to live
Si está tomando contigo	If she's drinking with you
Te dice, "Espérame aquí"	And she says, "Wait for me here"
Te deja y se va con otro	She leaves you and goes off with another
Y tú, como on pariguayo al fin	And you, like a pariguayo after all
Pariguayo, aprende a vivir	Pariguayo, learn to live
Cuando por ti le preguntan	When they ask her about you
Le dan ganas de reír	She feels like laughing
Ella dice que te trata	She says she treats you
Como un pariguayo al fin	Like a pariguayo after all
Pariguayazo, aprende a vivir	You big pariguayo, learn to live
Cuando te ve por la calle te dice,	When she sees you on the street she says,
"Estoy buscándote a ti." ¡Mentira!	"I've been looking for you." Lies!
Ella le está buscando, y tú	She is looking for him, and you

Como un pariguayo al fin	Like a pariguayo after all
Pariguayo, aprende a vivir	Pariguayo, learn how to live
Piénsalo bien patantún	Think about it carefully, dum-dum
Esa mujer no es un maíz	That women is no fool
Es machete de dos filos, y tú	She's a two-edged machete, and you
Como un pariguayo al fin	Like a pariguayo after all
Pariguayo, aprende a vivir	Pariguayo, learn how to live

These songs suggest that women were unreliable because they had no sense of self-control and therefore could not resist sexual desire. The idea of women's sexuality as a potentially dangerous natural force that can only be controlled by containment was part of the cultural baggage inherited from the country's Spanish/Mediterranean colonizers. Women's sexuality had been kept under control in the confines of patriarchal rural home and community settings but was unleashed when they discovered freedom of movement in the city. Because uncontrolled female sexuality could conveniently be blamed for most of the bachateros' problems, it absolved them from assuming any responsibility for failed relationships; songs almost never mention other possible reasons—for example, men's failure to provide affection, respect, faithfulness, or economic support—that a woman might leave a man.

Because there were fewer social or economic constraints binding a woman to unwanted relationships, men found that their power to make women change their behavior when they failed to fulfill men's needs or expectations became limited in urban contexts. When men's potency or prerogatives had no effect on women's behavior, men railed at women through bachata. As one young man explained to me, "Dominican men are machistas, they want their orders to be obeyed. But their women don't like to obey them, and from this come their conflicts. Bachata is a defense of men."

When a woman decided to establish a relationship with another man, men complained of *engaño* (deception)—one of bachata's most common themes. Unlike the early bachatas, in which abandonment caused extreme grief, bachatas from the 1980s responded with *despecho* (spite or indignation) and rage. The following song, a virulent expression of despecho, interestingly contains a rare mention of children, whose existence are invoked to draw attention to the woman's perfidy.

La allantosa
(Deceitful woman)
Singer: Luis Emilio Félix

Desde el día que te fuiste	Since the day you left
No habías vuelto	You haven't been back

Ahora vienes a llorar adonde mí	Now you come crying to me
Sigue, y sigue tu camino con quien quieras	Get going with whomever you want
Que este negro no quiere saber de ti	This *negro* doesn't want to hear about you
En el mundo hay mujeres desgraciadas	In this world there are miserable women
Pero tú, tú no tienes compañera	But you, you don't have a match
Abandonaste a tus dos hijos enfermos	You abandoned your two sick children
Y ahora vienes a pedirme que te quiera	And now you're asking me to love you
Las mujeres como tú no valen nada	Women like you aren't worth a thing
Tú no tienes nada, nada de valor	You've got nothing, nothing of value
Sólo un hombre que esté ciego o esté loco	Only a man who's blind or who's crazy
Puede dar una moneda por tu amor	Would give anything at all for your love

In bachata, men could also compensate for their inability to control women by bragging and other sorts of posturing that reaffirmed their masculine authority. Usually, boasting was directed at other men rather than at women—although presumably the boaster hoped that women as well would be impressed by the show of bravado. Bachateros boasted about a variety of features prized in a macho culture: their ability to attract many women and to satisfy them all sexually; their ability to physically challenge and overcome other men; and their ability to drink heavily. The following song by Bolívar Peralta expresses a common male boast that he is unfettered by responsibility or commitment to any one woman because he is charming enough to attract others.

Que venga otra mujer
(Let another woman come)
Singer: Bolívar Peralta

Mundo de amor y desengaño	World of love and disillusion
Hoy nada es raro para mí	Today nothing is strange to me
Y si uno hoy me ha olvidado	And if one has forgotten me today
Otra conmigo ha de venir	Another's bound to come along
Quien quiera ven, mira mi mesa	Whoever wants to, come to my table
Hoy siento ganas de brindar	Today I feel like toasting
Uno por la que ya se aleja	One for her who is leaving
Y otro por la que ha de llegar	Another for the one who will come
Me va la vida, pasó el ayer	My life goes on, yesterday passed
Si una me olvida, que venga otra mujer	If one forgets me, let another woman come
Junta tu copa con mi copa	Join your cup to mine
No hay diferencia, son igual	There's no difference, they're the same
Si trago a trago ella se agota	If drink after drink it gets empty
Hasta el presente ha de pasar	Even the present will pass

The pain of separation and disillusion was also expressed in bachata as *amargue*, a word that literally means bitterness—specifically the bitterness caused by deception, not the more generalized feelings of sadness brought on by unrequited love or separation due to causes other than deception. The concept of 'amargue' is similar but not identical to the U.S. concept of 'blues.' Blues suggest a certain emotional depression, even despair, perhaps caused by a woman, but they can also be caused by the hopelessness of the singer's socio-economic reality. Amargue, on the other hand, is an emotional state caused by women: a man who is *amargado* (embittered) is one who has been deceived, who has lost a presumed innocence at the hands of a treacherous woman. Indeed, so many bachata songs expressed this bitterness that in the early 1980s, bachata began to be called *música de amargue* (see Chapters 1 and 6). The embittered man typically consoles himself in a bar, drinking with friends who commiserate with his plight, as the following song by Confesor González illustrates:

No te amargues por ella
(Don't get bitter over her)
Singer: Confesor González

Ya me desengañé	I've lost my illusions
De toditas las mujeres	About all women
Porque a un amigo mío	Because I saw what happened
Yo vi lo que le pasó	To a friend of mine
El confiaba en su señora	He trusted his wife
Y le daba hasta la vida	He would have given her his life
Y fue tanta la confianza	And he trusted her so much
Que con otro lo engañó	She betrayed him with another
Ya no creo en ninguna de las mujeres	I don't believe in any woman anymore
Porque cada día ellas se ponen peor	Because every day they get worse
Ellas se vuelven mariposas en los jardines	They become butterflies[5] in the garden
Y van cogiendo el sabor de cada flor	And take the flavor from each flower
Amigo mío, siéntate en mi mesa	My friend, come sit at my table
Que te voy a brindar un trago de licor	I'm going to offer you a toast of liquor
No te amargues por ella	Don't get bitter over her
Que un hombre vale más que una mujer	A man's worth more than a woman

While we must consider the verbal denigration of women as a form of violence, physical violence towards women—which certainly occurred—was seldom if ever mentioned in song texts. When physical violence was mentioned, it was directed at other men who threatened to interfere with a man's control over a woman. Songs in which men boast about their ability and willingness to fight other men were not particularly common in other Caribbean popular musics—although they were in one of bachata's important antecedent genres, the Mexican ranchera. The following song exemplifies this sort of macho bravado.

El cañón
(The cannon)
Singer: Silvestre Peguero

Voy a comprar una pistola	I'm going to buy a pistol
Con cuarenta cargadores	With forty rounds
Para quitarles la vida	To take away the life
A todos los hombres traidores	Of all treacherous men
Es que yo la quiero mi amigo	It's just that I love her, friend
Es que yo la amo	It's that I love her
Y no quiero ver	And I don't want to see
Otro aquí a su lado	Another here at her side
Lo digo por el vecino	It's because of the neighbor
Que es un hombre traicionero	Who is a treacherous man
Ahora quiere quitarme	Now he wants to take away
La mujer que yo más quiero	The woman I most love
Y si con esa pistola	And if with that pistol
No lo puedo resolver	I can't resolve the problem
Voy a compraime [sic] un cañón	I'm going to buy me a cannon
Para defender a mi mujer	To defend my woman

While most of this boasting aggressively asserted the singer's sexual and physical prowess, in a few cases unfettered male sexuality was celebrated with noncombative, pastoral imagery, as in following verses sung by Sijo Osoria:

El negro más bello
(The most beautiful black man)
Singer: Sijo Osoria

Yo soy el negro más bello	I'm the most beautiful black man
Que reside entre las flores	Who lives among the flowers
A las mujeres picando	Nibbling at women
Y ellas me dan sus amores	And they give me their love
Nunca me siento amargado	I never feel embittered
Me chupo aquellas flores	I suck those flowers

In others, the metaphor for sexual prowess was thoroughly urban:

Yo soy como el dólar
(I'm like the dollar)
Singer: Manuel Chano

Yo soy como el dólar	I'm like the dollar
Que vale en el mundo entero	That's valued all over the world
Y dondequiera que voy	And wherever I go
Consigo lo que yo quiero	I get what I want

Ando p'arriba y p'abajo	I wander here and there
Enamorando mujeres	Seducing women
Y por mi forma de ser	And because of the way I am
Consigo la que yo quiero	I get the one I want
El amor y el interés	Love and interest
Son dos cosas parecidas	Are two similar things
Y yo por una mujer	And me, for a woman
Me atrevo a perder la vida	I'd risk losing my life
Yo me encuentro ser dichoso	I'm a happy man
Dichoso soy de verdad	Truly happy I am
Yo no le pido a ninguna	I don't ask women for anything
Y todas me quieren dar	And they all want to give to me

Interestingly, the arena of struggle between the sexes transcended the material world and extended into the realm of the supernatural. Dominicans, especially those of rural origins, firmly believe that spirits, or *misterios* (see Davis 1987), can be enlisted in the effort to either obtain (or retain) a partner or, conversely, to resist the efforts of enemies to manipulate them through similar magical strategies. In the following song a man boasts that his magical powers are stronger than those of an unfaithful woman he has abandoned, who has been using magic to try to get him back.

No soy un maíz
(I'm no fool)
Singer: Sijo Osoria

La mujer que yo tenía	The woman I had,
Amigo mío, la boté	My friend, I threw away
Por andar de bochinchera	Because she ran around
Yo por otra la cambié	I exchanged her for another
La que quiera traicionarme	She who betrays me
La boto lejos de mí	I'll throw far away from me
Porque aunque a veces me desgrano	Because while I might lose my kernels [come apart]
Pero no soy un maíz	I'm no fool
Tú creíste muchachita	You thought, little girl
Que por ti me iba a morir	That I'd die for you
Pero te has equivocado	But you were wrong
Ahora es que estoy feliz	It's now that I'm happy
Ahora tú te estás muriendo	Now you're the one who's dying
Porque no te tengo a ti	Because you don't belong to me
No me importa que tú llores	I don't care if you cry
Tu llanto me hace feliz	Your tears make me happy
De nada te valieron tus mechitas	Your little candles were useless
Soy más malo que el demonio Lilí	I'm worse than the devil Lilí

El dinero que le diste al brujo	The money you gave the witch
Junto con él, mujer, me lo pedí	Together with him, woman, I asked for it
He sabido que lo está vendiendo todo	I hear you are selling everything
Para a las fuerzas tenerme junto a ti	To forcefully keep me at your side
No me des risa, mujer, te lo repito	Don't make me laugh, woman, I tell you again
No botes tus cheles, yo no soy un maíz	Don't throw away your money, I'm no fool
Hablado: No me importa que tú digas que ando detrás de ti. Quiero que comprendas que tú, tú no estás en nada, y tú ya no significas nada para mí	Spoken: I don't care if you say I'm after you. I want you to understand that you, you are nowhere, and you don't mean a thing to me

The economic basis of male-female relationships in the shantytown context was evident in bachateros' frequent references to being the *dueño* (owner) of a woman, suggesting that women were considered an economic resource much like any other possession; "owning" a woman bestowed upon a man all sorts of benefits of which her sexuality was only one. In some cases, the references to ownership implied a pimp-prostitute relationship, but it could also refer to any man involved with a woman who was supporting him, even partially. If a man lost a woman, it meant an economic as well as an emotional loss and, moreover, dealt a serious blow to his social status and self-esteem. The following song (whose title and singer are not identified on tape) typifies the references to a man's ownership of a woman and the necessity of defending his "property" from usurpation by others.

Sabes que soy tu dueño	You know I'm your owner
Y que vengo prendí'o	And that I've come here inflamed
No quiero nada de él, no	I don't want anything of his
Yo reclamo lo mío	I'm demanding what's mine
Quizás hay otro con ella	If there's anyone else with her
Va a haber tremendo lío	There's going to be big trouble
A nadie lo soporto	I won't put up with anyone
Que juege con lo mío	Playing with what's mine
A mí no tengo moda	I don't care
Porque me vean prendí'o	If people see me inflamed
Sabes como me pongo	You know how I get
Por defender lo mío	Defending what's mine
Mis amigos me dicen	My friends tell me
Que ya estoy perdí'o	That I'm already lost
Yo vengo a partir brazos	I've come here to break arms
A rescatar lo mío	To reclaim what's mine

Other bachata songs revealed a different, more acceptable model of male dependence on women: that of child to mother (*mami*). Mami was capable of fulfilling a man's every need and could be the source of well-being when she lavished her attention on a man. The following song expresses the bachatero's deep satisfaction with a woman/mother who unquestioningly fulfills his needs.

Ay mami
Singer: Marino Pérez

Que mujer tan chula	What a great woman
La que yo tengo	The one I have
Siempre me paga	She always pays
Lo que yo me bebo	For whatever I drink
Si me voy a la barra	If I go to the bar
Pido una botella	I order a bottle
Si yo no la pago	If I don't pay for it
Me la paga ella	She'll pay it for me
Espero que vuelva	I hope she comes back
Que de verdad me quiere	Because she really loves me
Para que me sobe	So that she can rub me
Adonde me duele	Where it hurts
A veces de noche	Sometimes at night
Me da mi traguito	She gives me a little drink
Para que le cante	So that I'll sing to her
Con el quejaíto	With a little moan
Yo te quiero mucho	I love you a lot
Mi dulce negrita	My sweet little negra
Nunca te me vayas	Don't ever leave me
Negra de mi vida	negra of my life

While the use of the word *mami* as a term of endearment is very common in the Dominican Republic, in bachata it was emblematic: dozens if not hundreds of bachata songs contain calls to "mami!" either in verse or in the spoken phrases uttered between verses, such as the following phrases called out by Marino Pérez in one of his songs:

> Mecho! [nickname for Mercedes] Mecho my darling, mami, I love you so much I can't forget you! I won't forget you; come soon, I'm dying for you, my love! I love you very much, *chichí*, mami, I love you too much; I dream of you all night long. How could I leave you, my love, how could I forget you, if you are my only delirium in life, darling? Tell me, love, tell me.

Many of the calls to mami expressed deep fears of abandonment, because if mami were to leave, men would be deprived of her comfort and support; for example, Tony Santos cries out, "¡Regresa, mami! ¿O acaso es que no me quieres, mami mía? ¡Vuelve, mami!" (Come back, mami! Is it that you don't love me, mami? Come back, mami!).[6]

Vendiendo Huevo: The Packaging and Selling of Sex

During this same period (late 1970s and 1980s), another category of bachata song became widely popular—*canciones de doble sentido* (double-entendre songs) which were unconcerned with the social or emotional
consequences of sex. They were very much interested in sex itself, however: most of them were extended narratives in which sexual activity was
graphically described by replacing the words for body parts or sexual
acts with words for ordinary objects or activities. The explicit sexual references in these songs clearly distinguished them from both the romantic
bachatas by the likes of Luis Segura as well as from the baladas listened
to by the middle classes, in which singers might make veiled allusions to
a night of bliss or mention a woman's beautiful lips or eyes, but they
would never—like the later bachateros—refer to her sexual organs.

In spite of their sexual subjects, these canciones de doble sentido
were not only about sex; they were also about the mutability and impreci-
sion of language as well: composers played a game of making words
mean what they wanted them to mean, subverting what they were supposed to mean. Listeners, in turn, derived pleasure as much from appreci-
ating the composer's ability to manipulate language as from the sexual
subject of the song itself. Several bachateros specialized in these songs,
among them Tony Santos, Blas Durán, and Julio Angel, and it was they
who produced the most commercially successful bachata songs in the
1980s; clearly there were economic rewards for producing this type of
song. Double entendres had been fairly common in the spicy, topical merengue (mostly in the traditional merengue típico and occasionally in the
orquesta merengue as well), but they had not been used in romantic
music, nor had they been as deliberately (and successfully) used as a commercial strategy.

Interestingly enough, it was not always men's needs and pleasure,
but the woman's as well, that were the subject of these songs. Female
sexual desire in itself—when not complicated by emotional and social
considerations—seems to have been accepted as natural, fun, even if
physically exhausting: doble sentido songs often referred to sexually vo-
racious women who besiege the hapless singer with endless sexual demands. But this seems to have been considered a humorous rather than a
threatening situation. The following example by Tony Santos was typical
of the period:

El aparato de mi mujer

(My woman's gadget)

Singer: Tony Santos

Los vecinos de mi casa	My next-door neighbors
Fueron a la policía	Went to the police
A poner una denuncia	To make a complaint
En contra de la negra mía	Against my negra
Ellos no pueden dormir	They say they can't sleep
Ni de noche ni de día	By night or by day
Porque mi morena vive	Because my morena always
Con la música subí'a	Has the music turned up loud
Y la negra, incomodada	And negra, irritated
Así se puso a gritar	Started to cry
Ella por darme cachú	In order to [ ]
Así se puso a gritar, "Papi	She started to cry out, "Papi!
Súbeme el volúmen	Turn up the volume
Que aquí nadie está asustado	No one here is frightened
Que este aparatico es mío	This little gadget is mine
Yo no lo cogí presta'o"	I didn't borrow it"
Yo le bajaba el volúmen	I turned down the volume
Sin que ella se diera cuenta	Without her realizing it
Pero ella me gritaba	But she cried to me
"Sube hasta que amanezca"	"Turn it up until dawn"
Yo se lo desconectaba	I disconnected it
Y en eso el brazo caía	And the tonearm dropped
Y la negra con sus manos	And negra with her hands
Ella volvía y lo ponía	Put it back again

While these songs certainly objectified women and their bodies, men's organs were objectified as well. Moreover, they also revealed a humorous and frank approach to sexuality very different from the tragic, violent, and contemptuous songs about emotional loss that characterized some of the "straight" songs. In fact, double-entendre songs were never used to condemn women or their sexuality. The following canción de doble sentido by Blas Durán is interesting because it makes explicit reference to a man who, because he cannot find work, has nothing to give his woman but his virility.

El huevero

(The egg man)

Singer: Blas Durán

Hablado: ¡Señores, llegó el huevero, a diez centavos los vendo!	Spoken: Gentlemen, the egg man has arrived, I sell them for ten cents!
Como no encuentro trabajo	Since I can't find a job
Me dedico a vender huevo	I sell eggs

Y a mi morena querida	And it's that way
Con eso yo la mantengo	That I support my dear morena
Todos los días por la mañana	Every day in the morning
Cuando le doy desayuno	When I give her breakfast
Quiere que le busque huevo	She wants me to get her eggs
Y que se lo dé bien duro	And to give them to her real hard
Con pique o sin pique	With or without spice
Yo vendo mis huevos	I sell my eggs
Y bien sabrositos	And very tasty
Que yo tengo mis huevos	My eggs are
Y a la hora de las doce	At the noon hour
Cuando empezamos a comer	When we start to eat
Quiere que le dé más huevo	She wants me to give her more egg
Esa bendita mujer	That blessed woman
Esa mujer que yo tengo	That woman that I have
Le gustan los huevos grandes	She loves big eggs
No le gustan los chiquitos	She doesn't like little ones
Porque se queda con hambre	Because they leave her hungry
Hablado: Lo que tiene uno que hacer para ganarse la vida	Spoken: What one has to do to earn a living!

In the bachatas de doble sentido, women's sexual organs were typically represented by fruits and other foodstuffs (e.g., *ñame* [a tropical tuber], coconut, onions, cotton), while men's penises were more often represented by mechanical devices such as cars, combs, light bulbs, and record players. This suggests that women were considered as belonging to the natural world, while men belonged to the cultural world of man-made objects. On the other hand, although I could not find a single example of a woman's organs being represented by a manufactured object, men's organs were represented not only by mechanical devices but by natural objects as well. For example, penises could also become birds, sticks, or trees, as illustrated in the example below, suggesting that men, unlike women, can straddle the natural and man-made (i.e., cultural) domains.

El pichoncito comelón
(The hungry little pigeon)
Singer: Sergio Correa

Yo tengo un pajarito	I have a little bird
Un pichoncito comelón	A hungry little pigeon
Pero yo vivo solito	But I live all alone
Yo no tengo	I don't have anyone
Quien me atienda mi pichón	To take care of my pigeon

Todos los días bien temprano	Every day very early
Yo tengo que trabajar	I have to go to work
Y él levanta la cabeza	He lifts up his head
El quiere desayunar	He wants some breakfast
El pajarito tan comelón	Such a hungry little bird
Pero yo no tengo	But I don't have anyone
Quien atienda mi pichón	To take care of my pigeon
Yo le pedí a una muchacha	I asked a girl
Comida para el pichón	For food for the pigeon
Pero ella le cogió miedo	But she got scared
Al verlo tan cabezón	When she saw his big head
Estoy buscando una morena	I'm looking for a morena
Que lo sepa comprender	Who will understand him
Para que él coma de noche	So that he can eat at night
Y siempre al amanecer	And always at dawn

That women's sexual organs were substituted by items such as coconuts, onions, cotton, and ñame is related to the common Spanish Caribbean practice of referring to women as food, who are eaten by men in the sex act. This could be seen as crass sexism, with men wishing to obliterate women by consuming them, but other ideas also might be resonating as well. Fruits and vegetables are living, growing things, and hence suggest fertility—unlike manufactured items which offer no possibility of growth or reproduction. The images of fertility and assimilation could be the bachateros' way of symbolizing their relationship with the natural world: by equating women with natural objects and assimilating them, they reestablished their connection with a natural world from which they were becoming increasingly alienated.

The bachatas de doble sentido, like the songs of drinking and carousing, were severely criticized as immoral and indecent. But these songs also represented bachateros' resistance to the double standards of a society obsessed with sex but that feigned respectability by masking its lasciviousness with the trappings of luxury. For example, when the Puerto Rican *vedette* (sex starlet) Iris Chacón visited Santo Domingo in 1987, the major newspapers displayed large photos of her famous ample and shapely buttocks that were worthy of any pornography magazine. Advertisers also consistently employed explicit sexual images to sell products, often using visual double entendres; for example, one television beer commercial alternated pictures of scantily clad women with a beer bottle transparently representing a phallus. Clearly, what determined whether sexually explicit material was accepted or rejected was the class of its consumers rather than the content of the images themselves. As Janice Perlman has pointed out, what is accepted as main-stream or rejected as marginal is "determined less by what is done by the numerical majority or minority, and more by what is done specifically by the middle and upper classes. If the criteria for normalcy were preva-lence-determined rather than class-determined, then playing the numbers would be called mainstream, while attending the opera would be mar-ginal. Clearly this is not the case" (Perlman 1976: 92). Thus, a nearly nude, blonde white woman publicly displaying her body in sexually suggestive poses in an elegant Santo Domingo hotel and in newspaper photographs was acceptable and normal, but the candid, earthy images of sexuality expressed in bachata lyrics—for example, comparing the female genitalia to vegetables—were considered vulgar and deviant.

It is important to remind the reader that while in the 1980s more angry songs of despecho and doble sentido were being produced than in the 1960s, romantic bachatas resembling those of the 1960s continued to be released; using the bachata records I collected in 1986–87 as a sample, about one-third were still of the romantic variety. These romantic songs, however, tended to be extremely tragic, and death was a constant theme:

Dime que me quieres
(Tell me you love me)
Singer: Luis Segura

No sé qué hiciste de mí	I don't know what you've done to me
Para adorarte haces falta	I miss adoring you
Ni de día ni de noche	Neither by day nor by night
Dejo de pensar en ti	Can I stop thinking of you
Aunque estemos distanciados	Although we may be far apart
No sé si piensas en mí	I don't know if you think of me
Porque dicen que otro hombre	Because they say another man
Se ha hecho dueño de ti	Has become your owner
Dime que no es cierto	Tell me it's not true
Dime que es mentira	Tell me it's a lie
Que sólo me quieres a mí	That you love only me
Dime que me quieres	Tell me you want me
Dime que me amas	Tell me you love me
Dime que sí, corazón	Tell me it's so, darling
Aunque digan que eres falsa	Even if they say you are false
Yo no te dejo de hablar	I won't stop talking to you
Tú te has metido en mi alma	You have gotten into my soul
Y no te puedo olvidar	And I can't forget you
Me está matando este amor	This love is killing me
Me está llevando al abismo	Its taking me to the abyss
Desde que te conocí	Since I met you
Me estoy muriendo de amor	I'm dying of love

Because songs such as these still adhered to the generalized roman-tic tradition of the love song and did not invoke the realities of urban shantytown life, they were considered more "refined," more "decent," and these singers themselves tried to disassociate themselves from those who made the "vulgar" bachatas. Nevertheless, while their songs were in fact less sexually explicit than those of their counterparts, they still displayed the exaggerated emotionality and the popular language (as well as the guitar-based music) that defined the genre. The following song by Leonardo Paniagua begins with a poetic and quintessentially romantic lament by a man abandoned by his lover. But in the last verse, the song loses its poetic refinement and expresses sentiments that would be highly unlikely in a balada or bolero.

Tú sin mí
(You without me)
Singer: Leonardo Paniagua

Acuérdate	Remember
Del amor que has cortado	The love you have scorned
De las cosas que eran	The things that were
Todas para ti	All for you
De las últimas caricias	The last caresses
Que me diste	You gave me
Del silencio que dejaste	The silence you left
Al despedirte	When you said good-bye
De las noches que faltaban	The nights that were yet
Por vivir	To be lived
Acuérdate	Remember
¿Quién eres tú sin mí?	Who are you without me?
Acuérdate	Remember
De las luces que se apagan	The lights that are turning out
De la soledad del alma	The solitude of the soul
De lo grande que es tu cama	The wideness of your bed
Sin mi amor	Without my love
De lo largo que es un día	How long a day is
Sin palabras	Without words
De lo triste que es saber	How sad it is to know
Que no te aman	That you are not loved
Del cariño inmenso que te di	The immense affection I gave you
Acuérdate	Remember
¿Quién eres tú sin mí?	Who are you without me?
Dando vueltas por el mundo	Going around the world
A buscar otro querer	Looking for another love
Tú sin mí	You without me
Como perro vagabundo	Like a vagabond dog
Esperando que comer	Looking for something to eat
Tú sin mí	You without me

The Silent Voices: Women in Bachata

Readers will note that I have referred to bachata composers and singers as if they were always men, and my discussion has been focused on perceptions of women expressed by men. This is because, with but a few exceptions, most bachatas were (and continue to be) written and sung by men. I was able to collect the names of several women bachateras: Carmen Francisco, Alida Liranzo "la Chiquitica del Norte," Leonida Alejo, Lisette (a very young woman recording in 1987), Leonida y la Mischer, and Carmen Lidia Cedeño "Zorangis la Soberbia" (Zorangis the arrogant one—who sang with a group called Los Reyes del Este, from San Pedro de Macorís). Only two bachateras, however—Mélida Rodríguez and Aridia Ventura—have become widely known. Otherwise, most bachateras have made so little impact that no one knew much about them, and it was difficult (and in some cases impossible) to locate their records.

Interestingly enough, Mélida Rodríguez, undeniably bachata's most unique and powerful female voice, emerged in the 1960s, bachata's formative period. In addition to having an extraordinarily expressive voice, Mélida composed her own songs. Unfortunately she recorded only one LP and a few singles before she died young sometime in the late 1960s or early 1970s. Nevertheless, the songs she left are truly haunting and compelling statements of her experiences of social and economic dislocation, which, according to Mélida, were suffused with solitude and suffering. In the following song, she alludes to leaving her small hometown to go to the city, where she ends up alone, in a bar, cut off from all family supports.

La solitaria
(Solitary woman)
Singer: Mélida Rodríguez

Ya no te quiero	I don't love you anymore
Tú bien lo sabes	You know it well
No quiero un hombre	I don't want a man
Que me haga sufrir	Who makes me suffer
Me voy de tu lado	I'm leaving your side
Me voy para siempre	I'm leaving for good
Y salgo un día	I'm leaving one day
No nos volvamos a ver	We won't see each other again
Oye, mi amiga	Listen, my friend [female]
Oiga un consejo	Hear this advice
Tú no sabes	You don't know
Lo que me ha pasado a mí	What has happened to me
Míreme los ojos	Look at my eyes

Que ya no tienen lágrimas	They have no more tears
Que por los hombres	Don't let yourself
No se deje sufrir	Suffer for men
No tengo madre	I have no mother
No tengo padre	I have no father
Ni un hermanito	Not even a brother
Que me venga a acompañar	To come and keep me company
Yo vivo triste	I live in sadness
Vivo solitaria	I live in solitude
En mi barquito	In my little boat
Yo me voy a navegar	I'm going to sail off
Dejé a un pueblito solitario	I left a lonely little town
Entré a una barra	I went into a bar
Y me puse a tomar	And started to drink
Ey, cantinero	Hey, barman
Sírvame otra copa	Serve me another glass
Porque mis penas	Because I've come here
Aquí las vengo a ahogar	To drown my troubles

The fact that most of Mélida's songs are situated in the bar was highly unusual, given that most songs by her male counterparts at the time were still in the indefinite and nebulous space of romantic love that I discussed above: in her songs, the bar clearly emerges as a symbol of urban alienation. Mélida also openly embraces drinking (which even today women seldom do publicly) not only as a panacea for emotional pain but as a way to have fun.

Esta noche me quiero emborrachar
(I want to get drunk tonight)
Singer: Mélida Rodríguez

Esta noche me quiero emborrachar	Tonight I'm going to get drunk
Para ver lo que puedo encontrar	To see what I can find
Tengo un hombre muy bueno	I've got a good man
Me da todos sus besos	He gives me all his kisses
Me entrega sus cariños	He gives me his caresses
Y todo el corazón	And all his heart

Even more extraordinarily, she openly discusses her decidedly non-traditional sexuality. She makes quite clear that her sexual behavior is her personal prerogative—she is seeking pleasure—and it is independent of the constraints imposed by men or family. She admits, however, that sexuality cannot substitute for the kind of emotional intimacy and support she desires:

La trasnochadora
(The night owl)
Singer: Mélida Rodríguez

Dicen que soy trasnochadora	They say I'm a night owl
Porque vivo tomando de bar en bar	Because I live drinking from bar to bar
Lo que busco son mitad de cariño	I'm looking half for affection
Y dinero que me puede remediar	And half for money that can heal me
Vivo en un mundo de placeres	I live in a world of pleasures
Perdida en esta oscuridad	Lost in this darkness
Pero se lo pido al infinito	But I ask the infinite
Que me guíe por la claridad	To guide me to the light
Yo no sé lo que me pasa a mí	I don't know what's happening to me
[ ] que yo las tengo así	[ ] I have them this way
Le pido al señor que me acompañe	I ask the lord to stay with me
Y me quite este mal de mis pesares	And to take away this burden of sorrows

In another song she openly admits she engages in extramarital sex (she stops short of declaring herself a prostitute), but she adamantly rejects the social stigma attached to women who are sexually active and refuses to equate a woman's value with the nature or extent of her sexual activity.

La sufrida
(Suffering woman)
Singer: Mélida Rodríguez

Ya no me importa	I don't care anymore
Que me digan qu'estoy mala	If they tell me I'm bad
En esta vida yo me siento feliz	In this life I feel happy
En la otra vida	In another life
Que es la que llaman la buena	The one they call good
Yo sufrí mucho	I suffered a lot
Y por eso la cambié	And that's why I changed it
Ahora me culpan	Now my friends blame me
Mis amigos porque ignoran	Because they don't know
Lo sufrida que yo he sido	The suffering I've endured
Por ser buena	For being good
Yo sólo sé la amargura que se pasa	Only I know how bitter it is
Siendo buena y que me culpen de mala	To be good and be blamed for being bad
Yo soy mala	I'm bad
Y seguiré siendo mala	And I'll keep on being bad
Porque es mucho	Because I suffered
Que sufrí por ser buena	Too much for being good
Es mejor ser mala	Its better to be bad
Y parecer buena	And seem good
Que ser buena	Than to be good
Y que me culpen de mala	And be blamed for being bad

Apart from Mélida, no other woman presented such direct challenges, both to the broad domain of traditional ideas about female sexuality, as well as to the more specific male domain of bachata; since her death, the only bachatera to achieve national stature was Aridia Ventura. While Ventura did in fact sing and compose songs from a female point of view, I was told that many of her songs were composed by others and had been selected by Radhames Aracena, upon whom she remained dependent throughout most of her career. Nevertheless, her songs did provide an alternative viewpoint to that of male bachateros. The following song, like many bachatas, expresses contempt for a former lover, but from a female point of view, and, moreover, it is situated in the feminine sphere—the home—rather than a bar.

La fiesta
(The party)
Singer: Aridia Ventura

Si es cierto que te vas	If it's true you're leaving
Voy a pedirte un favor	I'm asking you a favor
Que revises bien la casa	Check the house well
Lo que te vas a llevar	For what your taking with you
Que no se te olvide nada	Don't forget anything
No tengas que regresar	So you won't have to come back
Y si puedes darte prisa	And if you can, hurry up
Que voy a usar el lugar	I'm going to use your place
Si es cierto que te vas	If it's true you're leaving
Te lo pido por favor	I ask you please
No te tomes tanto tiempo	Don't take such a long time
Cuando vayas a empacar	When you pack
Que no se te olvide nada	Don't forget anything
Que puedas necesitar	You might need
No vaya a ser que por eso	So that to get it
Se te ocurra regresar	You even consider coming back
Si es cierto que te vas	If it's true you're leaving
Una fiesta voy a dar	I'm going to give a party
Porque la verdad sea dicha	Because if the truth be said
Ya no te aguantaba más	I couldn't stand you anymore
Y no intentes regresar	And don't try to come back
Con mi fiesta en la mitad	In the middle of my party
Que pueda ser que te atienda	The one who answers the door
Quien ocupa tu lugar	Could be the one taking your place
Si con alguien tú me ves	If you see me with someone
No te pongas a botear	Don't have a fit
Porque fui tuya sola	Because I was yours alone
Y no me supiste aprovechar	And you didn't appreciate me

Puedes seguir tu camino	You can keep going
Por aquí no vuelvas más	Don't come back here
Porque yo ya tengo en lista	Because I already have on the list
Quien ocupará tu lugar	Someone to take your place

The songs recorded by another bachatera, Carmen Francisco, on the other hand, sometimes echoed the male voice in bachata, condemning women for being treacherous creatures that disturb social order.

Mentirosa y traicionera
(Liar and traitor)
Singer: Carmen Francisco

Tú me vives criticando	You're always criticizing me
Porque soy de esta manera	Because I am the way I am
Dices que no andas conmigo	You say you won't be with me
Porque soy una cualquiera	Because I'm a nobody [i.e., slut]
Pero tú siendo casada	But you, being married
Eres falsa y traicionera	Are false and treacherous
Que teniendo tu marido	Having a husband
A otro hombre te le entregas	You give yourself to another man
Sabiendo que a dos personas	Knowing that for two persons
L'estás buscando problemas	You are creating problems
Y yo mejor prefiero	I'd much rather
Ser de esta manera	Be this way
No quiero ser	I don't want to be
Una señora placentera	A lady of pleasure
Como eres tú	Like you are
Mujer de conciencia negra	Woman of black conscience
Eres mala y mentirosa	You are bad and a liar
Y traicionera	And treacherous

I cannot offer adequate explanations as to why women have been so peripheral in bachata. It has nothing to do with a cultural prejudice against women making music: in fact, the Dominican Republic probably has more women making commercial music than any other Latin American country—and I do not mean just singing and composing, which women commonly do all over Latin America—but playing instruments and constituting the core of the musical ensemble. There have been several all-women merengue orquestas, among them Las Chicas del Can, La Media Naranja, and Las Chicas del País; and in merengue típico, both Fefita la Grande and María Díaz play the lead instrument—the accordion—and the bands go by their names. While some songs sung by these women musicians have been written by men, many have been composed by the women themselves and reflect the female point of view; furthermore, these women, playing trombones, saxophones, congas, accordions, and the other instruments traditionally played by males, have offered a highly potent visual and auditory image of women as artistic creators.

The absence of women in bachata is especially noticeable when compared to other Latin American popular musics associated with the underclasses, in which women have had a more prominent voice. For example, in the guitar-based Colombian *música carrilera* (see Chapter 7)—in which songs were also situated principally in the bar/brothel context—*carrilera* was sung as often by women as by men, often mincing no words in commenting on the irresponsible behavior of men.[7] In bachata, however, women never achieved similar levels of participation.

Moreover, while Dominican men were able to articulate their emotional pain, their vulnerability, their frustrations, and their anger through bachata, women did not have comparable opportunities to voice their concerns and grievances. Given that both men and women experienced the difficulty and anguish of shantytown life, it seems peculiar that bachateros manifested no solidarity with women, no interest in cooperating with them in order to cope with their shared social and economic troubles—as can sometimes be found in rock songs, for example, in which singers invoke the power of a couple's love to overcome economic hardship or social prejudice. On the contrary, women in bachata songs were frequently portrayed as the aggressors and men as victims. Bachateros complained about betrayal, alienation, and hopelessness, yet they did not blame these problems on the economic and political elite who had indeed betrayed and abandoned the poor as a class, but on women. Men certainly knew that even if they could no longer control women as they once had, they nevertheless exercised more power over their own lives than could women, who were even more vulnerable and exploited than men. In bachata songs, men explored the tensions between male and female, owner and property, aggressor and victim, freedom and control, order and chaos. But in failing to understand that the root problems were economic exploitation, unemployment, poverty, overcrowding, and social disruption, these tensions remained unresolved, and women have remained the silent subjects of men's commentary.

Chapter Six

*F*rom the Margins to the Mainstream

s artist and cultural observer Juan Valoy noted, bachata in the 1980s expressed "rage, depression, anguish, conflict, and knives; it smelled of sewer, of street, rum, mud—in short, it was urban music" (personal communication). Bachata's coarseness scandalized the country's middle classes and justified its continued exclusion from the mainstream media and music industry. Nevertheless, bachata would not go away. Throughout the 1980s it continued to grow in popularity and to push against the social and economic barriers that kept it marginalized, breaching them briefly in 1983 and, after being forced back into invisibility by the middle of the decade, breaking through them at the end of the decade. By the early 1990s, bachata had finally become a socially acceptable and economically profitable genre able to compete, if not equally, at least more favorably with other genres of popular music. While today it is indisputable that bachata has "arrived" socially, there is considerable disagreement about who was responsible for bachata's improved status, why it happened, and what it will mean for the future of bachata. In this chapter I address these changes, beginning with a brief survey of the popular music landscape in the early 1980s and then analyzing some of the key events that have contributed to bachata's still ongoing social transformation.

The Music Industry in the 1980s

While the economic crisis of the early 1980s had devastated the country's poor majority, those in the higher end of the music business clearly benefited both from the economic restructuring and later, from the flow of capital that the IMF package brought into the country. For example, when import restrictions were removed, 24-track recording equipment was brought into the country and became available to the well-financed producers of orquesta merengue. In 1982 Tin Valdés, a Cuban immigrant with prior experience in the music business, was the first to bring such equipment to the Dominican Republic, where he established a modern recording studio, Estudios Quisqueya (Tin Valdés, interview). A year later Mrs. Damaris de Peña, owner and president of the advertising agency Young, Rubicam, and Damaris (a subsidiary of the U.S. advertising firm of Young and Rubicam), purchased the facilities of Estudios Fabiola, one of the country's oldest recording studios, adding a modern 24-track recording studio and changing its name to Estudios EMCA. Around 1984 the country's other older studio, Estudios Mozart, was purchased by a company called Audiolab, which introduced the country's third 24-track recorder (July Ruiz and Miguel Pichardo, interviews).[1] These new studios notably benefited the large twelve- to sixteen-piece merengue orquestas because the equipment allowed each instrument to be recorded separately and then mixed according to the preferences and creativity of professional producers and sound technicians. The improved sound quality greatly improved merengue's ability to compete in the international marketplace.

The new recording facilities, however, were not particularly beneficial to bachateros. Since the early 1960s, many bachateros had recorded in Fabiola's relatively inexpensive 8-track studio; but when EMCA upgraded its facilities in 1983 and eliminated the old studio, bachateros were forced to rent the more expensive 16-track studio. After the currency devaluations increased the cost of vinyl and other materials, it became much more difficult for individual musicians and small-scale producers to independently finance recordings, making them more dependent on the established bachata producers such as Radhames Aracena, Rafael Mañon, and José Luis. At the same time, these producers began taking fewer risks with new or unknown musicians. José Luis, for example, became more reluctant to invest in production costs and concentrated on buying finished tapes, leaving it to the musicians to finance their own recording. Whereas this option may have been more profitable for well-established musicians like Luis Segura who could pay for recording costs and then demand better prices for their tapes, aspiring bachateros with no capital were clearly hurt by the new conditions. In many cases, the only alternative was to work with Guarachita, because even though Aracena paid the musicians next to nothing, he did pay for the production process from beginning to end, and Radio Guarachita provided their records with valuable national exposure.

Partly because of their limited capital and partly because they were unfamiliar with the full range of possibilities offered by modern recording technology, bachata producers usually rented only the absolutely minimum time and equipment necessary to put out a record and did not (or could not) pay for studio rehearsals or for extensive post-production mixing. Even when using 16-track equipment, they often did not know how to take advantage of the creative possibilities of the expanded multitrack recording. For years bachata ensembles had recorded simultaneously, using only two or four microphones; in other words, rather than constructing a finished product by layering one track over another as is done in modern recording, bachata songs were recorded in one shot by the whole ensemble. Often, because they did not consider it necessary to use so many tracks for the small—at most six-person—bachata ensemble and because it saved money, some bachateros took advantage of the unused tracks by recording several songs on the same length of tape.

Occasionally the studio's sound engineer made up for producers' lack of technical expertise and served not only as a sound technician but also as a mediator between the musicians' experience and expectations and those of the modern music business. EMCA's sound engineer Miguel Pichardo, for example, occasionally corrected musicians' grammar and pronunciation. Moreover, knowing that bachateros preferred an echolike quality over the dry, clean sound preferred by merengue musicians, Pichardo tried to accommodate them by giving their recordings that particular sound. But most importantly, he was also aware that many bachata musicians had trouble understanding the demands—and opportunities—of the modern recording studio: he advised the musicians on how to improve their recordings by picking up mistakes in musical execution and explaining that they could be easily corrected by rerecording only the problem areas. I personally observed a recording session in which Pichardo explained the concept of sound editing to a musician and tried to get him to repeat a few bars of a song where he had made a small mistake in the first attempt. The musician, whose experience was playing by ear with accompaniment by other instruments, stumbled when trying to replicate only those measures in which he had made the mistake because he lacked the acoustical cues and support he was accustomed to getting from the ensemble as a whole. Clearly, multitrack recording separately presupposed a conceptual leap from traditional ways of thinking about music as a whole to thinking about a song as a composite of separate pieces. Learning to fragment and manipulate the parts of music was part of a larger process of learning to manipulate the reality of social and cultural fragmentation demanded by urban life.

Record pressing was done in the country, either at Guarachita (where it was cheaper) or at Discomundo. Cost-saving measures in this stage of production further reduced the quality of bachata records; for example, producers often used a single stamper for far more pressings than it could properly reproduce, resulting in very poor sounding records. Another practice—used mainly by pirates, but sometimes by producers who for whatever reason no longer had the original stamper—was to make a stamper from a record rather than from a master tape, with truly awful sound quality as a result. The final quality of bachata records, produced in the cheapest possible way, was far inferior to that of records released by the merengue orquestas.

Once records were ready, they were distributed via the informal bachata economy described in Chapter 4. They did not, however, receive any exposure via mainstream media. Like recording studios, the country's broadcast media had been enhanced by sophisticated equipment imported during the 1980s. These improvements, however, benefited only those musics whose producers and promoters were well situated both socially and economically. High-quality recordings of orquesta merengue alternated with the similarly well financed salsa, balada, and rock on the country's fifty-two FM radio stations (Mahan and Straubhaar 1985: 9), most of which were located in urban areas. These radio stations worked only with payola: in order to get a record played, producers or the musicians themselves had to pay the disc jockeys or station managers a certain sum of money. Radio stations, of course, never admitted to these practices, although occasionally something would happen to expose the system. For example, in 1987 Haitian-born merenguero Felicumbé publicly complained that after spending five thousand pesos on payola, the radio stations still refused to play his record; he attributed the boycott of his record to a rival orquesta merenguero, Aníbal Bravo, who supposedly paid the same disc jockeys *not* to play Felicumbé's record.

While bachata musicians or producers were able to buy studio time and manufacture their records when they managed to scrape together enough money, they could not, however, buy (even if they could have afforded the payola) access to urban-based broadcast media that refused out of principle to play bachata because of its low-class associations. It was certainly true that the poorly produced and manufactured bachata records did not sound well on FM, but the barriers to bachata were unquestionably the result of class bias. Luis Medrano, a prominent producer of national and international music, acknowledged the prejudices against bachata that radio station owners and managers held:

> The reasons for this are sociological. It's a division of society, of classes, that is real, that exists. For example, La Z [a major Santo Domingo FM station], which is merengue, won't play you a guitar-based merengue. A station like Radio Mil can't play you a bachata, because it is directed at a determined public. One program director of a radio station played Paniagua when "Chiquitita" was released in 1979. He

put it on against the wishes of the station director and everybody else, and he was criticized severely. (Interview)

Because of these prejudices, those bachateros who did not work with Radhames Aracena were deprived of any opportunity to promote their music to the country's large urban population and had to settle for whatever air play they could get on rural radio stations. As a result, bachata producers and sometimes the musicians themselves who were able to finance trips traveled to towns all over the country, personally visiting radio disc jockeys willing to play bachata and encouraging them—with small cash payments—to play their records. Even in those areas, bachata was often limited to specific shows at certain times of day—usually at odd hours such as very early in the morning.

Bachata was also excluded from television, which was worse than its exclusion from radio because there were no analogs to small rural radio stations to provide it with alternative broadcast outlets. Dominicans of all economic strata watched television—in 1984 there were over 550,000 television sets for a population of approximately 6 million (Mahan and Straubhaar 1985: 2)—making it the most effective vehicle for exposing music to the widest possible public. The country had seven color television stations, plus direct cable service from the United States in some urban and tourist areas. Almost 20 percent of Dominican programming was music (Mahan and Straubhaar 1985: 13), most of which consisted of performances by merengue orquestas and balada musicians. Among the most popular programs were noon-hour variety shows featuring merengue orquestas promoting their current hits and their upcoming live performances, which gave them invaluable nationwide publicity.

Although television did provide broad public exposure for merengue orquestas and balada singers, live performances were becoming a privilege reserved for the elite. Except for annual events such as the fiestas patronales and Santo Domingo's Festival de Merengue—when municipalities paid the sizable band fees—most live performances by merengue orquestas took place in exclusive clubs that most Dominicans could not enter because cover charges and beverage costs were excessively high, and dress codes requiring elegant attire were strictly enforced. In 1987 the average fee to enter a nightclub along Santo Domingo's fashionable *malecón* was 15 to 25 pesos (3 pesos equalled US$1), while a special performance at one of the luxury hotels might cost 30 to 40 pesos. Ticket prices to performances by international balada singers appearing in Santo Domingo were even higher, ranging from 60 to 150 pesos per person.

The print media was as active as television and FM radio in promoting orquesta merengue—and excluding bachata. All the major newspapers included daily entertainment sections in which merengue industry

news figured prominently, and weekly hit parade lists, dominated by orquesta merengue (followed by balada, and then by rock and salsa in
about equal proportions), announced current hits. These lists, however,
did not reflect the numbers of records sold, but rather—according to
many individuals who worked in the music business—the amount of
payola that had been paid: a number-one spot on a given newspaper's hit
parade cost a certain amount of money, second place somewhat less, and
so on. While the extent of payola in the Dominican Republic has not been
documented, the fact is that no matter how many tens of thousands of
records a hit bachata may have sold, no bachata *ever* appeared on a hit
parade list. Even if bachata musicians or producers could have afforded
the costs of being included on such lists, the disreputable bachata would
never have been allowed to appear side-by-side with the other socially
acceptable musics.

Because bachateros never received any royalties from sales of their
records, they had to depend on live performances to survive. In the 1980s
almost all the bachateros who had achieved any stature resided in the
capital, but they traveled frequently to the provinces, where they were
much in demand. Interestingly, musicians actually were paid better and
played in better venues in the provinces than they did in Santo Domingo—a deviation from the general rule that musicians do better playing in the city than in provincial areas. When performances did take place
in Santo Domingo, they happened in small, often seamy bars located in
very poor neighborhoods and were almost never announced in the newspapers or on major radio stations; they were strictly neighborhood affairs.
Such low-class establishments, even those having certain features that
gave them more "class" (e.g., revolving mirrored balls on the ceiling, public-address systems, murals painted on the walls), could not charge their
clients more than a two- or three-peso cover charge. Limited to such cash-
poor venues, most bachata musicians, even the more successful ones,
never made much money and remained, on the whole, as poor as their
fans. In the mid-1980s, for example, even Luis Segura—who had sold
hundreds of thousands of records in the course of his career—could be
found playing in sleazy brothels.

There was one other frequently overlooked aspect of the Dominican
music business in which bachata was also at a distinct disadvantage compared to merengue—the *patrocinio* (sponsorship) system, which consolidated a mutually beneficial relationship among popular music, the
advertising industry, and its largest clients: the beer, rum, and cigarette
industries. The close relationship between popular music and the cigarette and alcohol industries in the Dominican Republic is hard to overem-
phasize: they are advertised together, consumed together, and support
each other economically. Almost every musical event of any importance

(as well as sports events and other sorts of public gatherings such as art gallery openings and academic conferences) is sponsored by companies manufacturing these products. In the patrocinio system, alcohol and cigarette companies sponsor musical events by providing advertising in exchange for an agreement that the host establishment will sell only their brand of rum, beer, and/or cigarettes at that performance; beverage companies often include a few free cases of liquor for the establishment to sell as well.[2]

Patrocinio was most often offered for performances by merengue orquestas because of their social status and economic importance. Yet it is telling that, in spite of the fact that the country's largest consumer group liked bachata, the alcohol and cigarette companies and their publicity agencies made few attempts to appeal to them by sponsoring their preferred music. Because the advertising companies were interested in creating images of sophistication, glamour, fantasy, and spectacle, they shunned association with bachateros, who had little to offer the image-making process. As a result, sponsorship of bachata events was not only less frequent but less generous as well. According to publicist Manuel Rodríguez, the companies and agencies did not usually seek out bachata ensembles; when they did sponsor bachata performances, it was usually by request of the musicians, who hoped that the free publicity (and the possibility of a few cases of free liquor) would encourage club owners to contract them. The company would not, however, provide the same level of publicity in the media as they did on behalf of the orquestas (interview).

It is worth digressing here to note that the liquor companies cynically took advantage of the increasing despair within that large segment of the population (70 percent) that was at or below the poverty line by asserting, through their advertising campaigns, that their products offered solace and escape. Not surprisingly, in spite of worsening economic conditions that characterized the late 1970s and 1980s, production and consumption of alcohol rose dramatically. In this context, it seems hypocritical that bachata songs such as Teodoro Reyes' "Homenaje a los borrachones" (Homage to drunks) (cited in Chapter 4), which celebrated drinking, were considered so offensive to polite Dominican society. Clearly, the directness of Reyes' lyrics posed a deliberate challenge to the values of a society that criticized bachata's association with drinking yet accepted the advertising industry's aggressive promotion of alcohol for profit.

The combination of less sophisticated recording techniques; poorer manufacturing quality; the inability to obtain nationwide exposure and effective media promotion; and the low profits available to bachata musicians, producers, and distributors all left bachata at a disadvantage in relationship to orquesta merengue. As a result, bachata's musicians, producers, promoters, and consumers were circumscribed within a single socio-economic class and context. In contrast, orquesta merengue, improved by technological advances in musical recording and favored by extensive exposure via the mass media, underwent a period of rapid expansion. In the 1980s, merengue achieved an unchallenged hegemony in the national market as well as among Dominican migrants in the United States, where many orquestas gained access to the lucrative international Latin music market. The number of orquestas increased dramatically as musicians and their promoters jumped on the bandwagon: in 1975 there were forty merengue bands registered with the musicians' union, AMUCABA; by 1987 there were over eighty. Transcending class and even national boundaries, the more successful bands obtained performance contracts not only in New York City and Puerto Rico, but also in Panama, Colombia, Venezuela, even Europe, eventually surpassing salsa as the most popular Latin dance music. These orquestas, no longer just musical ensembles but incorporated businesses, set up luxurious offices from which to coordinate their recording, performance, and promotional activities. Merengue's international success was so extraordinary that people began referring to it as "el boom de merengue" (Fernández 1986).

Monday Night Fever: La Fiebre de Amargue

Much as those in the mainstream music business might have wished bachata would go away, its popularity kept on growing among the country's poor majority, competing ever more successfully with the socially acceptable musics they were promoting such as orquesta merengue, salsa, and balada. In 1983 Luis Segura released a highly melodramatic but enormously successful record entitled "Pena" (Grief), which outsold every other recording in the mainstream market, sending bachata—for a brief time—into middle-class venues, thereby encroaching into merengue and balada's domains. For almost two years, bachata musicians were able to enjoy limited access to venues that had been closed to them in the 1970s. As bachata made its entry into society, however, its name was first changed to *música de amargue* (music of bitterness), thereby disassociating it—and its new middle-class listeners—from the social stigma associated with the disreputability of bachata. For example, one journalist noted: "For the last few months a number of songs and musical arrangements have been heard that conform to the artistic style called *amargue*, which is also qualified by others as *bachata*, although in our way of thinking it doesn't necessarily mean the same, because the first term denotes pain and sorrow and the second, carousing and vulgarity" (Vicioso 1983, translation mine).

A number of explanations can be offered for bachata's change in fortune. Some have attributed it to the success of Luis Segura's "Pena," which reportedly sold over 200,000 copies, crossing over into the mainstream and bringing bachata to the attention of the media. Luis Dias, however, speculated that the bitterness expressed by the bachateros resonated with the suffering being experienced by segments of the population who were feeling the effects of the IMF-induced economic crisis and feeling out of touch with the increasingly glamorous and international orquesta merengue while their own fortunes were declining (interview). Longtime bachata guitarist Edilio Paredes, on the other hand, claimed that it was he, Ramón Cordero, and Ramón Cabrera "el Chivo sin ley" (the Outlaw goat) who not only gave bachata its new name, but who were responsible for introducing bachata into the social mainstream via a regular Monday-night show, featuring bachata, that they organized in a more upscale restaurant than had been typical for bachata performances:

> That Monday I started thinking. . . . Let me talk to Ramón [Cordero], because we should start a show somewhere, a show with Ramón Cordero, the Chivo playing güira, with me and other singers of the genre. And we formed the show. Then Cuco Valoy's sound technician said, "I'll get the place." We started the show in Los Minas, in the Alma Rosa area [a working-class neighborhood] on Venezuela Avenue, at a restaurant called El Túnel [the tunnel]. And that's where that kind of music started. Here they call it bachata. The meaning it had been given was like they wanted to lower it. One night we were resting there in Los Minas. It was full of people. After we started the show, some girls went by and asked, "What's happening here?" and I say, "The bachateros are here." That weighed a lot on me because I know what bachata is and that its meaning is a little party, a pastime. But here it was given a very low meaning, something else, different. And I said to Ramón, "Compadre, let's change the name. Let's call the show 'Lunes de amargue' [Amargue Monday]." And that's how we started the "Lunes de amargues." And the name bachata has been disappearing. Now we are amargue singers, but before we were bachateros. (Paredes, interview)

Shortly thereafter Edilio Paredes left for New York with Leonardo Paniagua, leaving the show in the hands of his brother Nelson Paredes, Ramón Cordero, and Ramón Cabrera. The musicians they invited to participate in the Monday shows at El Túnel were those who had already established a name for themselves, such as Aridia Ventura and Oscar Olmo. Shortly thereafter, the media noted that amargue singers were being contracted to perform in other middle-class restaurants in the center of the city: Ramón Cabrera played in El Rincón, Luis Segura nearby in Ricardo's, and some, including Tony Santos, even played in the elite Sheraton Hotel. That same year, 1983, a *disco-piscina* (a club/bar with an outdoor dance floor and a swimming pool) in the nearby town of San Cristóbal began hiring musicians such as Tony Santos for group shows known as "Viernes de Amargue" (Amargue Friday) which were well attended by the local elite as well as by clients who came all the way from Santo Domingo. A flurry of newspaper and magazine articles on bachata appeared and referred to the phenomenon as *la fiebre de amargue* (amargue fever).

Bachata musicians who had previously been denied access to television suddenly became invited guests on variety shows. The motives for giving television air time to bachata musicians, however, were questionable. Some people suggested that including bachateros on television shows was a populist move to attract more viewers from bachata's wide audience. Others claimed that bachata musicians were put on the air as *bufeo* (buffoonery), to add a comic touch to the shows through the not-so-subtle technique of pretending to take them seriously but clearly mocking their exaggeratedly tragic lyrics and their attempts to project urban sophistication. (I myself saw a videotape of one such show and can attest that the musicians were in fact ridiculed, being used as foils for the interviewer to display his wit.) A magazine article by José Rafael Sosa commenting on bachata's presence on television reveals the extent to which the media pundits still scorned bachata: "The production of the so-called Festival de Amargue early this year on 'El show de mediodía' [the noon-hour show] revealed the preference of the middle class for the amargue song. In this festival—a sort of musical comedy—the amargue song was parodied, and it was through the same means [i.e., parody] that the name appeared referring to that type of music" (Sosa 1983, translation mine).

At no time did anyone suggest that the music had any inherent value and therefore the same right as any other music to be on the air. Nevertheless, regardless of the motives television producers may have had to include bachata in their shows, these television appearances unarguably gave bachata and its musicians a level of national public exposure they had never had.

At the height of the amargue boom, Luis Segura was invited by students to give a concert at the Universidad Autónoma de Santo Domingo, the nation's largest public university. A second concert that was to include Luis Segura and "el Chivo sin ley" was planned by the employees' union but was prohibited by the dean on the grounds that such music was unacceptable in a university setting. The controversy that followed gave those journalists who came to bachata's defense the opportunity to decry the economic injustices and deep social cleavages that existed in the country. These may have been crocodile tears shed for the benefit of a reading public hostile to urban intellectuals, but it did put journalists, at least for a while, on the side of bachata and its constituency.

Bachateros did not absorb the criticism passively. Tony Santos released a merengue de guitarra referring to these attacks:

A vida o muerte
(To life or death)
Singer: Tony Santos

Nuevo decreto han tirado en el país	A new decree has been made in the country
¡Ay señores, póngale mucha atención!	Gentlemen, pay attention!
De fusilar la gente de guitarra	To shoot the guitar people
Qu'están acabando con los combos	Who are wiping out the [merengue] combos
Y con los show	And the shows
Tienen orden de fusilamiento	They have orders to shoot
Ay señores, qué barbaridad	Gentlemen, what barbarism
Tienen orden de fusilamiento	They have orders to shoot
Pero este plan no se les va a dar . . .	But this plan isn't going to work . . .
¡Que estamos aquí, pegados!	We are here, sticking fast!

Throughout 1983 the print media commented frequently on "amargue fever," although not in the entertainment section along with the trade news on merengue and balada but, rather, in essays commenting on the sudden appearance of bachata in "polite society," which revealed the deep contradictions and insecurities people felt about being in contact with a music so long associated with the underclasses. Clearly, while the phenomenon could be dismissed either as a momentary fascination with the forbidden, as comic relief, or as an antidote to a difficult economic situation, bachata challenged mainstream society's comfortable representations of itself, where it came from, and where it was going. Journalist Carlos Batista's musings on the meaning of the amargue boom are particularly interesting in this regard: he acknowledged the fact that many people were familiar with bachata and that this reality should legitimize listening to the music; nevertheless, he continued to express hostility toward the music, which he clearly feared might actually establish itself among the middle classes:

> Bachata fever, is it falling or rising? Today amargue is on its feet, but the indifference into which it is falling is notable. And this is because all fevers fall. The high tide of bufeo recedes, leaving bachata in its previous place, normalcy. If it is in fact true that all of us have a trace of nostalgia inside, the mark of one or another bachata that once delighted or gladdened us in the past, it is no less true that much of the expectation and expansion that the genre took constituted an escape door for the middle class, which saw or sees itself marginalized from

expensive shows. And that's the way it is because, although the middle class likes it, they do not consider, nor do we believe that they will consider, bachata to be their favorite music, and much less will they hold their performers as models or paradigms. Their desires and aspirations, generally ascending, in truth do not correspond to the situation that bachateros express. (Batista 1983, translation mine)

Amargue fever, unfortunately, did not last very long. While the regular Monday and Friday amargue shows continued for a while, by 1984 amargue was no longer newsworthy, and shortly thereafter the amargue shows in middle-class venues were discontinued. It is hard to ascertain whether the amargue boom was a creation of the media, whether it resulted from a cluster of particularly successful songs, or whether there were sociological reasons for its temporary acceptance. On one hand, I resist crediting bachata's success in 1983–84 to the media's marketing strategies rather than to the recording and performing accomplishments of the musicians; but on the other, the amargue boom was so short-lived that it is hard to escape the conclusion that it was, in fact, a simple case of media exploitation, after which bachata was again relegated to what Batista euphemistically called "normalcy."

As for why the boom was so short, it is quite likely that those interested in promoting the rising orquesta merengue actively worked to remove the increasingly successful bachata from the competitive arena. A statement by disc jockey Willie Rodríguez reveals how threatening bachata had been to merengue in 1983: "In '83 the merengue achieved the highest sales and surpassed the bachata, the worst of enemies, for the first time" (Rodríguez 1986: 26, translation mine).

When Rodríguez made this statement in 1986, he knew quite well that bachata was no threat to merengue, because by 1985 bachata had been pushed back into its working-class contexts and to its inferior and almost invisible status in mainstream Dominican society. It was receiving absolutely no air play on Santo Domingo radio stations (with the exception of Radio Guarachita) or on Spanish-language radio in New York. Bachata performances were almost never announced in newspapers, and were seldom broadcast on television, much less ever presented to tourists as an example of local folk culture. In fact, bachata was so invisible that tourists could easily visit the country and never even detect its existence. This exclusion was not accidental, but actively enforced, as the following personal anecdote reveals. In 1986 I was eating dinner in a pleasant but by no means luxurious restaurant in a tourist section of the city of Puerto Plata when two guitar players entered and made the rounds of the tables, singing old guitar favorites and asking for contributions. When they arrived at our table and I requested a bachata, the musicians replied that while they themselves liked and played bachata they were forbidden by the manager to play it for the customers.

Bachata was not the only music excluded from competing equally in the marketplace: the rural merengue típico, a music that shared a comparable niche in the music business, was confronted with many of the same obstacles to its dissemination. Nevertheless, most Dominicans still held merengue típico in fond regard as a quaint symbol of the country's rural past. Bachata, on the other hand, was an uncomfortable reminder that there were many—far too many—who had not benefited from the country's rapid modernization and technological progress. Bachata's performers and audience exhibited none of the tasteful sophistication and discrete worldliness that the dominant classes would have liked the country as a whole to display as evidence of its progress and modernity; nor did they display the predictable traditional values and social deference of peasants in former times. These people lived in shantytowns in ramshackle houses constructed of discarded materials, they dressed in cheap, unfashionable clothes, and they sought escape and entertainment not by listening to sophisticated music in the privacy of their homes or private clubs, but by listening to bachata at neighborhood colmados or in seedy bars. In response, the dominant classes created negative stereotypes with which to justify their indifference to the plight of those who were economically destitute and whose social world had been turned upside down by the experiences of migration and urbanization: they charged that the poor were ignorant, violent, vulgar, tasteless drunkards and whoremongers, and they used their preference for bachata as proof of their degeneracy. One unashamedly explicit articulation of disgust for bachata's practitioners was made by disc jockey Willie Rodríguez to a group of media figures and entertainment journalists in 1986: "Are we going to allow the bachata to continue to be our maximum representative on an international level? . . . I prefer the Spanish caricature of el Záfiro [a merenguero who sang in flamenco style] to the distortion and alienation of our things that Luis Segura brings, of inciting violence, alcohol consumption, a series of negative things, and fomenting pain at the same time" (Rodríguez 1986: 22, translation mine).

Bachata, far from being an international representative of the Dominican Republic, was a virtual pariah in its own country. Rodríguez's motives for making such a patently unfair and untrue statement seem clear: to rearticulate and reaffirm the prevailing social disapproval of the genre and to insure and justify its continuing exclusion from the mainstream media and marketplace.

Bachata Persists

In 1987, one journalist wondered about the meteoric rise and fall of bachata in an article entitled "¿Qué es de ellos?" (What has become of them?). Yet, as the author noted, bachata was still widely popular among the country's poorest and most dispossessed citizens:

> It's been a while since I've heard anything from the bachateros. But they are there. Selling records and performing. Their song, which corresponds to what the sociologists calls subculture, has a flavor of the people not given by the musically sophisticated balada. Bachata has its idols, and what's curious is that the idols are the most lewd in their songs, which are almost always composed by them. Although it's only fair to acknowledge that there are idols, such as Luis Segura, who have "refined" songs. There were others in the recent past, such as José Manuel Calderón and Inocencio Cruz, who achieved leadership with songs with decent themes. (*Tarde Alegre,* January 10, 1987, translation mine)

Indeed, in spite of the continuing obstacles and handicaps that bachateros encountered in their efforts to produce, promote, and distribute their music, bachata was surprisingly successful: major hits sold 50,000 copies, while average hits sold around 10,000; even minor hits sold about 2000. Moreover, bachata frequently outsold orquesta merengue and balada in the domestic market, as merengue producer Luis Medrano observed in 1987: "The middle/lower class are 45 percent if not 50 percent of the market in record sales. The distribution of bachata is better than that of balada and salsa. . . . A Paniagua sells more records than José José or Julio Iglesias or any other national soloist" (interview).

Unlike Medrano, many Dominicans involved in the music business did not care to acknowledge the ability of bachateros to sell records. Entertainment journalists, for example, announced the sale of 25,000 orquesta merengue records as if it were a major accomplishment. Yet when bachateros had major hits such as Leonardo Paniagua's late 1970s "Chiquitita" or Luis Segura's 1983 "Pena," each of which sold far more than 50,000 copies, they neither appeared on a hit parade list nor were mentioned in a music review.[3]

The informality of the bachata business made it difficult to assess bachata's performance in the marketplace with any precision. Record vendors, for example, saw no reason to keep careful records since they bought their stock in very small quantities and turned it over quickly. I did meet one owner of a somewhat larger stall in Santo Domingo who kept a list of what he sold in a school notebook, but he reported that when the notebook filled up, he threw it out and began a new one. Producers were more likely to know or approximate how many of their records were actually sold because they could keep track of the number of disks pressed; the smaller producers, however, did not keep such records. The pressing companies, which were formal businesses with more thorough accounting procedures, might know how many copies of a particular bachata record had been produced in their facilities; but because it was not unusual for bachata producers to take the stampers to different companies for successive pressings, their figures might not reflect total sales. Complicating any efforts to arrive at exact sales figures, several stampers of the same record might be owned by different individuals, each of whom would order his own pressings. (This was the case, for example, with Luis Segura's major hit song "Pena," of which nobody knows for sure how many copies have been sold.)

Only Radhames Aracena was likely to know exactly how many records he sold because his company was in every way a well-organized and well-financed participant in the formal economy. Nevertheless, he absolutely refuses to discuss these figures with anyone, and he is said to have shunned TV interviews because he does not like being asked specific questions about his business. In the extensive interviews he gave me, he was very forthcoming about the details of Guarachita's history, but he never once mentioned a sales figure. I asked José Luis, whose expanding business seemed to be in transition between the informal and formal economies, about his sales figures; he answered, "Yo no trabajo contabilizado" (I don't work with accounts).

Musically, the bachata songs that were popular in the 1980s sounded very different from their predecessors. Most of them were still based on the classic four-four bolero rhythm, but many were speeded up, giving the music a completely new sense of time. These songs were highly danceable—not in the slow and dignified embrace that characterized dancing to *música suave* (soft, romantic music)—but in an entirely new style in which dancers could engage in the sort of choreographic display typical of merengue dancing such as turns, elaborate footwork, and exaggerated pelvic movements. Bachata had become *música bailable* (dance music) as well as *música romántica*.

In addition to increasing the tempo of the bolero-based bachatas, bachata conjuntos began enlivening their performances by including guitar-based merengues in their repertoires. Blas Durán was one of the pioneers of this innovation: more than any other bachatero, he was responsible for dramatically altering the sound of both bachata and merengue and for popularizing the modernized bachata-merengues on a mass scale. Durán himself did not play an instrument, but he was a brilliant composer, masterfully combining the streetwise, picaresque quality of merengue lyrics with bachata's earthy double entendres. He was also an inspired performer, taking advantage of being unfettered by an instrument to work the audience with jokes and antics, and he understood the appeal of novelty:

> I like to mix music to see what comes out. Not to tire the audience. The public can't always be singing the same thing. And notice that

the orquestas that have always played the same thing have fallen. You have to vary for the public, even though it may be with the same voice, but varied. Give them something cheerful, give them a little something sad, give them something else with applause, give them this with jokes. You see, even marriages get tired, if the man is always in the house. (Durán, interview)

Durán first experimented with an electroacoustic guitar on his 1985 single "El motorcito" (The little motorcycle), a sexual double entendre in a fast bolero rhythm that did not make a significant impact. In 1987, however, he put together an expanded ensemble of eight musicians with the name Blas Durán y los Peluches, and released an electric guitar-based merengue, "Consejo a las mujeres" (Advice to women). Durán jokingly introduced this song with the phrase "¡Fuera de ancho, que llegó el estrecho!" (Out with the wide, make way for the thin!). This seemingly nonsensical wisecrack, however, cloaked a David-to-Goliath message to the mainstream music system that they had better move over to make room for bachata. As he explained: "Wide means fat people, and narrow a skinny one. In other words, you get out, because I've arrived, and I'm better than you are" (interview). Durán's boast was right on the mark: his new style of bachata—electric, energetic, sassy, and danceable—touched a nerve in bachata's audience, and "Consejo a las mujeres" became one of bachata's biggest hits. Moreover, by successfully incorporating the long-popular merengue into bachata, Durán directly challenged the orquestas on their previously exclusive turf.

"Consejo a las mujeres" was a milestone for several reasons. Durán had begun his recording career in 1969, but unlike other bachateros, he had also worked as a singer in orquesta merengue ensembles. As a merengue musician he had learned the basic techniques of multitrack recording and sound mixing from his producer, Bienvenido Rodríguez. When Durán recorded "Consejo a las mujeres," he did not have the band record simultaneously, as bachata ensembles had always done before, but rather, he laid down the rhythm track and later added the voices, as he had seen done by merengue orquestas. He had his guitarist play an electric guitar and emphasized its twangy sound in the mix.[4] He also used the brighter, more metallic güira instead of a maraca, and he added an electric bass and a tambora to the ensemble. His double entendre lyrics were bawdy but clever and humorous, and he spiced up the song with catchy phrases, including the "¡mujeres hembras!" (female women) that came to identify the song. The end result was a record with a novel and fresh—however unpolished—sound that took the country by storm. The record became one of the best-selling records of the decade (second only to Luis Segura's "Pena"), selling over 100,000 copies in the Dominican Republic alone, and many others in the United States and Puerto Rico

(Blas Durán, interview). In 1988 he released another electric guitar-based merengue called "La arepa," which also featured a prominent (and cheap-sounding) electric keyboard. Durán's new electric sound—and its extraordinary success—inspired others to imitate his style, including a younger generation of bachata musicians who became bachata's superstars in the 1990s.

By the end of the 1980s electric guitar-based merengue had become a staple, with most bachateros routinely including it in both their recordings and live performances.[5] In order to play merengue, many bachata ensembles simply added a tambora and güira to their existing instrumentation, using them only when they played merengues. Others, however, eliminated the bongo and maracas altogether and substituted merengue percussion instruments—playing the tambora upright instead of sideways to approximate the sound of the bongos and imitating the sound of the maracas with the güira. The appearance of these guitar-based merengues had two important consequences. First, the guitar-based merengue, which had been practically forgotten in urban contexts, was reintroduced as a viable style of popular music. Second, the modern guitar-based merengues blurred the previously cleaner distinctions between bachata as slow romantic music that was contrasted with the faster dance merengue.

Including both fast and slow bachatas as well as merengues in bachata performances allowed bachateros to better compete with merengue orquestas, whose star had risen throughout the 1980s, but which had begun losing some of those qualities, such as its locally based themes and language, that had made it so appealing to Dominican audiences. Merengue groups had also begun incorporating sophisticated new instruments, particularly synthesizers, into their ensembles, which altered the music's sound textures. Moreover, rather than using original material, many orquestas resorted to recording cover versions—arranged as merengues—of foreign music, especially baladas, that had already proven successful abroad (a practice locally known as *fusilamiento*). These strategies were intended to appeal to diverse international audiences, but they gave merengue a homogenized, formulaic sound that in the opinion of many merengue fans was moving merengue too far from its roots. The ambivalence of Dominican audiences toward the increasingly internationalized merengue presented bachata with new opportunities, which bachateros were quick to exploit. But more important, at a time when the cost of attending dances with live merengue orquestas had become unaffordable for many, bachata met a real need for live dance music in the barrio. As Blas Durán observed:

Any rag of an orquesta charges 4, 5,000 pesos, whereas a small group of ours, a good one—because I'm not saying that all are good; some guitar groups are turkeys that no one could listen to, but there are good groups, with quality, with class—and we play for 1600, 2000, and here in the capital they pay less, 600, 800 [pesos]. To get together 500 pesos [for a band] is not easy. But you have to play for the people, the people want to dance, too. If the people can't dance with these orquestas that charge so much money, well, they take a Blas Durán, a Luis Segura. And people dance, because these musicians have a name, and the people like that. (Interview)

As the 1980s proceeded, bachata hits continued to appear, such as Julio Angel's 1985 "El salón" (The salon), Tony Santos' 1986 "Amarilis, échame agua" (Amarilis, throw water on me), and then Blas Durán's 1987 mega-hit "Consejo a las mujeres." The media could no longer completely ignore these immensely popular bachatas, and as a result, their performers were very occasionally invited to appear on television, and they received a little air play on a few of the major radio stations as long as their popularity lasted. Long-playing records (never 45 RPM singles) by bachateros Leonardo Paniagua and Luis Segura, whose romantic lyrics were not found to be offensive to middle-class tastes, began to appear in some (but by no means all) mainstream music stores—although these records were never displayed prominently along with the other recent releases. By the end of the 1980s bachateros like Durán and Segura who had hit songs—and business savvy—were obtaining distribution contracts with U.S.-or Puerto Rico-based Latin labels such as Kubaney or Borinquen in order to market their music to Dominican migrants abroad; and they began traveling to New York City, where they played to Dominican audiences in small restaurants and clubs, usually serving as opening acts for merengue and salsa orquestas.

Winds of Change

While writing the conclusions to my dissertation in 1989, I speculated about the potential of Durán's style: "It is too early to know what effect Durán's new sound will have on the bachata genre as well as on merengue (which has never before used the electric guitar—although given the proven success of Durán's formula some merengueros might well experiment). But because of the insistent urban feel of Durán's recent songs, I predict that if bachata ever 'crosses over' it will be through songs such as his." Within a year of that statement, bachata was indeed "crossing over" in formerly unimaginable ways, and within another two years, bachata had become widely accepted and even fashionable not only within the Dominican Republic itself, but in other Latin American countries and Europe as well.

The stylistic innovations introduced by Durán and his successors certainly contributed to bachata's widening popularity among its tradi-

tional consumers, but they were not by themselves responsible for bachata's improved social status; help came from unexpected sources. In the
1980s, bachata's steady and growing popularity among the country's
poor majority and its periodic irruptions into the national consciousness
began attracting the attention of four musicians—Luis Dias, Sonia Silvestre, Víctor Víctor, and Juan Luis Guerra—all of whom were part of a gen-
erational cohort of progressive intellectuals, artists, and musicians who
had come of age in the 1970s and were collectively referred to as La Generación de los 70 (the '70s generation). With the exception of Guerra (who
was slightly younger than the other three), these musicians had begun
their careers in the nueva canción movement, performing together or separately in avant-garde venues such as Casa de Teatro and La Junta and
participating in the 1974 Siete Días con el Pueblo Concerts (see Chapter
4). Many of the artists and intellectuals among the Generación de los 70
had been raised in rural areas and were familiar with bachata, but at the
time no musician took bachata seriously as an idiom for his or her own
work. They occasionally sang it in informal gatherings, however—"partly
to laugh, although we also enjoyed it" (Sonia Silvestre, interview).

Even though nueva canción had declined as a musical and social
movement by the 1980s, Silvestre, Dias, and Víctor Víctor had individually emerged with reputations as political radicals and/or social noncon-
formists, but nonetheless as "serious" musicians. Silvestre had become a
successful singer, winning numerous music awards both within the country and abroad (e.g., Chile's Viña del Mar song competition). Víctor Víctor
had become well known as a canta-autor (singer-songwriter) as well as a
composer for other musicians. Silvestre and Víctor Víctor both worked
primarily in the ballad format, although their work continued to bear the
imprint of nueva canción styling. In contrast, Luis Dias, who in the 1970s
had been a member of the musical ensemble/study group Convite, had
turned his attention to musical experiments combining Dominican folk
genres with U.S. blues, jazz, rock, punk, and heavy metal, working with
some of the most creative and talented young musicians from the Generación de los 70. First with a group called Madora and later with another
band called Transporte Urbano, Dias performed audacious experimental
music that was much appreciated by his avant-garde colleagues but that
was incomprehensible both to the Dominican public at large and to the
mainstream musical establishment. Even though Dias was recognized as
a brilliant composer—well-known merengue musicians such as Fernan-
dito Villalona had major hits with his songs—he himself recorded very
little; moreover, his refusal to conform to mainstream musical aesthetics
and his unorthodox lifestyle made him the bête noire of the popular
music scene.

Juan Luis Guerra, born and reared in Santo Domingo, was still in his teens during the height of the nueva canción movement and at the time had been more interested in rock than nueva canción. As an aspiring young guitar player, however, he had moved in the same circles with and was influenced by the musicians and intellectuals of the Generación de los 70, and on numerous occasions he had performed with Silvestre and Víctor Víctor. After studying music in the Dominican national conservatory and then in Boston at the Berklee College of Music, Guerra formed an a cappella group in 1984 collectively known as "4:40" (referring to the standard practice of tuning A at 440 vibrations per second), whose vocal style was reminiscent of the U.S. group Manhattan Transfer. Guerra's arrangements, however, combined Dominican folk genres with U.S. and Brazilian jazz, clearly reflecting the intellectual influences of Luis Dias and Madora (Tejeda 1993). Juan Luis Guerra and 4:40's first recording, "Soplando," did not do well economically, but in 1985 the group signed with Karen Records, whose astute music producer Bienvenido Rodríguez encouraged Guerra to try something more economically viable—merengue.

Guerra, whose interests were inclined more toward jazz, was initially reluctant to work with the notoriously commercialized merengue, but he agreed to try. Applying his formal musical training to his compositions, Guerra produced merengues far more sophisticated and complex than the formulaic products recorded by other merengue orquestas. At the same time, by drawing on his intellectual roots in the nueva canción movement, his merengues were solidly based in regional styles, and his lyrics utilized the rich colloquial language of merengue's Dominican audience to comment on a variety of issues of concern to ordinary Dominican citizens, from the difficulties of obtaining a U.S. visa to the persistence of class divisions within Dominican society. By the end of the decade Guerra and 4:40 had released several long-playing recordings with Karen Records—*Mudanza y acarreo* (CDK 91/BMG 3234–2) in 1985, *Mientras mas lo pienso . . . tú* (CDK 105/BMG 3233) in 1986, and *Ojalá que llueva café* (CDK 126/BMG 3231) in 1987—that gave Guerra a reputation as a musician of outstanding quality and unimpeachable musical credentials who had successfully renovated the spiritually ailing merengue.

Of these musicians—Sonia Silvestre, Víctor Víctor, Luis Dias, and Juan Luis Guerra—Dias was the most firmly grounded in and connected to Dominican street and folk culture, and he was the first to direct serious attention to bachata as a genre worthy of working with. Dias had been interested in bachata since the late 1970s and had performed some experimental rock-jazz-bachata fusions with Transporte Urbano, although none were released as recordings. In 1984 Dias composed and performed a song called "La perdida" (Loose woman), whose music was a sort of rock-bachata fusion, but whose lyrics—about a man's desperation over his woman's promiscuous ways—were unequivocally those of a bachata. The song never came out as a record, although Dias made a music video of it that appeared within a television show on prostitution (Luis Dias, interview). In 1985 Sonia Silvestre recorded one of Dias's bachata-inspired songs, "Corazón de vellonera" (Jukebox heart), but it had been arranged in the bolero style by well-known Dominican arranger Jorge Taveras (also a member of the Generación de los 70) and little resembled a bachata. While these early incursions into bachata should definitely be considered seminal, they made little impact on the public at large or on the mainstream music industry.

Around 1988, musician and producer Cholo Brenes (who had organized the Siete Días con el Pueblo concerts in 1974) proposed to Sonia Silvestre and Luis Dias that they produce a record together; Dias agreed, but said he wanted to do it as a bachata. Given Silvestre's by then substantial reputation, this was a radical proposal, but she liked the concept: "It was an idea I agreed with totally when he presented it to me. It seemed extraordinary, especially the way he wanted to do bachata . . . to make bachata without shame and without problems, to make bachata seriously" (Sonia Silvestre, interview). Dias wrote the bachatas, and Jorge Taveras did the arrangements, but this time—for the first time in his career—Taveras tried to capture an authentic bachata sound. For her part, Silvestre deliberately tried to imitate the bachateros' emotional style of singing. Her backup musicians (all of whom were part of the Generación de los 70) agreed to jettison their prejudices against bachata in order to collaborate on the project. The final long-playing recording, released a year later, was called *Quiero andar* (I want to keep moving); it contained five bachatas, one salsa, one balada, and, bowing to the producer's wishes, one lambada, all of which—except the lambada—had been written by Luis Dias (Sonia Silvestre, interview).

The bachatas on this Silvestre-Dias-Taveras collaboration sounded very different from those of bachateros such as Luis Segura or Blas Durán. The instrumentation relied on synthesizers, partly to keep production costs down, but also because of Dias's predilection for musical experiments: with the exception of the bongos and the guitars, all the instrumental parts were created with synthesizers—even the maracas. Moreover, in all but one of the bachatas the lead instrument was a synthesized accordion rather than the guitar—a deliberate attempt by Dias to fuse the sounds of merengue típico and bachata. An electric guitar was used in some of the pieces, but as a rhythm instrument, not for lead, as in street-level bachata; in only one song, "Andresito Reina," was an electroacoustic guitar played in a way that approximated bachateros' guitar style. The resulting sound texture of *Quiero andar* was, as Silvestre phrased it, *tecno,* but nevertheless, the bachatas had an earthy quality to them, and Dias' lyrics spoke to the difficult and sometimes violent lives of people who inhabited bars and the streets, that clearly distinguished the songs from baladas and boleros. Dias, well aware that these bachatas were quite different from those he had been inspired by, coined the term *bachata madre* (mother bachata) for the original bachata and the term *tecno-bachata* or *tecno-amargue* for the more sophisticated bachatas he and his colleagues were making.

In contrast to the all-too-common practice of mainstream musicians who co-opt grass-roots music for their own purposes without acknowledging their sources, Silvestre and Dias wanted to use their stature as recognized professionals to validate bachata, as well as to explore its possibilities for artistic expression. Silvestre recalled her own feelings about the project: "I wanted to interpret a genre that was popular, original, and that allowed me to communicate directly with the popular sensibility. Our intention was to valorize this manifestation as an expression that was authentic, that had quality, value, originality, and we felt the necessity to identify ourselves with popular musical values, without complexes" (interview).

As veterans of the nueva canción movement, they anticipated that their work would make a strong impact on a society that had held bachata in such low esteem for so long: as Silvestre said, "It was a way of confronting, in an agreeable way, conventional and reactionary thinking. We enjoy scandalizing people" (interview). In interviews with the media, Silvestre declared she was a bachatera and insisted that bachata was a worthwhile form of music. She even made the assertion—surely outrageous to some—that all Dominicans had a bachatero hidden inside, whether they wanted to acknowledge it or not. Surprisingly, the critical response to *Quiero andar* was quite positive. In terms of sales it was a modest success, selling fewer than five thousand copies, but culturally it made a tremendous impression: as Silvestre said, "The record was decisive because I had made it, a serious woman singing bachata." In the wake of *Quiero andar*, the doors to social acceptance that had been closed to bachata began opening.

In the late 1980s, the Barceló rum company initiated a highly praised and successful ad campaign which replaced the usual images of scantily clad women and glitzy social contexts with images highlighting Dominican traditional and folk culture and urging natural resource conservation. In 1989 Juan Luis Guerra, who was still supplementing his income by composing and arranging commercial jingles, arranged a folk tune that had been "discovered" by Dominican folklorist Fradique Lizardo for one of these Barceló commercials (Tejeda 1993: 201). As a reaction to the positive public response to the commercial, Guerra decided to expand the piece into a full-length song, and, encouraged by Silvestre's success with

Quiero andar, he arranged the first part of the song, entitled "Como abeja al panal" (As a bee to the hive), as a slow bachata; after a few verses, however, the song switched into a highly danceable salsa.

Musically, Guerra's first experiment with bachata in "Como abeja al panal" sounded much more like street-level bachatas than the Dias-Silvestre-Taveras production: Guerra's guitar work, while revealing his advanced training, imitated the bachateros' guitar style, and his vocal style subtly approximated their melodramatic way of singing. Guerra also used synthesizers to enhance the production, but they remained in the background, allowing the traditional guitar-maraca-bongo sound texture to be in the foreground. Four of *Quiero andar's* five bachatas, in contrast, had relied on the (synthesized) accordion and overall had a much more experimental flavor. Lyrically, however, Dias's songs, populated by people whose lives unfolded at night in bars and on the streets, were closer to the spirit of the original bachata than were Guerra's lyrics, whose images of love and courtship were chaste, delicate, and refined.

The two-part structure of Guerra's first bachata, "Como abeja al panal," however, suggested he was not quite committed to bachata. Indeed, Silvestre reports that just before Guerra himself had decided to arrange the first part of "Como abeja al panal" as bachata, he was somewhat dismayed when he saw what the *Quiero andar* project was about: "He was a little scandalized because we were making bachata, because 'Mi wachimán' [My watchman] and 'Quiero andar' [the title song] used the language of the street" (interview). After "Como abeja al panal" was released as a single in 1989 and became a hit, Guerra made a bolder venture into the still-suspect genre: it was entitled *Bachata rosa*. Completed in 1990 but not released until 1991, this recording contained four bachatas, "Como abeja al panal," "Burbujas de amor" (Bubbles of love), "Bachata rosa" (Bachata rose), and "Estrellitas y duendes" (Little stars and fairies). Guerra's longtime friends and associates, Sonia Silvestre and Víctor Víctor, provided some of the backup vocals.

Unlike "Como abeja al panal," Guerra's new bachatas were in the bachata idiom from beginning to end. While he enhanced his arrangements with synthesizers, the guitar was clearly the lead instrument, and the bongo and maraca percussion prominently marked their slow, bolerolike rhythm, similar to that of romantic bachateros like Luis Segura. On "Burbujas de amor" Guerra employed the bachateros' most notorious technique, the sexual double entendre, although his word play was sophisticated and metaphorical rather than earthy and direct. Comparing Guerra's lyrics to those she sang, Silvestre noted, "Juan Luis's bachatas were *rosa* [rosy], while mine were red" (interview). Their rosiness was exactly what made them so appealing to mainstream Dominican audiences.

Following Silvestre, Dias, and Guerra's experiments with bachata, Víctor Víctor released a recording entitled *Inspiraciones,* which included a bachata entitled "Mesita de noche" (Night table) that became a modest hit. Like Silvestre, Víctor Víctor wanted to use his position and reputation to break down the social barriers that had kept bachata marginalized:

> Being schooled musicians, we had more possibilities to permeate the mass media by knowing how to manipulate technology, by having been singers in the 1970s who had become very popular and who continued to be very popular. . . . I am a schooled musician, I've studied in conservatory, I've studied in Boston, and I make bachata. It is a different bachata, but a bachata that we've always acknowledged has been inspired by them, and we say so. We want to imitate the bachateros. (Interview)

Bachata Arrives

To everyone's astonishment and delight, *Bachata rosa* became a triumphant success in terms of record and concert ticket sales, not only in the Dominican Republic, but throughout Latin America, in the United States, and even in Europe. It also exceeded all expectations in terms of the level of media attention the group received: after breaking into the *Billboard* charts, Guerra's achievement was noted by major U.S. periodicals such as the *New York Times, Rolling Stone,* the *Village Voice,* and even the *Wall Street Journal.* Yet while *Bachata rosa* undeniably had outstanding musical and lyrical quality, its worldwide success must also be attributed to producer Bienvenido Rodríguez's renowned business and public-relations acumen. The recording's repertoire, for example, had been astutely chosen for the widest possible appeal: in addition to the bachatas, it included songs in other popular Latin American genres, from perennial favorites such as merengue, salsa, and bolero to nueva canción; other songs were influenced by French Caribbean zouk and Afropop rhythms. In spite of the fact that a bachata, "Burbujas de amor," was the most successful song on the recording, in reality, *Bachata rosa*'s achievements abroad were in many ways incidental to the bachata genre itself: given that almost nothing was known about bachata outside the Dominican Republic and that neither Rodríguez nor Guerra seem to have done much to educate their international audiences about its origins, non-Dominican fans had no way of knowing that there was something socially and culturally distinctive about the appealing guitar-based love songs it contained. They were simply great love songs with a simple, earthy quality.

In the Dominican Republic, on the other hand, it mattered a great deal that these songs were bachatas. With the likes of Juan Luis Guerra, Sonia Silvestre, Luis Dias, and Víctor Víctor not only working in but celebrating the value of bachata, it could no longer be considered a forbidden, outlaw music; and there could be no further justification for obstructing its access to the mainstream media and market. This opening could not have happened at a more propitious time, because at street level, bachata was ready for the mainstream.

Blas Durán, who had pioneered the use of electric guitars in his bachata-merengues, continued to release outrageous but enormously popular double entendre bachatas and bachata-merengues. But, following in his footsteps, a younger generation of bachateros imitating his style were finding even greater success. Two of these, Luis Vargas and Antony Santos (not to be confused with Tony Santos), would have been successful in bachata's traditional market under any circumstances, but they were fortunate to launch their careers at a moment when the mainstream media and audiences were willing to listen to their music. Vargas' and Santos' bachatas still displayed some of the qualities that mainstream society had always criticized about the genre: the musicians themselves were poor, unsophisticated, and of rural origins, their lyrics were direct and raw, the language was vernacular, and their musicianship was rather primitive. Unlike the bachata of their predecessors such as Luis Segura and Marino Pérez, however, their music sounded different—younger and more confident: the electric guitars gave their music a more modern and assertive feel, and their repertoires, which included about equal measures of bolero-bachatas and bachata-merengues, met the public's need for both romantic and dance music.

Moreover, a few savvy bachata producers such as José Luis and Rafael Mañón were beginning to realize the importance of paying attention to improving the production quality of bachata if they were to appeal to wider audiences. In the studio, they began to take better advantage of multitrack recording and sound mixing. They completely discontinued 45 RPM vinyl singles, for years the most popular format among poor consumers, but whose notoriously low quality had been unacceptable to FM radio stations. Instead, recordings were released on inexpensive cassettes for bachata's traditional consumers and on CDs (compact digital discs) for the more affluent and for FM radio stations. They also began paying more attention to artistic management and marketing techniques, dressing their musicians in more sophisticated clothing, investing in good-quality photographs of the groups for publicity purposes, and providing more money for payola to radio stations.

The increasing social acceptance of bachata initiated by the work of Silvestre, Dias, Guerra, and Víctor Víctor, combined with the bachateros' vigorous new musical style and bachata producers' greater attention to production quality, gave bachata a level of access to the major FM radio and television programs—and to the middle- and upper-class audiences that they reached—that would have been inconceivable just a few years earlier. Middle-class audiences, tiring of the increasingly formulaic merengue orquestas and no longer so embarrassed to listen to bachata, welcomed the energetic newcomer to the musical arena.

The trajectory of one bachata song that became a nationwide hit in the early 1990s clearly demonstrates bachata's rapidly changing fortunes. In 1992 Antony Santos released a romantic song in a lively bolero-son rhythm called "Voy pa'llá" (I'm going there), in which he vows to take his girlfriend away from her parents because they have forbidden them to marry. "Voy pa'llá" first became a hit among bachata's traditional constituency, but it was not played on major FM stations until Las Chicas del Can, an all-woman merengue ensemble, recorded it. Their version, like Guerra's "Como abeja al panal," had a two-part structure, beginning as a guitar-based bachata sounding much like the original (however, with the gender of the narrator and beloved reversed), but then the verses were repeated as a fully orchestrated merengue. Because Las Chicas del Can was a well-established merengue orquesta, their version of "Voy pa'llá" received extensive air play on the major radio stations immediately after it was released, and it became a hit. When it became public knowledge that it had originally been a bachata, Santos' version—available in a well-produced CD—began to receive air play as well, and sales of his cassette went through the roof. While bachata sales figures have never been kept, Santos' version of "Voy pa'llá" was widely considered to be the year's biggest hit.

The boom was on. Journalists rushed to display themselves as open-minded and hip by writing favorable commentaries about bachata and its performers. By the end of 1992, bachata, no longer the object of scorn, could be heard on major FM radio stations, a change that producer José Luis described as "un logro maravilloso" (a marvelous achievement): "Before, bachata couldn't be heard on FM. Luis Segura was the first with 'Pena,' but now Antony Santos with 'Voy pa'llá,' Luis Vargas, then Raulín, and now practically all those who are successful. It's not total, but there are many FM stations looking to play bachata—the original bachata. Now there are FM radio programs playing all kinds of bachata" (interview).

The fact that bachata recordings could be purchased without embarrassment or shame gave bachata access to a nationwide, classwide market. José Luis reported that while in the 1980s an average bachata hit sold about 20,000 to 30,000 copies, in the 1990s it could sell 60,000 to 100,000 copies. (These figures are more dramatic when taking into consideration that the earlier figures were for 45 RPM singles, while the later figures were for the more expensive cassettes.) Bachata's economic potential was not lost on mainstream musicians. Merengue orquestas began including bachatas in their repertoires (either performing them as merengues or adding electric guitars to perform them as bachatas), among them Wilfrido Vargas, Jossie Esteban y la Patrulla 15, and Primitivo Santos. Similarly, vocalists such as Anthony Ríos, Alex Bueno, and Valeria began recording bachatas that sold well, and other even more unlikely singers such as the quintessentially mainstream diva Charytín Goico announced their intentions to include bachatas in future recordings. Jumping on the bandwagon, Sony's Latin music division compiled songs from their catalogue that had been hits in other genres, and paid well-known Dominican arranger Manuel Tejada to arrange them as bachatas. The recording was entitled *Bachata Magic*—although its slickly arranged and orchestrated songs actually bore little resemblance to bachata. Blas Durán cynically observed:

> Now bachata is bigger than merengue. I say that they wanted to eliminate bachata here, because it was hurting many interests and many orquestas. Sometimes those [bachata] records used to come from below and become even bigger hits because they were bachatas. They called it names, like música de guardia and música cachivache. When they saw they couldn't finish bachata off and that we kept going—because bachata always had its public—those high-profile singers decided to sing bachata as well. (Interview)

The bachateros and their producers were well aware that the incursions of people like Guerra and Silvestre into bachata had been helpful because their music was no longer stigmatized and barred from the mainstream media and marketplace. On the other hand, they knew that bachata had always been popular with the country's poor majority, and they could not help but note that the newcomers were clearly benefiting from something the bachateros had created. Bachata producer Rafael Mañón, for example, observed:

> Bachata had meant low category, but when *Bachata rosa* came out, the ugly name became a nice name, because someone of his international category helped. . . . But they didn't do it thinking of helping bachata, they did it thinking commercially. . . . They took advantage of the strength that bachata was gaining to raid it themselves. Who could have told those people when Luis Segura, Marino Pérez, and those people first started out that they would be recording bachatas? No one could have told them, because they wouldn't record it. But seeing the strength that bachata was gaining, they raided it. (Interview)

Blas Durán made similar observations:

> Bachata was a very low music, belonging to bars, the countryside, cabarets. When the moment came that those gentlemen recorded bachata, people looked at it another way, saying, "No, wait a minute, Juan Luis Guerra is singing it, Sonia Silvestre, Víctor Víctor." Now they think it's pretty and think it's great. Now all bachata is great. Nobody in the fancy parts of the city paid any attention to it, power-

ful people didn't pay attention to it, because it was sung by poor people, from below. But when artists of high caliber sing it, now they have a different attitude. (Interview)

While mainstream musicians continued to jump on the bachata bandwagon, another young bachatero, Raulín Rodríguez, made a meteoric entrance into the musical marketplace. Raulín had begun his career in 1987 when he was only fifteen, singing and playing guitar with his friend Antony Santos' group. While most of their predecessors lived in Santo Domingo, both Raulín and Santos had been born and reared in the countryside, near the northwestern town of Montecristi. After five years with Santos, Raulín established his own group, and shortly thereafter released a recording entitled *Una mujer como tú* (A woman like you) that contained a song, "El dolor" (The pain), which became one of the biggest hits of 1993. Unlike his colleagues Antony Santos and Luis Vargas, who continued to use sexual double entendres, Raulín composed romantic lyrics without a trace of the sort of sexuality that had been considered so offensive in other bachateros. With his youthful energy and boyish, wholesome demeanor, Raulín was highly appealing to middle-class audiences who may have liked bachata musically but were still uncomfortable with its explicit sexuality. Raulín was widely recognized in the press as a major new talent who could take the "original" bachata to new heights of popularity and economic success.

In December 1993 a milestone in bachata's development took place: for the first time, bachateros appeared on the same stage with the tecno-bachateros. Two concerts called De Bachata en Bachata (From Bachata to Bachata) were held in the country's two principal cities, Santo Domingo and Santiago. Organized by Víctor Víctor, the concerts included performances by Luis Segura, Raulín, Sonia Silvestre, Víctor Víctor, and a recently formed merengue orquesta as an opening act. They were held in large venues—each city's sports arena—and ticket prices were kept low— twenty and fifty pesos (6 pesos equalled US$1)—to draw an audience of all social classes. The Santiago concert was well attended, but the Santo Domingo concert exceeded Víctor Víctor's expectations: it was almost packed. Silvestre sang her bachatas from *Quiero andar,* as well as Juan Luis Guerra's "Estrellitas y duendes"; Víctor Víctor sang some sones and three bachatas he had composed and recorded. Raulín generated a great deal of excitement and got the audience dancing. But it was Luis Segura, whose long career symbolized bachata's struggle for legitimacy and whose presence on the stage manifested its long-overdue acceptance into Dominican society, who received the most applause. In an act of symbolic importance, Víctor Víctor accompanied Segura in a duet of "Pena."

In organizing these conceptually progressive concerts, Víctor Víctor and Sonia Silvestre indicated that they had redefined their vision of political activism with respect to music: rather than singing about the masses, they were singing with them. The concerts had two distinct goals. First, they wanted to remove the distinctions between the grass-roots bachateros and middle-class bachateros like themselves. As Silvestre noted, "We must achieve that . . . to break these divisions" (interview). Second, they wanted to express their solidarity with the original bachateros by helping them secure a larger space in mainstream venues. In order to do this, they had to eliminate any remaining middle-class prejudices against bachata, which they tried to accomplish by exerting whatever personal and professional influence they had.

> It was a concert that didn't have many pretensions of breaking attendance records, because people are still ashamed to go to these things. People are clandestine bachateros—but they buy the records, right? The intention was to break that barrier . . . so that the people who control the media, those who write, those who speak on the media lose their fear of being a clandestine bachatero . . . because I know how to fight. The bachateros don't know how to fight, they get squashed. (Víctor Víctor, interview)

In addition to these concerts, Víctor Víctor and Silvestre planned other ways of bringing bachata into the mainstream. In early 1994 Víctor Víctor was recording a compilation of classic Dominican songs, arranged and sung by himself, that would receive extensive publicity and distribution. Two of the songs on this recording were bachatas—Luis Segura's "Pena" and Bernardo Ortiz's "Dos rosas." This, he claimed, was a radical project, because for the first time, bachata songs were being included within the canon of "classic" Dominican songs. Silvestre was also working on a new recording on which her band, while still instrumentally "tecno," was trying to approximate more closely the sound of street-level bachata. As of this writing, however, neither Sonia Silvestre nor Víctor Víctor nor any other tecno-bachateros had ever invited a bachatero to sing or play with them on a recording. As Víctor Víctor responded when I asked him about this, "I'm going very slowly on this, because you can't mess around with things that are well established. If we rush in, we'll lose" (interview).

While the tecno-bachateros' commercial future looks quite rosy, the fate of the majority of street-level bachateros is more uncertain. Of the older bachateros, Luis Segura, whose intensely romantic songs had never been tainted by sexual references, has fared the best in bachata's new social context. Well remembered as the sobbing singer of the blockbuster song "Pena," Segura easily appealed to the aesthetic preferences of bachata's new middle-class audiences. Moreover, in the media's rush to acknowledge and historicize the recently "discovered" bachata, Segura emerged—quite rightfully—as the "Father of Bachata" and has been almost lionized, invited repeatedly to perform on television, and interviewed widely by the press. After years of barely eking out an existence, Segura's new star status has finally translated into economic rewards. It is interesting—given that he remained so traditional in his style throughout the 1970s and 1980s—that he recently invested in the full complement of instruments and equipment required for a merengue orquesta in order to form a new group, Luis Segura y su Orquesta, in which several of his sons are musicians. Segura claims to prefer his old style of romantic music to the faster bachatas and bachata-merengues he has added to his repertoire in the past few years in response to the demands of younger audiences. Nevertheless, the recording he was working on in early 1994 included salsas and baladas as well as slickly arranged bachatas, clearly attesting to his interest in exploring the possibilities of mainstream commercial music. How well he can compete with merengue orquestas remains to be seen.

Blas Durán is also doing well, partly because he already had a strong following, and partly because he has an undeniable knack for lively and catchy—if often bawdy—songs that appeal to Dominicans' love of language and wordplay. However, he has been branded in the press as a "dirty" bachatero and has not achieved the same level of acceptability among the middle-class audiences as Raulín and Luis Segura. Always sensitive to the winds of change, Durán has begun writing "clean" songs that will more easily get FM air play, although he says he will continue to compose the humorous double entendres upon which he has built his career. Leonardo Paniagua, on the other hand, is still singing romantic songs in his former style, but has been unwilling to sing merengues. As Luis Segura said of him, "He hasn't wanted to change; he's still in the antiquity of before. That's why you don't see much of him. But he still has yesterday's public" (interview).

In the past, bachata's low social and economic status engendered a certain egalitarianism—all bachateros were poor. Even Luis Segura, bachata's most revered figure, never made enough money to break out of working and living in roughly the same low-status contexts as his audiences. As bachata enters the mainstream, however, it will almost certainly conform to the mainstream's "star" system, in which a handful of individuals such as Raulín will be able to ascend socially and economically, while the majority of bachata musicians, still poor, unpolished, and technically illiterate, will continue to languish in poverty and obscurity. While bachata as a whole is no longer scorned and ostracized as it was in the past, musicians like Ramón Cordero and Bolívar Peralta, who still play in small acoustic ensembles and who do not have the kind of managerial support that has helped Raulín and Anthony Santos mask their poor rural origins, will not likely gain access to better-paying middle-class venues.

Indeed, in 1994 only five bachateros had managed to fully "cross over" into the mainstream marketplace: Raulín Rodriguez, Antony Santos, Luis Vargas, Luis Segura, and Blas Durán. Their recordings were available in Santo Domingo's better music stores, but those of other bachateros such as Marino Pérez or Bolívar Peralta were still available only at street stalls.

Tellingly, none of the bachateros who have "made it big" in the 1990s are recording with Guarachita, whose centrality to bachata has been fading steadily since the late 1980s when the more talented or established musicians began seeking out other producers, such as José Luis or Rafael Mañon, who paid them better and who paid more attention to recording quality. Moreover, as urban FM radio stations began to play bachata in the 1990s, Radio Guarachita's ability to reach nationwide audiences—for which bachateros had been willing to forego payment for recording—began losing its appeal. Radio Guarachita went over to the FM format in 1988, but Aracena only minimally upgraded its equipment, which had been in continual use since he purchased it in the 1960s. As a result, Radio Guarachita's sound quality remained well below that of other FM stations, making it less attractive to listeners now accustomed to better-sounding radio. Even the station's 1987 move from its downtown facilities into a modern new building along an industrial strip on the northern outskirts of Santo Domingo undermined Guarachita's formerly close relationship with its audience, because visitors now must make a special trip instead of being able to drop by. Furthermore, the new building's more corporate design (especially the lack of a radioteatro from which to view the broadcasts) contrasts sharply with the shabby but familiar ambiance of the old facility, and discourages the sort of spontaneous visits that listeners used to make in the past. The likelihood is that when Radhames Aracena retires, Empresas Guarachita will disappear.

The shift from vinyl to cassette technology has affected all bachateros and bachata producers, including Radhames Aracena. Vinyl singles, long the standard format for bachata, had been highly advantageous to poor musicians: even if they could not find a producer to finance them, all they needed to release a record was enough money to pay the studio rental and manufacturing costs for two songs. Now, musicians must record at least ten songs for a cassette, which has substantially increased the costs of production. From the viewpoint of poor consumers, while cassette technology is cheaper overall than vinyl, a vinyl single was still cheaper than an entire cassette; moreover, vinyl singles allowed them to purchase only a singer's hit song rather than an entire recording. As for the owners of bars and colmados who depend on recordings to provide music for their customers, cassettes hinder their ability to easily select a desired song from their music collections, whether it be a current hit or a favorite classic. CDs offer the selectivity that vinyl records had, but because they are not produced in the country and must be imported from the United States at a cost of approximately twenty dollars each, they are too expensive for most proprietors.

Cassette technology also stimulated changes in bachata distribution practices. In the 1980s bachata cassettes were generally low-quality reproductions of long-playing records. As long as the 45 RPM vinyl single was still the most popular and widely used format, cassette piracy was not a serious threat to bachata producers; piracy mostly took the form of unauthorized compilations of current or former hits. However, when vinyl records were discontinued, bachata producers releasing their products on cassettes had to compete with pirated versions sold at lower prices than the originals. In response, some bachata producers sought to undercut the pirates by selling their cassettes at such a low price that it was not worth it for pirates to duplicate them. These low-price—and low-quality—cassettes sold by the producers themselves were called *cassettes corrientes* (ordinary cassettes), and they were almost indistinguishable from the pirate versions: the recording tape itself was of unknown origin and questionable quality, the artwork on the labels was very poorly reproduced, and the cassettes were not cellophane wrapped. Both the pirate and corriente cassettes were sold via street stalls, and customers had no way of knowing which was a pirate and which was its close relative, the corriente—nor did they care.

Middle-class consumers, however, would not accept the poor-quality packaging of either the cassette corriente or pirate cassette, so bachata producers began offering the music of their more successful bachateros such as Raulín—those likely to be distributed through record stores—as *originales*, which were supposedly comparable in quality to the "original" cassettes of mainstream musicians released by the major record companies (i.e., the tape quality was supposed to be superior, they would be wrapped in cellophane, and the label would be of better quality). Although originales were sold at more than double the cost of a corriente, the difference in price between them did not necessarily indicate differences in tape quality: one major bachata producer and cassette manufacturer confessed to me that all the cassettes he manufactured—even the originales he sold wholesale to mainstream record stores—were identical except in their packaging.

Now that all bachata is released on cassettes, it is almost impossible to find a vinyl bachata record for sale in Santo Domingo. This means that most bachata production prior to about 1990 is now unavailable—with the exception of those older songs that have become "classics," which, because they are still money makers, are being rereleased on cassettes and even on CD. Radhames Aracena, whose Empresas Guarachita has long been well organized and managed, will almost certainly have stored

Guarachita's substantial and significant output reaching back into the 1960s. It is doubtful, however, that most of the smaller bachata producers, whose enterprises have always been casual and small-scale, will have stored their master tapes or even copies of their vinyl recordings. As a result, bachata's non-Guarachita recorded history will soon be disappearing as people begin to discard both their record players and the vinyl records they used to play on them.

While bachata's past may indeed disappear from the historical record, the future of the genre as a whole looks bright indeed—particularly if it follows the historical trajectories of other similar grass-roots musics that have become widely popular and commercially viable. Merengue, for example, also began as a low-class, low-status, rural music but was later accepted by all Dominicans as a symbol of their national identity. As merengue moved into new social contexts, however, it changed dramatically, raising the possibility that bachata may also lose its former character as it moves into the mainstream. On the other hand, in spite of the fact that only one variant of merengue—orquesta—achieved hegemony in the commercial arena, both traditional accordion-based merengue típico and modernized accordion-based típico moderno ensembles are still evolving within a community of listeners who identify with provincial rather than urban Dominican culture. Manuel Peña documented a similar process of stylistic bifurcation in Texas-Mexican conjunto music, where the more traditional style coexisted with a more modern orquesta variant that emerged to satisfy the needs of an increasingly middle-class-oriented segment of its audience (1985). It is quite possible, then, that while the newer tecno-bachata style that appeals to middle-class audiences may eventually predominate commercially, recordings by "traditional" acoustic guitar-maraca-bongo bachata ensembles will continue to circulate among the rural and urban poor. Young bachateros such as Raulín Rodríguez, however, hold open the promise that bachata can cross over to mainstream audiences—and perhaps international audiences—without losing its connection to its original grass-roots consituency.

In the 1970s and 1980s, male shantytown residents increasingly sought escape and entertainment in bars.
By Deborah Pacini Hernandez

"YO QUIERO ANDAR"
SONIA SILVESTRE

Lado A: YO QUIERO ANDAR / HASTA UN PUNTO ES QUE SE RUEGA / LIMBO Y CONGA / MI WACHIMAN

Lado B: MELODIA DE AMOR / NAUFRAGIO / SIN COMPETENCIA / ANDRESITO REINA

Sonia Silvestre's first bachata recording.
By Oi Records

Luis Segura and Víctor Víctor sing a duet on "Pena" in the 1994
De Bachata en Bachata concert.
By El Nacional

Avant-garde musician Luis
Dias was the first to
experiment with bachata.
By Laura Sklar

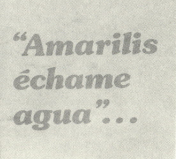

In the 1990s bachata still circulates via street stalls, but only on cassettes.
By Deborah Pacini Hernandez

"*Amarilis échame agua*"...

Tony Santos' 1986 hit record, "Amarilis, échame agua."
By Unidad Records

Blas Durán played revitalized
bachata with spicy
bachata-merengues using
electric guitars.
By J & N Records

Juan Luis Guerra's 1991 recording *Bachata rosa*
was an international success, giving bachata a
new social legitimacy.
By Karen Publishing

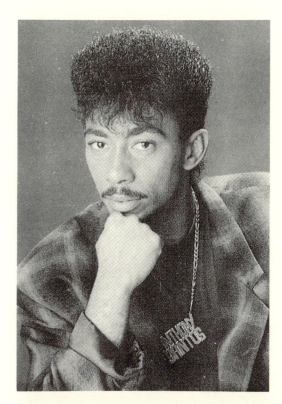

Younger bachatero Antony
Santos' 1992 hit "Voy pa'allá"
crossed over to mainstream
audiences.
By RM Records

Raulín Rodríguez's romantic lyrics and expanded ensemble have made him
enormously appealing to young middle-class audiences.
By Deborah Pacini Hernandez

Chapter Seven

*C*onclusions

*I*n looking at bachata's more than three-decade-long trajectory, it is important to ask why it emerged as a style at all. Most Latin American and Caribbean countries have some sort of tradition of guitar-based trios and quartets, and many of them are modeled after Cuban groups, such as the Trío Matamoros, that became enormously popular throughout the region in the 1940s and 1950s. Haiti, for example, has a musical tradition known as *twoubadou* (troubadour) that is almost identical to the Dominican Republic's tradition of guitar-based music: its instrumentation consists of two guitars, maracas, and a *marimbula* (thumb bass), and differs from its Dominican counterparts only by the presence of a conga-like *tanbou* (drum played with the hands) rather than bongos (Averill 1989: 212–13). Why, then, did the Dominican Republic's tradition consolidate into a distinct style while traditions elsewhere, as in Haiti, did not? In this concluding chapter, I address this question, as well as others related more specifically to style formation in the sort of urban contexts from which bachata emerged.

Stylistic and Social Contours: A Summary

Charles and Angeliki Keil, commenting on the issue of style consolidation, noted that "each style exists as a counter force to rapid cultural change rather than a stimulant" (Keil and Keil 1987: 75). When bachata emerged in the 1960s, poor Dominicans of rural origins were migrating by the thousands into urban areas, where they had to cope with a potent mix of economic exploitation, official neglect, and profound social disruption. The cheerful merengue típico, although grounded in rural culture, was inappropriate for expressing the suffering and alienation experienced by people living in extreme poverty in unbearable shantytown conditions. The glitzy orquesta merengue that dominated the popular music landscape was even less capable of reflecting or speaking to their particular lifestyles and problems. Bachata, in contrast, combined familiar elements of rural culture (such as the guitar-bongo-maraca ensemble) with the ability to articulate a variety of emotions; moreover, bachata could be made by anyone with a guitar, some friends to provide backup percussion, and the desire to tell a story through song. The resulting musical style—structurally simple, linguistically raw, and narratively direct—so faithfully articulated the experiences and concerns of the poor that it shocked and repulsed mainstream Dominican society. Denied a voice in the mainstream musical arena, bachata's practitioners resisted by carving out a space for their music at the margins and secured it by establishing the small-scale but effective economic networks that ensured its circulation and survival.

Bachata emerged and flourished within shantytown contexts, suggesting that musical developments may be greatly influenced by the type of physical environment in which people live. Santo Domingo's crowded shantytown conditions made the kind of family gatherings that had been traditional in rural areas difficult to replicate, so most bachata "events" consisted of listening and dancing to recorded music in public places such as colmados and, particularly, bars. The fact that the latter were male-oriented, not family-oriented spaces, imprinted bachata with the language and imagery of the bar and street rather than that of family and work. In order to better understand the relationship between musical development and physical environment, one can compare bachata with the historical trajectory of polka. Polka events are family- and community-oriented festivities (e.g., weddings or parish dances) that take place in working-class neighborhoods in locations such as churches, rented halls, or lawns. Polka lyrics reflect the family orientation of these social contexts; they are intended to provoke laughter and merriment, but even when slightly "off-color," they are appropriate for the whole family (Keil, Keil, and Blau 1992). Dominican shantytowns were not socially disorganized localities—their residents did indeed create extensive social and economic networks in order to cope with their situation—but unlike working-class Polish neighborhoods they were physically dysfunctional: they lacked the infrastructure necessary to provide even basic needs such as clean water and garbage disposal, much less amenities such as church halls or lawns, that allow family- and community-building musical events such as parish dances to take place.

Until 1990, bachata was undeniably the black sheep of the country's music business. The kind of radio station that played bachata (only provincial or minor AM urban stations), the time of day bachata was aired (generally at dawn), the kind of venues open to live bachata performances (low-class bars), the kind of places bachata records could be purchased (street stalls in working-class shopping districts), the kind of places recorded bachata could be heard in public (colmados, barras), the amount of money that could be made commercializing bachata (a fraction of what merengue musicians made)—all these prevented bachata from competing in the mainstream musical marketplace and from being heard beyond the confines of the spaces inhabited by the country's underclasses.

The dominant socio-economic sectors of Dominican society justified bachata's marginality by asserting that bachata was lacking in any aesthetic or social values. Thomas Turino has noted that "it is, of course, common for superordinate groups to block social assimilation to protect their favored position. This is largely done through the use of distinguishing cultural forms, practices and tastes while the cultural resources of subordinate groups are disparaged as a part of the overall pattern of domination" (Turino 1988: 128). In the 1990s, however, when establishment musicians and music companies realized that money could be made in bachata, the prejudices against bachata began to melt away, and within two years bachata was transformed from a musical pariah to an icon of radical chic.

In response to the economic obstacles confronting bachata in its early years, its practitioners developed a widespread network of social and economic relations for making and disseminating bachata that was only minimally connected to the mainstream music industry, but which provided a source of income for all those who participated in it. The small-scale informal bachata economy was in many ways similar to the ethnically based "networks of marginality" described by Steven Loza, which developed within Los Angeles' Chicano community for ensuring the availability of Chicano music in a context of Anglo disinterest in disseminating and promoting it (Loza 1993: 274–75). The persistence of bachata musicians, producers, and promoters in making and disseminating their music was not just an act of economic survival, however; it was also an act of resistance and self-empowerment. Shantytown residents who managed to scrape together enough money to produce five hundred 45 RPM singles of their own music directly challenged Dominican society's claim that bachata was unworthy of being reproduced and disseminated. They also challenged the economic hegemony of those who would have barrio residents buy *their* musical products instead.

Bachata also empowered its practitioners and patrons culturally by articulating and affirming their own experience, thereby meeting their need for a music in which *they* were the subject. Each bachata record sung in the language of the barrio and reflecting the concerns and experiences of the country's poorest (although mostly male) citizens manifested a rejection of the dominant society's supposedly refined and superior musical offerings as well as of the middle-class values and aspirations they expressed. As Anya Peterson Royce has pointed out, "Even if one does not have the resources to define a situation positively, one may still have the power to define it negatively. Individuals and groups can and do resist. They sometimes simply refuse to abide by others' rules, or they may accept them on the surface but resist them on a deeper level" (Royce 1982: 4). In short, although one segment of society unquestionably had the power to dominate, control, restrict, and impose, the subordinate classes were not powerless: they had the power to refuse, to challenge, and to subvert.

Most bachata songs in the 1960s were poetic, though unschooled, statements about the pains and pleasures of love; in the 1970s bachata began to address a wider range of problems associated with love, sex, and gender relationships. In particular, bachata songs began to reflect the sorts of problems resulting from the breakdown of the traditional family structure, particularly in regard to the transient and money-mediated relationships that became more characteristic of the shantytown environment as the economic crisis deepened. The media interpreted these changes in the music as a regressive evolution from simple rural backwardness to urban depravity. While it is important not to romanticize the often flagrantly misogynistic statements articulated in bachata songs, neither the Dominican media nor the intellectual establishment acknowledged that these lyrics were the symptoms, not the causes, of social disintegration, which demanded conscientious analysis and fundamental structural changes, not facile moral condemnation.

Since 1990 bachata has undergone a series of significant changes. Some innovations, such as the addition of electric guitars, were introduced by bachateros themselves. Others were developed by middle- and upper-class musicians who have imprinted their class aesthetics on what was formerly an underclass music. With the intrusion of these musicians and their middle-class audiences into bachata's formerly single-class bounded domain, bachata can no longer be defined, as it had been in the 1980s and before, by the low social status of its practitioners and patrons.

In spite of the variety of new instruments introduced into the bachata ensemble, bachata's most consistent and conspicuous feature is still its characteristic texture, the product of its guitar-led ensemble with a bongo and güira (or maraca) rhythm section, and its highly emotional singing style punctuated by exclamations such as "ay, ay, ay" or "¡mami!" Tecno-bachateros such as Juan Luis Guerra have added synthesizers to their sophisticated arrangements, but their songs have been defined as bachatas because of their guitar-bongo-maraca instrumentation and fervent singing style. Even though old-timer Luis Segura has formed a merengue-like orquesta, complete with horn section, to accompany him in an expanded repertoire that even includes salsas, as long as he continues to play a guitar and to wail his melodramatic lyrics, his music will be called bachata. I might add here a speculation: in the future, precisely because bachata's lead instrument is the guitar—more specifically the electric guitar—bachata may be more successful in the world music market than merengue orquestas because international audiences are often more familiar and comfortable with guitar-led than horn-led styles.

Bachata stylistic boundaries have expanded considerably since it emerged in the early 1960s, when most bachata songs closely resembled the slow, romantic Cuban bolero. At present, bachata includes several subcategories distinguished by rhythm and instrumentation, as well as by lyrical content. The more romantic bolero-like songs are called bachatas románticas, canciones de amargue, or bolero-bachatas—and sometimes simply boleros. Songs that are too fast to be called boleros or bachatas románticas are sometimes classified rhythmically as bolero-sones, although they may also be categorized according to the content of their lyrics: for example, those with double entendre lyrics can be called bachatas de doble sentido, while those disparaging women may be called bachatas de desprecio. Those in merengue rhythm are called bachata-merengues, regardless of whether they are played with acoustic or electric guitars. Bachatas made by mainstream, middle-class musicians who expand (or replace parts of) the basic guitar-bongo-maraca ensemble with synthesizers are called tecno-bachatas or tecno-amargues. These categories sometimes overlap; for example, some of the faster bachatas may have romantic lyrics, but their rhythms may be too fast to be classified as bolero-bachatas. Furthermore, these terms are not used consistently; for example, bachateros such as Raulín who have added synthesizers—however crudely—into their ensembles are never called tecno-bachateros.

Complicating this picture is the fact that bachateros' repertoires still occasionally include the other guitar-based genres that have always been around, such as son, ranchera, guajira, and guaracha. While such stylistic diversity may create problems for those seeking to define and categorize the music, it has also given bachata a versatility and broad appeal that has allowed it to survive and flourish in spite of obstacles that until recently limited its full participation in the country's music business.

The content of bachata lyrics has often been brought to bear in attempts to define bachata. Some observers rightly point out that bachata has always been a part of a tradition of romantic music and that, therefore, it should be defined by its primary concern with love. According to this view, Guerra's romantic lyrics, while far more sophisticated than street-level bachatas, are well within that tradition. Others, however, insist that bachata lyrics must reflect their original social contexts such as low-class bars and brothels and must be articulated with barrio language and imagery. When writing bachatas for Sonia Silvestre, for example, tecno-bachatero Luis Dias did not use a guitar at all, but rather a synthesizer imitating an accordion, but nevertheless, his songs were presented and received as bachatas because the lyrics reflected the lives and language of people such as prostitutes and watchmen. Because bachata is still in the process of evolving at both the grass-roots and middle-class levels, it remains to be seen to what extent bachata's stylistic identity will continue to be tied to its original shantytown-related language, imagery, and stories. While likely, it is not at all inevitable that as bachata crosses over to middle-class audiences, its characteristically earthy lyrics will be replaced by the sort of sophisticated and refined lyrics of Juan Luis Guerra; blues, for example, expressed the same sort of emotions when directed at its original African-American audiences as it did when its audience later became increasingly white and middle class.

Bachata's original function as a romantic music has been changing as well, over time becoming a music for dancing as well as romancing. A bachata dance has developed, tempos have sped up, and more bachata-merengues have been added to the usual repertoire—although it is uncertain whether these changes were driven by dancers' demands or by the musicians themselves. However, because bachata is still considered to be primarily romantic music, bachateros' recorded or live repertoires always include a number of songs that feature romantic narratives and poetic verse, which give listeners an opportunity to think about love and dancers an opportunity to dance more intimately. Bachata's ability to serve for both dancing and romancing has given bachata a competitive advantage over musics such as merengue or balada, each of which can fulfill only one of these functions.

In spite of all these changes, bachata has retained its integrity as a style and will almost certainly continue to do so. Bachata is a vigorous new music, still very much in the process of developing and expanding. Unlike older grass-roots musics such as U.S. polka that are in danger of disappearing because younger generations are not sustaining them (Keil, Keil, and Blau 1992: 199), bachata has been embraced by a new generation of musicians who are keeping it alive and healthy by changing it, experimenting with new instruments, performance strategies, recording techniques, and other innovations that are enabling it to compete successfully with other popular musics such as merengue. Expanding performance opportunities and a larger, multiclass consumer market will ensure that young musicians continue making bachata.

If bachata is threatened by anything, it will be that bachateros, in trying to appeal to middle-class audiences, may abandon those class-specific qualities (such as barrio language and imagery) that made it aesthetically satisfying to its original constituents. This has already begun happening, as some bachata musicians are deliberately seeking to avoid social censure by eliminating sexual double entendres—even playful and humorous ones—from their lyrics. Similarly, Luis Segura's move into the orquesta format—even though he professes to prefer his old acoustic style—suggests he feels it necessary to don the trappings of middle-class respectability by adopting a mainstream performance style. More homogenization is certain to occur as bachata is interpreted more frequently by mainstream musicians who impose middle-class aesthetics on it. On the other hand, it is heartening to see that while middle-class musicians' experiments with bachata are indeed doing well commercially, it has not been at the expense of the street-level bachateros: bachata fans have largely ignored these interlopers in favor of bachateros like Raulín and Blas Durán who remain organically connected to the bachata community.

Style Formation in Urban Contexts: A Comparative Perspective

Bachata's evolutionary trajectory and its characteristic social contexts invite further comparisons with other musics that have emerged and developed under similar circumstances. Bachata clearly belongs within a category that Charles Keil has called "people's music," a term he coined to define a space between "folk" (with its strong connotations of "rural," "illiterate") and "popular" (with its denotation today of "mass mediated") (Keil 1985: 119); he also uses the term "working-class music" interchangeably with "people's music." Charles and Angeliki Keil point out that people's musics have emerged in the wake of massive and disruptive rural to urban migration. The litany of ills associated with these processes are precisely those that afflicted bachata's practitioners and patrons:

> Through a combination of industrial processes that seemed inevitable until very recently, the peasantries of the capitalist world were forced off the land and pushed to the bottom of the cities, there to suffer a kind of predictable, and therefore initially near total, oppression. The catalogue of slum problems is long, familiar, but always worth reciting: unemployment for men and women and children; new "freedoms" to consume and be consumed; a breakdown of traditional family and kinship patterns, adultery, illegitimacy, prostitution; malnutrition and diseases, dependence on alcohol and drugs; crowded housing and high incidence of crime; alienation, anomie and other high-sounding names for despair. (Keil and Keil 1987: 76)

The Keils also observed that migrants often resist the oppressiveness of rapid urbanization under conditions of extreme poverty by creating new musical styles that link their rural past with an urban present:

The former peasants who became the working class not only survive and build the industrial economy, the cities, and transportation networks, and so forth, but they also create distinctive cultures. . . . The strongest musical styles of the twentieth century have come from the formation of the working classes in various countries—Afro-American blues, jazz, rhythm n' blues, gospel; white American country and western; Trinidadian calypso; Jamaican reggae; Greek laika or rebetika; Cuban and Puerto Rican latin; Polish-American polka. In each of these styles, class factors (especially the relative importance of lumpen life styles and values) and various ethnic traditions blend differently, but each synthesis has the power to evoke strong resonances across class lines and ethnic lines so that the effort to commodify these styles is usually unrelenting soon after their birth. (Keil and Keil 1987: 75–76)

Keil noted that working-class musics began arriving on the scene after World War I (Keil 1985: 129): U.S. blues and polka, Nigerian juju, Greek rebetika or laika, and Trinidadian calypso all emerged over five decades ago. Even though their status was initially low, these musics and their musicians have eventually percolated up into mainstream, middle-class contexts. Nigerian juju, for example, emerged in the 1930s as the creation of poor rural migrants but was later played by people who were fully assimilated into urban life, who were part of an "intermediate urban wage force that includes laborers, artisans, drivers, sailors, railway workers, clerks and teachers" (Waterman 1990: 9); and for the past twenty years it has been associated with the Yoruba elite, serving to "defend and celebrate their gains" (Waterman 1990: 228). Similarly, Greek laika emerged in the 1920s within poor peasant migrant communities in the city, but it later achieved wide acceptance and popularity throughout Greece (Keil and Keil 1987). In terms of mainstream social acceptance, only polka has been an exception: it was fashionable in Europe and elsewhere in the mid-1880s, but its status later declined in the United States when distinct Polish-American styles were developed within the working-class Polish-American community; today, polka is still stereotyped as "corny" and "square" (Keil, Keil, and Blau 1992).

In Latin America, the simultaneous processes of migration, urbanization, and industrialization intensified in the 1960s, spawning a new generation of "people's musics," which included bachata in the Dominican Republic, *chicha* in Peru, *música carrilera* in Colombia, and certain regional styles categorized as *brega* in Brazil. These musics emerged at a time when the recording and broadcast industries were promoting hegemonic middle-class-oriented popular musics—some of which, such as orquesta merengue in the Dominican Republic and later salsa throughout Latin America, had started out as "people's musics" themselves. Compared to these older, well-established musics, the new arrivals initially appeared to be simply degenerate hybrids of antecedent rural forms or else poor imitations of modern urban forms, and as a result, they were repudiated by the mainstream.

Chicha (also known as *cumbia andina*) was the creation of second-generation Andean migrants living in Lima's vast squatter settlements, and as such, it expressed the transition from rural to urban culture that bachata, juju, and other musics did in their countries of origin. Like bachata, chicha was considered a very low-class music, and middle- and upper-class Limeños either ignored it or looked upon it with scorn. In the 1970s it was largely confined within the boundaries of the squatter settlements and could not be purchased in middle-class Limeño record stores. It received some air play on radio stations targeting the migrant population, but these were AM stations, and the programming tended to be at odd hours, such as at dawn (Llorens Amico 1983: 130–34). Later, however, the media took note of chicha's wide popularity among migrants, who represented a sizable market, and chicha began to find its way into the mainstream media—even though it was still despised by most middle- and upper-class people (Raúl Romero, personal communication). Moreover, politicians and businessmen astutely recognized chicha's potential to serve as a Pan-Peruvian symbol that could be strategically used to attract the attention of migrants regardless of their region of origin (Turino 1990).

Interestingly, unlike bachata or any of the other urban-born musics discussed in this section, chicha had ethnic as well as class associations. As a combination of traditional highland *wayno* music and modern Colombian *cumbia* played with electric instrumentation, chicha indexed biculturalism (Turino 1990). Chicha was by no means an "authentic" Andean music, but its strong wayno elements spoke to its roots in highland culture, and in the eyes of the Lima middle and elite classes who despised Andean culture, it was marked with the stigma of Andean ethnicity. Interestingly, chicha was also rejected by "traditionalist" migrants for whom it represented a degeneration of Andean culture (Turino 1990: 15). Chicha, then, was burdened with not only low-class but Indian attributes as well—even though chicha's ethnic character was the product of association rather than substance.

Colombian música carrilera is primarily a vocal music sung by trios or duos accompanied by guitar-led ensembles directly modeled after the Mexican rancheras and corridos that enjoyed immense popularity in Colombia in the 1940s and 1950s. Like bachata, carrilera is associated with people from the lowest strata of Colombian society such as maids and other unskilled workers, and with low-class social contexts such as shantytown bars and brothels. It is most popular in the Andean highlands, but it is also widely listened to in Amazonian frontier towns where *co-*

lonos (peasant colonizers) from highland areas have migrated. (Several anthropologist friends of mine who have worked in the Colombian Amazon have noted that carrilera is also popular among the Indians, who purchase cassettes when they visit towns or cities.) Like bachata, carrilera is disseminated from urban areas to both rural and urban constituencies, although it is not as directly connected to any one metropolis as chicha is to Lima. Carrilera is scorned by the mainstream with disparaging adjectives, but its audience is numerically substantial, and there are a large number of recording groups—many of whom, interestingly enough, are comprised of women—who earn a living from carrilera. Like bachata, carrilera songs are primarily about failed male-female relationships, sung in the earthy language and using the imagery of the very poor. To my knowledge, carrilera has not yet been transformed by electric instruments and still retains the distinctive rural flavor of its Mexican antecedents; nevertheless, like bachata, it is unequivocally *not* peasant or rural music, but rather a music that links the rural and urban poor.

In Brazil, attempts by musicians of poor and/or rural origins to endow their music with a modern veneer similarly provoked the scorn of mainstream audiences, who labeled such music—regardless of its genre or place of origin—with the term *brega* (see Araújo 1988). For example, in recent decades migrants from the rural area known as the *sertão* that surrounds the city of São Paulo have modernized their traditional *música sertaneja* (see Carvalho 1993) with electric instruments and urban themes and added elements from other Latin American popular musics (especially Mexican and Paraguayan) that were popular at the time; the new style was referred to as brega sertaneja. Brega did not refer to a musical genre, but rather to an aesthetic perceived as low-class—much like the English words *kitschy* or *tacky*—which included super-romanticism and elaborate instrumentation. The term had been used long before the 1980s by record companies to refer to the unpolished style of musicians of poor rural origins; the musicians themselves, however, did not refer to themselves or their music as brega. The term was applied in several of Brazil's culturally distinct regions to very different musics; and the only feature musics labeled as brega had in common, other than their trappings of urban modernity (such as elaborate orchestration), was the fact that although they were initially ignored by mainstream media and audiences, they were extremely popular among the poorer sectors of the population. In the 1980s, middle-class-oriented, emotionally overwrought ballads by artists such as Roberto Carlos and Nelson Ned were also referred to as brega. Because it has been used in so many different places and contexts, nowadays the word "implies a depreciative value judgment" rather than a definable musical style and "can be attached to anything or anyone" (Araújo 1988: 84).

In contrast to bachata, chicha, and carrilera, whose still-visible rural antecedents provoked much of the criticism, musics called brega were criticized because they sounded too (imperfectly) middle-class. Nevertheless, with the exception of carrilera, these styles have achieved a certain level of social acceptance, although perhaps for different reasons. Chicha and bachata were both eventually recognized by intellectuals as autochthonous forms of urban folk music, which were embraced as a political statement of solidarity with the urban poor. In the case of brega, the motivation appeared to be aesthetic rather than political—to adopt (with tongue in cheek) some of brega's "tackiness," to invert it, and to make it chic. Indeed, the term *brega* came to the attention of mainstream Brazilian audiences in 1984, when a rock singer named Eduardo Dusek released a recording called *Brega-chique, chique-brega* (Araújo 1988: 50).

It is important to note that the names of these recently emerged urban-oriented "peoples' musics" were branded with social meanings indicating the low-class status and cultural vulgarity of the music and its patrons. Araújo, for example, describes some of the meanings contained within the term *brega:*

> Brega as a musical term would mean *música periférica* ("peripheral music") for "the great masses of the interior," interior in this case, becoming much more an economic category (i.e., relatively distant from the metropolis) than a geographical one (a small coastal city or the poor neighborhoods and slums of a big city would be considered "interior" under this criterion). . . . As an extension of that sense, the term might also be applied to anything vulgar, dated, kitsch, or, in a more abstract way, to any "representation of nothing." (Araújo 1988: 52)

The term *brega* also conflated with the Portuguese word for the low-class occupation (made lower because it was female) of maid, *empregada doméstica* or simply *empregada*. Bachata was also linked to maids in public discourse, although the term used to symbolize bachata's low status—música de guardia—linked it to policemen or guards. Interestingly, the other meaning contained in the word *brega*, that of nothingness, was also implicit in another term used for bachata, *música cachivache* (knickknack music), which connoted triviality and insignificance. The word *carrilera* is related to *carril* (rails); the term *música carrilera*, then, links the music to the low-class railroad workers of the 1940s and 1950s who used to listen to Mexican rancheras and corridos. In the case of chicha, the term referred to the corn beer prepared by indigenous Andeans. While accepted without embarrassment by chicha's fans, to Peru's middle and upper classes the word symbolized the Indians' cultural backwardness (Raúl Romero, personal communication).

There is one other music—Jamaican reggae—whose emergence was reminiscent of the musics described above, but whose subsequent trajectory was markedly different. Reggae, which combined traditional elements such as mento rhythms and Afro-Jamaican drumming with new ones borrowed from contemporary U.S. rhythm and blues, emerged from Kingston's shantytowns in the mid 1960s but crossed over into mainstream audiences—not only in Jamaica but worldwide—within less than a decade of its appearance. Reggae had several significant advantages that facilitated its escape from the confines of Kingston's shantytowns and its entry into the not only socially respectable but highly lucrative international pop market. First, Jamaica's migrant community in London provided reggae with an additional and economically significant market. More importantly, reggae was more easily able to reach non-Jamaican consumers because it was in English and was based on the widely understood U.S. rhythm and blues and rock idioms. Finally, from practically its beginnings, reggae had an upper-class English promoter, Chris Blackwell, who was able to obtain access for reggae in the mainstream media. None of the other Latin American musics had similar qualities or advantages that facilitated their promotion to broader audiences even within their own countries, much less abroad—although bachata certainly received such a boost from Juan Luis Guerra in 1991. The extent to which these musics may later be influenced by interactions between the music scene in the country of origin and migrant communities abroad remains to be seen.

All these newer musics shared the features that the Keils associated with the emergence of older working-class musics such as juju and blues (Keil and Keil 1987). They emerged as creations of rural migrants living in urban shantytowns/squatter settlements, but they have been subsequently disseminated back into rural areas, giving them rural as well as urban constituencies. Their musicians served as cultural intermediaries, articulating a dialectic between tradition and modernity by combining older rural and/or community-based music styles and practices with newer urban and/or class-based ones. All of them were considered to be very low-class musics, partly because of their practitioners' and patrons' low socio-economic condition but also because of their cultural hybridity: the derogatory names given to them clearly expressed the upper classes' disdain for the incompleteness and inadequacy of their assimilation into urban culture. These musics also had in common the fact that they were excluded from the media at the point of their emergence. Nevertheless, they circulated widely among their constituents (well before the mainstream took note), often via informal networks of distribution relying on small-scale, usually locally based economic and social interactions (e.g., street stalls for retail vending or peripheral bars and social clubs for performance venues) that were only loosely connected to each country's mainstream music and culture industries.

The rejection of these musics at their point of emergence has not been incidental but deliberate and active, in each case being justified by claims that they were of poor musical quality. When their economic potential has been recognized, however, they have grudgingly been given at least limited access to the mainstream media, although this has not automatically cleansed them of their social stigma. Raúl Romero has observed, for example, that since the 1980s chicha has indeed been highly visible on Peruvian television but that middle-class people hate it, and it is heavily criticized in mainstream publications such as *Caretas* (personal communication). The level of social disapproval heaped upon these new urban musics appears to be most intense when they threaten the interests of the economic and political elite. This can be seen most clearly in the Dominican Republic, where the country's mainstream music industry sought to capture the entire mass market for the various middle-class-oriented musics—such as orquesta merengue and balada—that they were promoting. Bachata's overwhelmingly negative associations began to diminish only when those associated with the mainstream music industry began investing in it.

Musical Practice and Class Formation: Looking to the Future

When Charles and Angeliki Keil presented their concept of people's music, they situated the origins of urban popular musics such as juju, blues, and reggae in the working classes. The problem with this formulation is that the term *working class*, used in its classic Marxist sense (describing wage earners who do not own the means of production), conjures up people who have steady jobs in officially regulated enterprises and who enjoy at least a minimum level of government-mandated employee benefits such as a minimum wage. Most of those who make and consume musics like bachata, chicha, and carrilera, however, are not "working class" in this sense at all, because they work in the informal sector, in unsteady, low-paying occupations such as street vending and domestic service. It is tempting to use the word *lumpen* to distinguish them from the working class; however, this word, too, is problematic because technically it refers to people who are outside the labor force and/ or do not work within the official economy. In Latin American countries where over half the population earns a living in the informal sector, these people are by no means outside the labor force. The term *low class*, which is not tied to how people work but rather to their income level, is perhaps more inclusive, but it does not make important distinctions between the rural and urban poor, nor between poor working-class people who have steady, if low-paying, jobs and who can afford to live in adequate, if modest, housing, and those who are chronically unemployed or underemployed and so desperately poor they are forced to live in substandard housing in overcrowded shantytowns or squatter settlements. The term *underclass* is perhaps appropriate for describing the urban non-wage-earning poor; I would insist, however, on maintaining a distinction between the underclasses in Latin America and inner city residents in the United States who are sometimes referred to with this term, because the availability of both social services and institutions such as schools, libraries, and health centers accessible to U.S. inner city residents—however inadequate they may be—connect them to the country's economic, political, and social infrastructure in a way that shantytown residents in developing countries simply are not.

In Latin America (and other third-world countries as well), the large group of people that can be categorized as low class is not at all homogeneous, even after accounting for other variables such as race, region, age, and gender. The steadily working poor and the chronically underemployed and desperately poor do not necessarily share residential space or lifestyles, they do not necessarily share values and aspirations—and they do not necessarily share musical tastes. For example, orquesta merengue, while middle-class oriented, is solidly grounded in the Dominican Republic's working classes—the majority of merengue's consumers as well as its musicians are of working-class backgrounds. Yet, as I have discussed at length throughout this book, orquesta merengue differs profoundly from bachata in the ways it is recorded, performed, distributed, promoted, listened to, and used. In 1989 I referred to bachata as a "music of marginality" rather than a working-class music or a people's music as defined by the Keils, because I believed that the active exclusion of bachata's practitioners and patrons from the country's socio-economic infrastructure had created material conditions that were different from those of the working classes and that these differences had an impact on how the music had taken shape. I also made reference to Peruvian chicha and Colombian carrilera as being similarly distinguished by their active exclusion from the mainstream of their nations' cultural life. However, the term *music of marginality* ceases to be appropriate when a musical style created by musicians and fans who are economically and socially marginalized begins to be produced by the dominant elite and marketed to non-marginalized audiences, which happened in the 1980s to chicha and is currently happening with bachata.

While bachata's musical and social contours are directly related to its origins in its particular Dominican context, its similarities to other musics that have emerged from conditions of extreme urban poverty suggest that the relationship between socio-economic status, physical environment, and musical practice needs to be further interrogated. Are there any intrinsic differences between musics created by poor migrants in the post-World War I era and those created after 1960? Is the fact that many of the older working-class musics (e.g., juju, calypso) have by now become hegemonic within their country of origin simply the consequence of longevity, or is there something specific as to how and when they emerged? To what degree are a group's socio-economic status and living conditions relevant to the music-making process? Is there anything unique to people working in the informal sector and living in shantytowns/slums/squatter settlements that would distinguish their residents' music-making processes from those of working-class people living in relatively better-off working-class neighborhoods? Can a music be distinguished by virtue of being born and/or embedded in the circumstances particular to contemporary social and/or economic marginality? Are these distinctions even worth making?

I propose that these questions do matter, because it seems inevitable that the conditions that existed when musical styles such as bachata were created will be with us for some time, and it is important that we understand them. Given our present direction, our collective future will continue to be tainted by further destruction of the environment and the rural lifestyles that depended on it, thus worsening competition for even basic resources such as clean air and water, and by ever-widening social inequalities between those who have access to adequate and satisfying lifestyles and those who do not. Here in the United States, questions about the relationship between economic deprivation, deteriorating physical environments, and musical practice underpin much of the recent controversy about the content of rap lyrics. Bachata and other similarly situated musics suggest that we need to think much more about how the simultaneous experiences of overcrowding and deprivation of basic needs affect musical practice and all its various aesthetic and social functions—dancing, having fun, feeling good, forgetting, lashing out, fighting back, and hearing the sound of one's own voice.

Notes

Chapter One

1. Dias's name is often spelled in its more common form, Díaz. He himself refuses to designate either spelling as correct, telling those who ask that they can spell it any way they like.
2. Early criollas were composed for guitar, although later they were also composed for piano and larger ensembles. Among the early composers of criollas were the Cuban Sindo Garay and his Dominican partner Danda Lockward (Miguel Holguín, interview; see also Jorge 1982).
3. The *montuno* is "a vehicle for improvisation, based on a two- or three-chord pattern repeated ad lib under the instrumental or vocal improvisations" (Roberts 1985: 229).
4. According to Juan Valoy, the skills that are desired and admired in the barrio include: being sexually skillful, dressing well, and knowing how to manipulate language. The word for the ability to manipulate language—*pintar* (to paint)—suggests that it is perceived as an artistic skill. Two other words for desirable barrio behavior similarly suggest the concept of artistry: *dibujar* (to draw), for the elegant footwork in salsa dancing (this refers to male dancing only—women are supposed to mark time); and *figurear* (to make figures), which refers to showing off, or preening, usually with elegant clothes (personal communication).
5. According to sociologist Jorge Cela, in many barrios there was at least one colmado for every thirty-five families (interview).

Chapter Two

1. Dance "jazz bands" had existed since the early decades of the century (performing most frequently for the elite) but they had played principally foreign musics such as the *danzón, polka, vals, schottische,* and *mazurka* (Jorge 1982a: 31; Convite 1976: 16). Music historian Arístides Incháustegui observes that the name "jazz band" reflected the influence of the U.S. occupation but that Dominican jazz bands, which included violins and flutes, bore little resemblance to

their namesakes. Their most frequent venue was movie houses, accompanying silent pictures (interview).

2. Several Dominican provincial capitals still preserve the gazebos in central plazas in which the municipal bands once played. In a few towns—for example, in Puerto Plata—municipal bands still play on Sunday afternoons.

3. One Dominican observer, Lepe Collado (1985), claims there were from five to eight stations when Trujillo took power; however, I could find no corroborating evidence.

4. Incháustegui reports (1987: 3) that a 1915 La Vega newspaper mentioned some recordings of a Dominican violin virtuoso from Moca, but these early records have not been located.

5. Incháustegui claims that Mesa could be considered the first bachatero, based on the kind of raunchy guitar-based songs he recorded.

6. Most of Trujillo's opposition was in exile; two invasion attempts, one in 1949 and another in 1959, were organized from abroad (Maríñez 1984: 74).

Chapter Three

1. This conflict is sometimes referred to as a revolution, as an aborted revolution, as a civil war, or as a disturbance (*revuelta*); the preferred word will depend on the political inclination of the speaker, with nationalists preferring *revolución*, while moderates or pragmatists use the word *revuelta*.

2. Another merengue musician, Joseíto Mateo, is often credited with adding the energetic dance to the merengue performance.

3. Some of these early bachatas, such as Ramón Cordero's "La causa de mi muerte" (The cause of my death) and Bernardo Ortiz's "Dos rosas" (Two roses), have since become classics and are still listened to widely as well as reinterpreted by others; for example, "Dos rosas" has been recorded in merengue by Wilfrido Vargas and as a bachata by Víctor Víctor.

4. Many of the disc jockeys Aracena trained later went on to become well-known figures in Dominican broadcasting. As to slang, Aracena still forbids it. Today this represents a major difference in style between Guarachita and other popular radio stations, whose broadcast styles depend heavily on being up-to-date with—if not innovating—street-level slang and verbal intonations for giving their announcing a contemporary, urban flavor.

5. I observed that in club settings musicians as well as MCs always directed saludos to friends in the audience—which on many occasions included me—thus simultaneously connecting themselves to the audience and displaying their skills in executing formal greetings.

6. I suspect that the addition of news responded to the necessity to keep up with what was considered an essential component of a modern radio broadcast rather than to a deep commitment to public information. When the news segment was added, the station had no proper facilities for newscasts: I observed the two newscasters preparing their stories on ancient manual typewriters set up in a dusty non-air-conditioned cubicle, and reading the news from two microphones set up on a table in front of the disc jockey's console in the radioteatro.

7. Because Radio Guarachita was an AM station, this should read "amplitude modulated" instead of "frequency modulated." I am not sure if the mistake was made by Aracena when he composed this passage or by Brea when she transcribed it.

Chapter Four

1. According to Jorge Cela, a sociologist and Catholic priest active in Santo Domingo barrios, there was a geographical as well as temporal dimension to the migrations: the earliest migrants mostly came from the eastern areas, when sugar cane plantations were established; the second, the result of Trujillo's expropriations, came primarily from the south and southwest; the last, post-Trujillo migration was primarily from the Cibao (interview).
2. The term *bueno/a* used in these lyrics carries a deeper cultural meaning than the literal English translation "good" (or "fine") allows, referring to a woman with sexual attractiveness as well as good looks. Used in this way, *buena* is associated with popular/street language; it would never be used in polite society—although upper-class men might use it in informal circumstances in order to add more color and emphasis to a statement about a woman.
3. "Quisqueya" is the Indian name for the Dominican Republic.

Chapter Five

1. There are many levels of prostitution; not all prostitutes are "professional"—i.e., they do not practice full-time, and not all of them are connected with brothels. Some women act independently and simply expect some sort of payment for sexual favors. Others have some sort of arrangement with the owner of a bar, whereby the owner receives a fee (paid by the client) for allowing the woman to work out of his establishment, but he has no control over what the couple does or where they go. Some bars have rooms in the back that can be rented for the night or by the hour, but the women do not reside on the premises. Finally, there are brothels as we tend to think of them, with women residing at an establishment dedicated principally to prostitution, although there would probably be a bar associated with it (Juan Valoy, personal communication).
2. Not all barras were disreputable: in spite of their often seamy appearance, many were simply the only public spaces that offered barrio residents a place to dance and socialize. I witnessed children with their families sitting in neighborhood barras on Sunday afternoons, listening to bachata (and other musics), drinking sodas, and dancing; at night, of course, the environment became less familial. On the other hand, while patrons in a neighborhood bar certainly might know each other well, barras, unlike homes, are open to strangers, and they operate under a completely different set of social rules than do family homes.
3. The imagery linking the heat of sexual desire to the heat of a burning sugar mill clearly reveals the composer's rural origin.
4. Simon Frith and Angela McRobbie (1978: 4) develop this idea in relation to rock, claiming that rock is "a necessary part of understanding how sexual feelings and attitudes are learnt."
5. In Dominican street slang, *mariposa de la noche* (butterfly of the night) is a prostitute.
6. One could seek explanations for obsession with mami in several places. One possibility would be a Freudian analysis of mother-son relationships; another would be a consideration of what Franco Ferrán (1985) refers to as the typical Dominican sense of *orfandad* (orphanage), which has two roots: on the one hand, the abandonment by Spain and on the other, the orphaned Africans.
7. The following song, from a commercial Colombian cassette lacking song titles

or singers, shows what is possible when women are given a chance to express their anger:

Ojalá que te dé harta fiebre aftosa	I hope you get a bad case of hoof-and-mouth disease
Y te llenes de niguas las dos patas	And both your legs fill up with parasitic sores
Que se te llene to'itico el cuero 'e rollas	And that your whole body gets covered with fungus
Y la cabeza tupí'a de garrapatas	And your head fills with ticks
Que cuando 'tés por debajo de otra guasca	That when you're underneath another country girl
Me vea yo con l'alcahueta de tu mamá	I run into that procurer who's your mother
Pa' quebrarles a los dos el sentadero	So I can break both your butts
Con to'iticas las tablas de la cama	With the boards of the bed
Que pagues caro y sucia	May you pay dear and dirty
Tu amor negro y falsario	For your black and false love
Y que un veterinario	And may a veterinarian
Te ha de desahuciar	Pronounce you a hopeless case
Y que mis propias patas	And may my own legs
Te vea arrodillado	See you on your knees
Rogando que te quiera	Begging me to love you
Más que sea por caridad	If nothing else than for pity
Acordáte gran flechudo de la estera	Remember, you big prick, the pallet
Donde jurastes por la Virgen serme fiel	Where you swore by the Virgin to be faithful
Y mientras yo me mataba trabajando	And while I was killing myself working
Vos con los otros pasando luna 'e miel	You were off with others on a honeymoon
Y hoy que vas sinvergüenciando por la vida	And today you're bumming through life
Dando por nada el morrito de tu amor	Giving away free the scrap of your love
Ya te veré por la calle envilecí'o	I'll be seeing you filthy on the streets
Y hasta embutí'o entre las llantas de un camión	Stuffed below the wheels of a truck

Chapter Six

1. By comparison, Jamaica—far smaller and poorer—had at least seven 32-track recording studios, most of which had been established in the wake of reggae's international success (Wallis and Malm 1984: 277).
2. Another form of patrocinio provides musicians with a contract paying a certain amount of money a year in exchange for exclusivity at all their performances during the term. This type of sponsorship is less desirable, because musicians realize that their names may become too closely identified with one company, making it harder for them to obtain patrocinio from other companies later on. Another variation of patrocinio is the *ayuda social* (social assistance), which entails sponsoring a benefit; the company pays for the publicity, and the proceeds, after other expenses, go to charity.
3. In 1986 I asked *Ultima Hora* entertainment columnist Carlos Batista why he had never reviewed Blas Durán's work, given the enormous popularity of his song "Consejo a las mujeres." Batista refused to believe the sales figures I gave

him—50,000 copies—so I told him I'd check with the pressing factory, Discomundo. Discomundo's owner confirmed that he had in fact pressed that many records. When I reported this back to Batista, he changed the subject: he simply wasn't interested in information that challenged his comfortable belief that bachata was irrelevant to the music business as a whole.

4. Durán was not the first bachatero to record with an electric rather than acoustic guitar; other bachateros such as the Paredes brothers and Los Macopejes had used electric guitars, but not for merengue-bachatas.

5. Durán and his successors use electroacoustic rather than solid-body electric guitars.

Bibliography

Alberti, Luis. 1975. *De música y orquestas bailables dominicanas 1910–1950*. Santo Domingo: Editora Taller.

Araújo, Samuel. 1988. "Brega: Music and conflict in urban Brazil." *Latin American Music Review* 4 (1): 49–89.

Arvelo, Alvaro. 1983. "Alcoholísmo en RD." *¡Ahora!* January, no. 1000: 13–16.

Arzeno, Julio. 1927. *Del folklore musical dominicano*. Santo Domingo: Imprenta la Cuna de América.

Austerlitz, Paul. 1986. "A history of the Dominican merengue highlighting the role of the saxophone." Master's thesis, Wesleyan University.

———. 1993. "Local and international trends in Dominican *merengue*." *The politics and aesthetics of "world music": The world of music* 35 (2): 70–89.

Averill, Gage. 1989. "Haitian dance bands, 1915–1970: Class, race, and authenticity." *Latin American Music Review* 10 (2):203–35.

———. 1993. " 'Toujou sou konpa': Issues of change and interchange in Haitian popular dance music." In *Zouk: World music in the West Indies*, ed. Jocelyne Guilbault et al. Chicago: University of Chicago Press.

Báez, Clara. 1984. *La subordinación social de la mujer dominicana en cifras*. Santo Domingo: Dirección General de Promoción de la Mujer/INSTRAW.

Balaguer, Joaquín. 1983. *La isla al revés: Haití y el destino dominicano*. Santo Domingo: Fundación Antonio Caro.

Baron, Robert. 1977. "Syncretism and ideology: Latin New York salsa musicians." *Western Folklore* 36 (3): 209–25.

Barreiro, Teófilo. 1986. "La orquesta popular: vía de movilidad social." *Acroarte: Primer seminario sobre las orquestas populares en nuestro país* 1 (1): 42–53.

Un barrio estudia a sí mismo: Los Guandules. 1983. Santo Domingo: Ediciones Populares.

Batista, Carlos. 1983. "El Añoñaíto canta al amor y la amargura con finura." *Escala*, September 11.

Black, Jan Knippers. 1986. *The Dominican Republic: Politics and development in an unsovereign state*. Boston: Allen and Unwin.

Boggs, Vernon. 1992. *Salsiology: Afro-Cuban music and the evolution of salsa in New York*. New York: Excelsior Music Publishing Company.

Bosch, Juan. 1986a. *De Cristóbal Colón a Fidel Castro: El Caribe, frontera imperial*. 5th ed. Santo Domingo: Editorial Alfa y Omega.

———. 1986b. *Composición social dominicana: Historia e interpretación*. Santo Domingo: Editorial Alfa y Omega.

Brea, Ramonina. 1975. "Análisis de la programación de Radio Guarachita." *Ciencia* 2 (2): 77–88.

Brito Ureña, Luis Manuel. 1985. "La bachata, canción de amargue, o de guardia cobra'o." *¡Ahora!* June, no. 1083: 74–77.

———. 1987. *El merengue y la realidad existencial del hombre dominicano*. Santo Domingo: Editorial Universidad Autónoma de Santo Domingo.

Cabezas, Dagmaris. 1987. "Condiciones familiares de los Dominicanos en New York." Paper presented at Migración y Situación de los Dominicanos en Estados Unidos, a conference sponsored by the Asociación Pro-Educación y Cultura (APEC), Rutgers University, January 29.

Carvalho, Martha de Ulhoa. 1993. "Musical style, migration and urbanization: Some considerations on Brazilian *música sertaneja* (country music)." *Studies in Latin American Popular Culture* 12: 75–94.

Castillo, José del. 1979. "Las emigraciones y su aporte a la cultura dominicana (finales del siglo XIX y principio del XX)." *Eme Eme* 8 (45):3–44.

Castillo, José del, and Manuel A. García Arévalo. 1988. *Antología del merengue*. Santo Domingo: Banco Antillano.

Collado, Lepe. 1985. "Curso sobre comunicación e ideología—la función ideológica de la prensa radiofónica." Unpublished teaching material, Universidad Autónoma de Santo Domingo.

Convite. 1976. *Apuntes sobre el merengue*. Santo Domingo: Casa por la Cultura Antillana.

Coopersmith, J. M. 1949. *Music and musicians of the Dominican Republic*. Washington, D.C.: Pan American Union.

Coplan, David B. 1985. *In township tonight: South Africa's black city music and theatre*. New York: Longman House.

Cordero Regalado, Juan M. 1983. "Trujillo prohibió la prostitución." *¡Ahora!* October 3, no. 1036: 3–5.

Crassweller, Robert. 1966. *Trujillo: The life and times of a Caribbean dictator*. New York: Macmillan.

Cruz Triffolio, Juan Antonio. 1987. "La bachata: un género musical o un ambiente jaranero?" *Galería* (supplement of *El Nacional*), June 7, p. 15.

———. 1988. "Trujillo dio el "visto bueno" para ingreso de Rafael Colón a orquesta." *Galería* (supplement of *El Nacional*), June 12.

———. 1991. "Apuntes sobre la bachata." Unpublished program notes.

Davis, Martha Ellen. 1987. *La otra ciencia: El vodú dominicano como religión y medicina populares*. Santo Domingo: Editora Universitaria de la Univeridad Autónoma de Santo Domingo.

Díaz Ayala, Cristóbal. 1981. *Música cubana del areyto a la nueva trova*. San Juan, Puerto Rico: Editorial Cubanacan.

"Dominicanos gastan 600 millones en bebidas y tabaco." 1987. *Master* 1 (1): 3.

Duany, Jorge. 1984. "Popular music in Puerto Rico: Towards an anthropology of salsa." *Latin American Music Review* 5 (2): 186–216.

Duarte, Isis. 1980. *Capitalismo y superpoblación en Santo Domingo*. Santo Domingo: CODIA.

———. 1986. *Trabajadores urbanos: Ensayos sobre fuerza laboral en República Dominicana*. Santo Domingo: Universidad Autónoma de Santo Domingo.

Fernández, Enrique. 1986. "Is salsa sinking?" *Village Voice*, September 2.

Ferrán, Franco. 1985. "Figuras de lo dominicano." *Ciencia y Sociedad* 10 (1): 5–29.

Frith, Simon, and Angela McRobbie. 1978. "Rock and sexuality." *Screen Education* 34:3–19.

Galán, Natalio. 1983. *Cuba y sus sones*. Valencia: Pretextos.

García, Manuel de Jesús Javier. 1985. *Mis 20 años en el Palacio Nacional junto a Trujillo*. Santo Domingo: Editora Taller.

Gómez Carrasco, Carmen. 1984. "Consideraciones sobre el hacinamiento en la ciudad de Santo Domingo." *Población y Desarrollo* 2 (6): 3–9.

Hernández, Julio Alberto. 1969. *Música tradicional dominicana*. Santo Domingo: Colección Artistas Dominicanos.

Herrera, Miguel Angel. 1991. "La bachata: una manifestación que se inició . . . sin ser música." *Escala, Revista Artística*, October 27.

Incháustegui, Arístides. 1987. "El disco en la República Dominicana." *Isla Abierta* (cultural supplement of *Hoy*), May 26.

———. 1990. "La nueva bachata dominicana." *Isla Abierta* (cultural supplement of *Hoy*), September 22.

Jiménez, Ramón Emilio. 1927. *Al amor del bohío*. Santo Domingo: Virgilio Montalvo.

Jorge, Bernarda. 1982a. *La música dominicana: Siglos XIX–XX*. Santo Domingo: Editorial Universidad Autónoma de Santo Domingo.

———. 1982b. "Bases ideológicos de la práctica musical durante la era de Trujillo." *Eme Eme* 10 (59):65–100.

Kahl, Willi. 1980. "Bolero." In *The new Grove dictionary of music and musicians*, ed. Stanley Sadie. Washington D.C.: Macmillan Publishers.

Keil, Charles. 1966. *Urban blues*. Chicago: University of Chicago Press.

———. 1985. "People's music comparatively: Style and stereotypes, class and hegemony." *Dialectical Anthropology* 10: 119–30.

Keil, Charles, and Angeliki V. Keil. 1987. "In pursuit of polka happiness." In *Popular culture in America*, ed. Paul Buhle. Minneapolis: University of Minnesota Press.

Keil, Charles, Angeliki V. Keil, and Dick Blau. 1992. *Polka happiness*. Philadelphia: Temple University Press.

Kleinekathoefer, Michael. 1986. *El sector informal: Integración o transformación*. Santo Domingo: Fundación Frederich Ebert.

León Díaz, Homero. 1982. "Apuntes para la historia de la locución dominicana— o—los pioneros." *El Locutor* 3, no. 24.

Liriano, William. 1986. "Mercado y dimensión económica de las orquestas populares." *Acroarte: Primer seminario sobre las orquestas populares en nuestro país* 1 (1): 34–40.

Lizardo, Fradique. 1978. "El merengue como elemento etnográfico." Paper presented at the conference Encuentro con el Merengue, Santo Domingo.

Lloréns Amico, José Antonio. 1983. *Música popular en Lima: Criollos y andinos*. Lima: Instituto de Estudios Peruanos.

Lora Medrano, Luis Eduardo. 1984. *Petán: La Voz Dominicana, su gente . . . sus cosas . . . y sus cuentos*. Santo Domingo: Editora Tele-3.

Loza, Steven. 1993. *Barrio rhythm: Mexican American music in Los Angeles*. Urbana and Chicago: University of Illinois Press.

Mahan, Elizabeth, and Joseph D. Straubhaar. 1985. "Broadcasting in the Dominican Republic." Unpublished manuscript.

Manuel, Peter. 1988. *Popular musics of the non-Western world.* New York: Oxford University Press.

Maríñez, Pablo A. 1984. *Resistencia campesina, imperialismo y reforma agraria en República Dominicana.* Santo Domingo: Centro de Planificación y Acción Ecuménica.

Matos, Francisco. 1987. "Rum distiller's new advertising mix targets respectability and sophistication." *Santo Domingo News*, March 12–18.

Miniño, Manuel. 1983. *Merengues de Luis Alberti.* Santo Domingo: Editora de Santo Domingo.

Morris, Nancy. 1984. *Canto porque es necesario cantar: The New Song movement in Chile, 1973–1983.* Latin American Institute Research Paper Series no. 16. Albuquerque: University of New Mexico.

Moya Pons, Frank. 1992. *Manual de historia dominicana.* 9th ed. Santo Domingo: Editora Corripio.

Nolasco, Flérida de. 1939. *La música en Santo Domingo y otros ensayos.* Ciudad Trujillo: Editora Montalvo.

Núñez del Risco, Yaqui. 1986. "La importancia de las orquestas populares en la producción de un espacio de T.V." *Acroarte: Primer seminario sobre las orquestas populares en nuestro país* 1 (1): 6–12.

Oliven, Ruben George. 1988. " 'The woman makes (and breaks) the man': The masculine imagery in Brazilian popular music." *Latin American Music Review* 9 (1): 90–108.

Ortiz, Fernando. 1974. *Nuevo cantauro de cubanismos.* Havana: Editorial de Ciencias Sociales.

Pacini Hernandez, Deborah. 1989a. "Social identity and class in bachata, an emerging Dominican popular music." *Latin American Music Review* 10 (1): 69–91.

———. 1989b. "Music of marginality: Social identity and class in Dominican bachata." Ph.D. diss., Cornell University.

———. 1990. "*Cantando la cama vacía*: Love, sex and gender relationships in Dominican bachata." *Popular Music* 9 (3): 351–67.

———. 1991. "*La lucha sonora*: Dominican popular music in the post-Trujillo era." *Latin American Music Review* 12 (2): 105–23.

———. 1992a. "Bachata: From the margins to the mainstream." *Popular Music* 11 (3): 359–64.

———. 1992b. "Merengue: race, class, tradition and identity." In *Americas: An anthology,* ed. Mark Rosenburg, A. Douglas Kincaid, and Kathleen Logan, 167–72. Oxford: Oxford University Press.

———. 1993. "Dominican popular music under the Trujillo dictatorship." *Studies in Latin American Popular Culture* 12: 127–40.

Peña, Manuel. 1985. *The Texas-Mexican conjunto: History of a working class music.* Austin: University of Texas Press.

Pérez Sanjurjo, Elena. 1986. *Historia de la música cubana.* Miami: La Moderna Poesía.

Perlman, Janice E. 1976. *The myth of marginality: Urban poverty and politics in Rio de Janeiro.* Berkeley: University of California Press.

Rico Salazar, Jaime. 1988. *Cien años de boleros: Su historia, sus compositores, sus intérpretes y 500 boleros inolvidables.* Bogotá: Centro de Estudios Musicales de Latinoamerica.

Rivera González, Luis. n.d. *Antología musical de la era de Trujillo 1930–1960.* República Dominicana: Publicaciones de la Secretaría de Estado, de Educación y Bellas Artes.

Rivera Payano, Andrés. 1983. "Un comentario sobre el género amargue." *¡Ahora!* August 29, no. 1031: 40–45.

Roberts, John Storm. 1972. *Black music of two worlds.* New York: Praeger.

———. 1985. *The Latin tinge: The impact of Latin American music on the United States.* Tivoli, N.Y.: Original Music.

Rodríguez, Willie. 1986. "Impactos de las orquestas populares en la programación de las radio-emisoras del país." *Acroarte: Primer seminario sobre las orquestas populares en nuestro país* 1 (1): 15–26.

Rodríguez Demorizi, Emilio, ed. 1975. *Lengua y folklore de Santo Domingo.* República Dominicana: Universidad Católica Madre y Maestra.

Rondón, César Miguel. 1980. *El libro de la salsa: Crónica de la música del Caribe urbano.* Caracas: Editorial Arte.

Royce, Anya Peterson. 1982. *Ethnic identity: Strategies of diversity.* Bloomington: Indiana University Press.

Safa, Helen I. 1974. *The urban poor of Puerto Rico: A study of development and inequality.* New York: Holt, Rinehart and Winston.

———. 1982. *Towards a political economy of urbanization in Third World countries.* Delhi, India: Oxford University Press.

———. 1995. *The myth of the male breadwinner: Women and industrialization in the Caribbean.* Boulder, Colo.: Westview Press.

Silfa, Nicolás. 1980. *Guerra, traición y exilio.* Barcelona: Nicolás Silfa.

Singer, Roberta. 1983. "Tradition and innovation in contemporary Latin American music in New York City." *Latin American Music Review* 4 (2): 183–202.

Sosa, José Rafael. 1983. " 'El Añoñaíto' del amargue." *¡Ahora!* August 1, no. 1027.

Tarde Alegre. 1987. "Qué es de ellos?" January 10.

Tejeda, Dagoberto. 1978. "La experiencia de Convite." Paper presented at the conference Encuentro con el Merengue, Santo Domingo.

Tejeda, Darío. 1993. *La historia escondida de Juan Luis Guerra y los 4:40.* Santo Domingo: Ediciones MSC, Amigo del Hogar.

Tolentino Dipp, Hugo. 1992. *Raza e historia en Santo Domingo: Los orígenes del prejuicio racial en América.* Santo Domingo: Fundación Cultural Dominicano.

Turino, Thomas. 1988. "The music of Andean migrants in Lima, Peru: Demographics, social power, and style." *Latin American Music Review* 9 (2): 127–50.

———. 1990. "*Somos el Perú* (We are Peru): *Cumbia andina* and the children of Andean migrants in Lima." *Studies in Latin American Popular Culture* 9: 15–32.

Valverde, Sebastián Emilio. 1975. "De nuestro folklore: el amor en la copla y en la décima." In *Lengua y folkore de Santo Domingo,* ed. Emilio Rodríguez Demorizi, 79–83. República Dominicana: Universidad Católica Madre y Maestra.

Veloz Maggiolo, Marcio. 1991. "Cómo eran las bachatas." *El Siglo,* January 11.

Ventura, Johnny. 1978. "El merengue en el presente." Paper presented at the conference Encuentro con el Merengue, Santo Domingo.

Vicioso, Virginia. 1983. "Auge, desarrollo y consequencias del fenómeno llamado 'amargue.' " *Hoy,* August 25.

Wallis, Roger, and Krister Malm. 1984. *Big sounds from small people.* New York: Pendragon Press.

Waterman, Christopher. 1987. "Juju performance practice and African social identity in colonial Lagos." Unpublished manuscript.

———. 1990. *Juju: A social history and ethnography of an African popular music.* Chicago: University of Chicago Press.

Ysalguez, Hugo Antonio. 1976a. "El merengue." *¡Ahora!* January 19, no. 636: 50–51.

———. 1976b. "Merengue se deriva de contradanza española." *¡Ahora!* no. 637: 48–50.

Discography

The following discography contains bachata recordings that readers in the United States will be able to obtain, rather than an inclusive list of important bachata releases since the 1960s. Although such a list would be historically useful, readers would be unable to locate most of the entries, because until the late 1980s most bachata was released on vinyl singles and the records circulated only in the Dominican Republic via the informal sector. At present, most bachata in the Dominican Republic circulates on cassettes, because CDs are too expensive for most of bachata's consumers. In the United States, however, a small but growing number of bachata musicians—either those with current hits (e.g., Raulín Rodríguez) or those with long-lasting careers (e.g., Leonardo Paniagua)—are released on CDs, which can be purchased in record stores (mostly located in large Eastern Seaboard cities) that cater to Dominican consumers. Bachata is not, however, stocked by music chains such as Tower Records, so readers who wish to obtain bachata recordings but do not live in cities with large Dominican communities may have to purchase by mail from distributors of Dominican music.

The following is a small but reasonably representative selection of (mostly recent) bachata recordings that are currently available in the United States. With the exception of Mélida Rodríguez's *16 éxitos de la Sufrida*, all of them are available on CDs as well as cassettes (although the CD catalogue numbers are listed here). Very little bachata recorded prior to the 1990s is available on CD because few rereleases of older material have been made; however, Luis Segura's *Perdido* and Mélida Rodríguez's *16 éxitos de La Sufrida* both date from the late 1960s. (Not all the recordings list dates.) Younger bachateros such as Luis Vargas and Antony Santos are perhaps overrepresented on this list because, as recent arrivals, they have benefited the most from bachata's new profitability and respectability. The compilation CDs, however, contain examples by important bachateros such as Marino Pérez and Bolívar Peralta who have not had similar luck in crossing over to mainstream audiences, but who have been important figures in bachata since the 1970s.

Collections

Bachatazos Vol. 1. José Luis Records. CDJLR 116. 1991.
Bachatazos Vol. 2. José Luis Records. CDJLR 151. 1992.
Cosecha Vol. 1: De merengues típicos y guitarras. Guitarra Records. CDG 1020. 1988.
Cosecha Vol. 2: De merengues típicos y guitarras. Guitarra Records. CDG 5007.

Individual Musicians

Bautista, Juan. *El jinete.* José Luis Records. CDJLR 154.
Cordero, Ramón. *Para todos.* José Luis Records. CDJLR 161.
Durán, Blas. *Bachata pueblo.* J & N Records. JN 758CD. 1992.
Durán, Blas. *El carnicero.* J & N Records. CDJN 10000. 1991.
Durán, Blas. *El piogán.* J & N Records. JN 789CD. 1993.
Durán, Blas. *15 éxitos.* Guitarra Records. CDG 5013.
Estévez, Víctor. *Como Adán y Eva.* José Luis Records. CDJLR 152.
Estévez, Víctor. *Sus 20 super éxitos.* José Luis Records. CDJLR 06.
Guerra, Juan Luis, y 4:40. *Areíto.* Karen Records. KCD146. 1992.
Guerra, Juan Luis, y 4:40. *Bachata rosa.* Karen Records. KCD136.
Paniagua, Leonardo. *El divorcio para que.* Luis Rivera Records. CDLCR 027.
Paniagua, Leonardo. *Pequeña.* Luis Rivera Records. CDLCR 023.
Paniagua, Leonardo. *Por ti amor.* Luis Rivera Records. CDLCR 021.
Rodríguez, Mélida. *16 éxitos de la Sufrida.* Gemini Records. 1076.
Rodríguez, Raulín. *Una mujer como tú.* Plátano Records. Plátano CD5012 (Note: contains "Qué dolor").
Rodríguez, Raulín. *Regresa amor.* Plátano Records. Plátano CD5025. 1993.
Romero Santos, Eladio. *Me quiere casar.* José Luis Records. CDJLR 149.
Santos, Antony. *La batalla.* Plátano Records. Plátano CD5009.
Santos, Antony. *La chupadera.* Plátano Records. Plátano CD5001 (Note: contains "Voy pa'llá").
Santos, Antony. *Corazón bonito.* Plátano Records. Plátano CD5026.
Santos, Tony. *El chiqui chiqui.* José Luis Records. CDJLR 148.
Segura, Luis. *El Añoñaíto Luis Segura: 15 éxitos.* Guitarra Records CDG-1009 (Note: good collection of Luis Segura classics).
Segura, Luis. *Perdido.* Artillera Records. CDSA 11 (Note: rerelease of older record).
Silvestre, Sonia. *Quiero andar.* Oi Records. PR 200.
Vargas, Luis. *En serio.* José Luis Records. CDJLR 172.
Vargas, Luis. *La maravilla.* José Luis Records. CDJLR 112. (Note: contains his first hit, "La traicionera").
Vargas, Luis. *Sin hueso.* Aramis Records. Mundo CD028.
Víctor Víctor. *Inspiraciones.* Polydor 3145210872. (Note: contains his first tecno-bachata "Mesita de noche"; also, this catalogue number is for cassette version, although it is available on CD).
Víctor Víctor. *Tu corazón.* Sony Tropical. DCC 809034–469546. 1993 (Note: contains "Bachata blues").

While under ordinary circumstances it would be inappropriate for an author to add the name of a music distributor to a discography, in this case it can be justified because bachata is still difficult to obtain for those people without access to a Dominican-oriented music store. New York-based J & N Distributors is one of the largest wholesale distributors of Dominican music in the United States, but it will process small retail orders as well. Their address is 766 Tenth Avenue, New York, NY 10019; their telephone number is (212) 265–1313.

Index